CAPTURED BY EVIL

CAPTURED BY EVIL

THE IDEA OF CORRUPTION IN LAW

LAURA S. UNDERKUFFLER

Yale UNIVERSITY PRESS

NEW HAVEN & LONDON

Published with assistance from the foundation established in memory of Henry Weldon Barnes of the Class of 1882, Yale College.

Yale University Press books may be purchased in quantity for educational, business, or promotional use. For information, please e-mail sales.press@yale .edu (U.S. office) or sales@yaleup.co.uk (U.K. office).

Set in Meridien type by IDS Infotech Ltd., Chandigarh, India.
Printed in the United States of America.

Library of Congress Cataloging-in-Publication Data

Underkuffler, Laura S.
Captured by evil: the idea of corruption in law / Laura S. Underkuffler.
    pages cm
Includes bibliographical references and index.
ISBN 978-0-300-17314-7 (cloth)
1. Corruption—Philosophy.   2.   Good and evil—Philosophy.   3.   Law
    and ethics.   I. Title.
    K5261.U55 2013
    364.1'323—dc23
                                                          2012038657

A catalogue record for this book is available from the British Library.

This paper meets the requirements of ANSI/NISO Z39.48-1992 (Permanence of Paper).

10 9 8 7 6 5 4 3 2 1

CONTENTS

ACKNOWLEDGMENTS

Work on this book began in 1993 when I spent a research leave in Washington, D.C., at the Woodrow Wilson International Center for Scholars and the Overseas Development Council. I am grateful for the material support given to me by both institutions, as well as the opportunity for collegial discussion that was invaluable in the early stages of the project. I also want to thank colleagues and friends at Cornell University and Duke University for their comments and ideas throughout the project. I would like particularly to thank Greg Alexander, Allen Czelusniak, Thatcher Freund, Alon Harel, Bob Hockett, Judith Miller, Charles Norchi, David Nowlin, Pablo Ruiz-Tagle Vial, Joe Singer, Deb Tuerkheimer, Frank M. Underkuffler and Jennifer Wriggins for their assistance in so many ways. I am also grateful for comments received during the presentation of the project at workshops hosted by DePaul University Law School, Harvard Law School, the University of Maine Law School, Queens University Faculty of Law, Boston University Law School, the University of Alabama Law School, University of California–Davis Law School, the University of Virginia Law School, Michigan State University College of Law, and Indiana University, as well as comments received at the Annual Meeting of the European Society of Criminology in Cracow, Poland, the Corruption Conference at Hebrew University, Jerusalem, Israel, and the Conference on Issues in Democratic Governance at the Universidad de Chile, Santiago, Chile.

A précis of Chapter 2 was published in *Corruption, Global Security, and World Order* (Robert I. Rotberg ed., 2009) under the title "Defining Corruption: Implications for Action." An initial discussion of some issues discussed in Chapter 2 can also be found in "El Concepto de Corrupción" (The Nature of Corruption), in *Fracturas en la Gobernabilidad Democratica* (Raúl Urzúa and Felipe Argüero eds., 1998).

INTRODUCTION

Mephistopheles: But tell me, Faustus, shall
I have thy soul?

—Christopher Marlowe, *Dr. Faustus*

The subject of this book is corruption.

"Corruption" is one of the most powerful words in the English language. When (for instance) we think of corruption of food, human bodies, or other physical objects, we think of something that is fundamentally or revoltingly altered, impure, rotten, or worse. When we think of corruption in government—the subject of this book—the impact of this word is equally powerful. Charges of corruption in public life have condemned men, destroyed the lives of women, and accelerated the decline and fall of governments. Corruption is something that human beings instinctively loathe, and that we try to excise from our midst. The word itself conjures something that is powerful, insidious, and destructive of human lives and institutions.

The thesis of this book is that corruption, when used in law, is a troubled concept. The contemporary Western ideology of law assumes that law must operate within a universe of knowable and articulable standards, logical and demystified, that strive toward neutral content and operation. Corruption, I shall argue, defies these limits. It is, in its essence, a pre-Enlightenment, intuitive, and emotional concept that relies on "religiously" revealed ideas of good and evil, falsity and truth. It is, in philosophical terms, a "degenerate" or "incommensurable" concept. It contradicts the dominant theory or "way of knowing" of law, and is something which that dominant theory cannot explain.

This character of corruption is illustrated by the efforts of theorists to reduce it to something that is knowable, rational, and "methodologically respectable."[1] In recent years, with increasing awareness of the costs of corruption and allegations of corruption for economic development, political stability, and other world goals, theorists have attempted to articulate the precise nature of political corruption in an avalanche of theoretical writing. Political scientists, legal academics, economists, and others have grappled with the meaning of this concept and advocated understandings of corruption such as the violation of law, a public servant's breach of a public duty, an agent's betrayal of a principal's interests, the denial of political equality, the subversion of the public interest, economic rent seeking by public officials, and others.

All of these attempts meet the implicit goal that legal concepts—and ideas of corruption—should be knowable, articulable, logical, and demystified. However, these attempts to capture the essence of corruption, as it is commonly understood, have met with little success.

Traditional theories fall into three broad categories: what I call "shell theories," which simply define corruption using some other unrelated and unexamined normative basis (law, public duties, and so on); "substantive theories," which assert their own norms on the basis of political or sociological theory; and economic theories, which define corruption in economic terms.

When examined, shell theories—such as corruption-as-illegality or corruption-as-breach-of-duty—are both radically overinclusive and underinclusive, and have little true substantive content beyond the unexamined norms on which they rely. Often corrupt acts will fall into these categories, but it is not the illegality or breach of duty that identifies the corrupt nature of the action. Substantive theories—citing betrayal, secrecy, inequality, and the subversion of the public interest—go further, by identifying elements that are often important characteristics of corrupt acts. However, these characteristics, alone or in combination, fail to capture all that corruption involves. Not all acts involving betrayal, secrecy, or inequality are corrupt, and there are corrupt acts that do not share these characteristics. Economic theories are a way to explain the incidence and effects of corruption, but they do not—of themselves—provide any new or unique way to identify the corrupt act.

Indeed, when they are examined, these formulations do not capture the deeper nature of corruption as even these theorists (as evident from their writings) often understand it. Corruption is more than lawbreaking; it is more than a breach of public duties. To say that "A is a thief" or that "A has breached his duty" is not to say that "A is corrupt." The latter is far more powerful, far more emotional, far more *essential* than the others. It is a searing indictment not only of A's act but also of A's character. It is a *dispositional* concept, which—in this context—establishes the foundational moral deficiency or depravity of the accused. It is a statement not only of what A has done but also of what A *has become*.

The idea of corruption that animates public contexts involves traditional ideas, but it is a far more complex idea. It is an explicitly moral notion, invoking notions of depravity and evil, human frailty and temptation. It imagines corruption as an external force, which attacks and undermines better human impulses. It is not simply an act, or a series of acts. It is the capture of individuals (and political systems) by corrosive, distorting, and decomposing forces. It is self-involvement, self-indulgence, and the loosening and discarding of the restraints of social bonds. It is (in the terminology that I shall adopt) the idea of the *capture by evil* of one's soul.

In this book, I argue that this idea of corruption is found throughout journalistic and other popular accounts of corrupt persons and corrupt acts. It also permeates the legal treatment of corruption by legislators, judges, and ethical boards. It appears in closing arguments, sentencing dispositions, and trial and appellate court opinions. It is not simply a common or cultural phenomenon (although it is that as well); it is a *legal* phenomenon, *a part of the law*, which colors the definitions of crimes, the invitations made to juries, and the legal and broader societal punishments meted out to those who are found to be corrupt.

The reason why this idea of corruption colors all settings, including legal settings, is obvious. It reflects, in an essential way, our deep, cultural notions of what corruption in fact involves. It drives our understandings of corrupt judges who, once revealed to be corrupt, we believe to be unfit for service on the bench. It drives our images of corrupt lobbyists or corrupt legislators, from whom we will accept no exculpatory moral account and for whom we can envision no genuine rehabilitation. It drives our understanding of corruption as a systemic effect and systemic influence, which presents institutional dangers that are far greater than other crimes, and which requires purgation rather than simple law enforcement.

The use of the idea of corruption as capture-by-evil in the design and enforcement of law carries many obvious dangers.

"Capture" and "evil" invite emotional responses, and are hardly justiciable concepts with known or accepted meanings. How can we have, as a part of law, the use of implicitly religious notions such as "evil" and "souls"? How can we embrace a concept which invites judges and juries to think in terms of "malevolence," "defilement," "perversion," and "sin"—emotionally laden concepts which are ripe for the fanning of hysteria, and which contradict, by their very nature, the idea of objective and dispassionate standards for the rule of law?

In addition, corruption as capture-by-evil is descriptive not of acts but rather of status—violating one of the most sacred tenets of criminal law. How can law employ a dispositional concept, which condemns moral degeneracy, when we believe—at the same time—that the focus of law's criminal powers should be *acts*, not the character of *persons*? To paraphrase what I have written in another context, we see the corrupt individual "not as a person who has done evil, but as someone who is possessed by evil."[2] As a result, we risk dehumanization of the offender, the denial of variable criminal culpability, and other excesses in criminal prosecution and punishment.

A degenerate or incommensurate concept may simply (and unacceptably) contradict a dominant and justified theory; or it may successfully challenge that theory in a way that illuminates its flaws. Which is the status of the idea of corruption as capture-by-evil? Is it simply an unacceptable relic of medieval ideas, or does it have a *legitimate function* in the contemporary administration of this difficult area of law?

In this book, I argue that the costs of the idea of corruption as capture-by-evil, for the rule of law, are real. However, to insist upon an understanding of corruption in more dispassionate or transactional terms has costs for the rule of law as well. The idea of corruption as capture-by-evil is not simply an idea of extreme moralists, or popular sentiment run amok; it is a recognition of the deep, systemic dangers that actual or suspected quid pro quo corruption, and the presence—in office—of those who have engaged in quid pro quo corruption, present for the *very idea* of the rule of law and its ability to control conduct. The corrupt politician, police officer, or judge does not simply threaten particular individuals with whom he might come into contact; his existence threatens the entire governmental system of reliance, trust, and the rule of law of which he is a part. Corruption as capture-by-evil explains why corrupt acts trigger systemic concerns, and why we find corrupt persons and acts so threatening, beyond the threat posed by other crimes. It explains what is meant by a "culture of corruption," and what it is about corruption that transcends cultural boundary lines. Corruption as capture-by-evil might threaten to perpetrate injustice in the treatment of individual criminal defendants; but it also, through its unequivocally moral nature, accomplishes systemic accountability in a way that other conceptions of corruption do not.

In short, corruption as capture-by-evil is both ubiquitous and degenerate in its use in law. As the pages of this book explain, any reckoning with this idea must consider both the dangers and the benefits that this powerful idea inherently involves.

1 EXPLORING CORRUPTION
The Inadequacies of Traditional Theories

Corruption, as an idea in politics and government, has been the subject of extensive academic analysis and commentary. For many years, political scientists, sociologists, and legal academicians—those groups that dominated the field—generally assumed a particular understanding of corruption and proceeded to study its causes, effects, and methods of prevention. Corruption, for instance, was assumed to be bribery and like acts, with little attention given to the precise contours of the idea or what the use of this idea added to the simple list of prohibited acts.

In the 1970s and 1980s this changed, and more sophisticated analyses began to appear. This was fueled by developments that were internal and external to the academic field. Political scientists such as Robert Klitgaard and economists such as Bruce Benson and John Baden began to focus on the nature of corruption as critical to how we see it, and whether it operates as a positive or a destructive social force. Legal academicians, prodded by a general movement toward the merger of the law with other disciplines, were no longer satisfied with the curt simplicity of statutory or other legal definitions. In addition, the sheer importance of corruption and allegations of corruption in national and international politics and governance made additional attention to the core concept inevitable.

No uniformity in understanding of the idea of corruption has emerged from these academic efforts. Although there is clearly a common understanding of corruption that is shared by politicians, journalists, and "the man on the street," academic theorists have advanced a multiplicity of meanings, with more or less scrutiny or explicit understanding. There are, however, several approaches that have become traditional in theorists' work and that can be readily identified. In this chapter we shall consider these theories and their ability to capture what, in "corruption," we believe to be at stake.

To begin, existing approaches to the idea of corruption fall into three broad categories: what I shall call *shell theories, substantive theories,* and *economic theories.* Briefly, these can be described as follows:

- *Shell theories* define corruption on the basis of specific acts that are deemed to be wrongful on some other, unrelated normative basis (e.g., "corruption as a violation of law," "corruption as a violation of duty," and so on). They do not, themselves, engage in the explication or evaluation of these underlying normative theories.

- *Substantive theories* define corruption on the basis of particular, substantive evils that the theories, themselves, identify (e.g., corruption as "betrayal," "secrecy," "violation of the public interest," and so on). They make normative judgments—rooted in political or sociological theory—that corruption, in their view, embodies.

- *Economic theories* are united in their view of corruption in economic terms. Generally, they combine shell theories (such as "corruption as illegality" and "corruption as breach of duty") with economic analysis, which provides substantive, normative judgments about the positive or negative nature of corrupt acts. They range from theories that maintain that corruption is a certain kind of economic evil, to those that argue that corruption is an economic good.

Let us now consider these theories, and their relative success in capturing what we believe corruption to involve, in more detail.

TRADITIONAL SHELL THEORIES

Shell theories have become extremely prominent in academic treatments of the idea of corruption. The two most powerful theories of this type are corruption as the violation of law and corruption as the breach of duty.

Corruption as Violation of Law

As James C. Scott's classic work in the field begins, "Corruption, we would all agree, involves a deviation from certain standards of behavior. The first question which arises is, what criteria should we use to establish those standards?"[1] If our concern is public corruption, perhaps the most obvious place to start is this: corruption involves the *violation of law*.[2]

This understanding is based upon a commonsense observation. When we think of corruption by government actors, we tend to think of crimes: bribery, fraud, extortion, embezzlement, and kickbacks on public contracts, and so on.[3] There seems to be a strong correlation between what we believe to be *illegal* acts and what we believe to be corrupt. Indeed, some observers would go further: if an official's act is prohibited by law, established by government, it is corrupt; if it is not so prohibited, it is not corrupt, even if it is otherwise undesirable.[4]

"Corruption-as-illegality" is a shell theory of corruption. Theorists who use this approach simply borrow the normative judgments made by law to establish what is or is not corrupt conduct.[5] For instance, in determining whether a payment to a public official is corrupt, the critical question under this approach is whether that payment is illegal (and, perhaps additionally, involves private gain or other described characteristics).[6] Legal norms are not evaluated or criticized; they are simply employed as the primary source for identifying what we believe to be corrupt acts.

The association of corruption with illegality has a tremendous advantage: it imports all of the safeguards that we associate with legal procedures and legal rules into our treatment of this phenomenon. For instance, by requiring that violation of the criminal law be proven, the idea of corruption as illegality ensures that corruption is pursued in accordance with the principles of notice, fair procedure, and other safeguards that are a part of the commitment to the rule of law. As stated by one commentator, "Lawyers will appreciate the virtues of this formal or positivist definition: it is clear, and officials, government employees, and ordinary citizens can be expected to know the requirements and prohibitions spelled out in statutes. . . . [T]he fact that something is illegal . . . provides something firm— something tangible."[7]

How useful is this theory in identifying the essence of corrupt behavior? When we examine the idea of corruption-as-illegality, we find serious problems. Consider, for instance, the following statements:

- A has broken the law.

and

- A is corrupt.

The meaning of these statements is clearly different. We do not consider burglars, bank robbers, perpetrators of assault, or even many white collar criminals (for instance, those who engaged in simple theft or tax evasion) to be corrupt. Although corrupt acts may be a subset of illegal acts, the meaning of these two ideas is clearly not the same.

Indeed, the lack of congruence between "illegality" and "corruption" is evident even when we limit our consideration to illegal acts that are of a type that we generally assume to be within an imagined core of corrupt conduct. Consider, for instance, payments made to induce an abuse of power for the achievement of private ends. As Scott observes, these would "include[] acts as diverse as a peasant's minute payment to a public hospital orderly to ensure his seeing a doctor and a large firm's generous bribe to a politician in return for his fiddling with the tax laws to its advantage."[8] Although both acts might be equally illegal, and within our general understanding of the kinds of acts that corruption involves, we would hesitate to call them equally corrupt—if, indeed, the first is corrupt at all.

It is apparent that notions of illegality are far broader than notions of corruption. In addition, and at the other end of the spectrum, what is illegal may fail to capture what we (nevertheless) firmly believe to be corrupt conduct.

An interesting example of the latter is illustrated by an Associated Press article reporting corruption-fighting efforts in China. This article, entitled "China Plans Crackdown on Media:

The Government Says It Wants to Stop Fake Reporters Soliciting Bribes," states:

> China announced Wednesday that it would carry out a wide-ranging crackdown on "fake news" and illegal publications.
>
> The crackdown . . . appears aimed at ratcheting up the ruling Communist Party's already tight media controls. . . . The party tries to tightly control the media in China and is sensitive to any criticism of its grip on power. . . .
>
> China has also struggled with problems of manufactured news stories and people posing as journalists seeking payoffs to suppress bad news.
>
> . . . .
>
> The announcement Wednesday in the Party's main mouthpiece, the People's Daily, and on a government Web site said the campaign will be aimed at bogus reporters who take bribes to produce positive stories and suppress negative news.[9]

Whether or not "bogus reporters" have something akin to legally enforceable, official obligations to be evenhanded in China, it is beyond dispute that (short of libel, fraud, or other tortuous conduct) they do not here. Someone posing as a reporter and accepting money to "produce positive stories and suppress negative ones" would not be engaging in illegal conduct in the United States. Yet, the idea that such conduct is unethical—even corrupt—seems to ring true to us as well. Clearly, condemnations of corruption do not depend upon legal grounding for their feelings of authenticity.

Indeed, the inadequacy of illegality as the arbiter of corrupt conduct haunts those theorists who attempt to adhere to this conception of corruption. Consider, for instance, Scott's treatment of corruption and machine politics. At the outset, Scott states an intention to adhere to an understanding of corruption that is rooted in the breach of "formal" or legal norms.[10] When later discussing "electoral corruption" and machine politics, however, he includes rewards such as "local development programs, pork-barrel legislation, loan programs, and legal patronage" within the "corrupt" ambit.[11] He acknowledges that in most instances these rewards are not illegal. Indeed, the lack of identity between corrupt and illegal acts is predictable, since the goal of the political machine is to control the organs of government and to institutionalize the corruption the political machine bestows.[12] When the actual configurations of public corruption are considered, there are quite obviously corrupt acts that the law (as presently constituted) does not reach. Indeed, if—as Scott assumes in this passage—the corrupt can capture the machinery of government, and can bend the products of government (the law) to their will, it is apparent that we cannot depend upon the legal or illegal nature of conduct to identify what is or is not corrupt. We cannot expect corrupt actors, who control the levers of legislative and executive power, to condemn themselves. If corruption can *infect* the law, it follows, as a matter of logic, that "corruption" and "legal status" cannot be the same.

There is, in short, no guarantee that the law will condemn all corrupt conduct. Nor is there any guarantee that the law will—as a fundamental matter—implement the values in which the common condemnation of corruption lies.[13] Although we generally assume that the law implements broader ethical or moral notions, there is no necessary connection between legality and what other, broader ethical or moral notions prescribe—a connection that "corruption" seems to demand. Indeed, as we have seen, the law itself can originate in corrupt practices, making reliance on the law for the articulation of normative standards a flawed and hazardous enterprise.[14]

Put another way, although a judgment of illegality may be placed on what we believe to be corrupt conduct, it is not the *illegality itself* that makes the conduct corrupt. Rather, we have other, preexisting reasons for condemning this conduct—preexisting reasons that the idea of illegality does not, of itself, capture. The stamp of illegality, even criminal illegality, does not *define* corrupt conduct; it is simply a societally determined consequence for engaging in the conduct that we believe to be corrupt, on independent grounds. The strictures of the criminal law might be useful in expressing (for instance) our judgment that corrupt conduct is by nature intentional or serious, or that prosecutions for corruption should be governed by the rule of law. It is not, however, the fact of illegality itself that supplies these judgments.[15]

In summary, the idea of corruption-as-illegality "suffers from being simultaneously too narrow and too broad in scope; all illegal acts are not necessarily corrupt and all corrupt acts are not necessarily illegal."[16] The unrelated normative basis that this shell theory borrows—that of *illegal* conduct—does not, of itself, identify the essential nature of the corrupt transaction. Clearly, some additional understanding is necessary to identify what corruption is.

Corruption as the Breach of Duty

If corruption-as-illegality is inadequate, perhaps *corruption as the breach of duty* will more successfully identify what—in corruption cases—is publicly at stake. Perhaps, through the idea of breach of duty, we can identify the particular character of public corruption that the simple idea of illegality cannot provide.

The breach-of-duty conception of corruption is very common in the legal academic and political science literature; writers from across the ideological spectrum identify breach of duty as the essence of the corrupt act. Formulations include the "misuse of authority";[17] the "lack of integrity in the discharge of public duties";[18] deviation from the "accepted norms"[19] or the "formal duties"[20] of a public role; the "violation of socially accepted norms of duty and [social] welfare";[21] "violat[ion of] responsibility toward . . . [a] system of public or civic order";[22] and so on. Duties can involve both acts and omissions. As one commentator has framed it, it is the "common understanding that a public official is corrupt if he accepts money or money's worth for doing something that he is under a duty to do anyway, that he is under a duty not to do, or to exercise a legitimate discretion for improper reasons."[23]

This theory, in its most popular form, is a shell theory of corruption; this theory does not of itself determine what the duties in question are, or whether they have been breached. The core, normative judgments that this theory recognizes are independently established by laws, regulations, personnel handbooks, customs, interpersonal understandings, ethical standards, or other sources.

There are, however, several implicit characteristics that a corrupt breach of duty is assumed to involve. First, it is assumed that this must be more than simple failure to act or negligent behavior. If a public official fails to process applications, fails to vote, or otherwise fails to execute her public functions, such failures are not, simply of themselves, "corrupt." Nor is simple misfeasance in office congruent with corruption. An office holder who makes errors in the execution of her duties is not, by virtue of that behavior alone, "corrupt." There must be more: there must be, at the least, *intentional* misconduct. As Robert Brooks has emphasized, "[C]orruption is *intentional*. . . . Failure to meet a recognised duty is not necessarily corrupt. . . . The corrupt official must know the better and choose the worse."[24]

In addition, the breach of duty in question must be of a serious nature: trivial acts of misconduct, even if intentionally done, are not "corrupt." There is, as was noted above, a loathsome quality to corruption. The breach of duty must be one that arouses the strong societal condemnation that we intuitively feel to be a justified response to corrupt acts.

Finally, there is the additional requirement—expressed by many courts and commentators—that the breach of duty must involve self-dealing or personal gain, by the actor, at the public's expense.[25] For instance, one commentator states that corruption "is a general term covering misuse of authority as a result of considerations of personal gain, which need not be monetary."[26] Another states that an act is corrupt when it "deviates from the formal duties of a public role because of private-regarding (personal, close family, private clique) pecuniary or status gains; or violates rules against the exercise of certain types of private-regarding influence."[27]

Thus, under this theory, we have identified the following core of corrupt behavior: it is the breach of a duty owed to the public, of an intentional and serious nature, which involves—as the result of that breach—anticipated private gain.[28] Have we, through this formulation, successfully captured what corruption involves?

There is no doubt—when we consider bribery, extortion, embezzlement, and other forms of public corruption—that intentional, serious breaches of duties by public officials, motivated by private gain, are involved. It is apparent that this pattern of conduct is clearly—perhaps necessarily—involved in these examples of corruption. However, are these elements sufficient to capture its meaning?

There are in fact serious problems with this approach. Consider, for instance, the following examples of intentional, serious breaches of duty, which involve the reaping of private gain:

- A driver stopped for speeding pays a police officer $20 to avoid arrest.

- A government official expedites or prioritizes a friend's visa.

- In response to the administration's promise to delay implementation of new regulations, an industry trade group issues an endorsement of the president in her reelection campaign.

- A legislator, gratefully remembering a campaign contribution, listens with particular attention to that contributor's concerns.

- A city attorney conceals remodeling in her home from a tax assessor.

- The city treasurer exaggerates her medical condition, and remains on city-paid disability leave.

- A city employee calls in sick, and goes to a ball game.

All of these actions seem to fall within the ambit of the breach-of-duty theory, which includes the violation of legal, social, and organizational norms. Yet, our conclusion that all are "corrupt" is far less certain.[29] In some cases, this uncertainty may be due to unresolved questions in our understandings of the duties involved—for instance, our notions of proper or improper rewards to political supporters and contributors are notoriously confused.[30] In other cases, the problem seems to lie elsewhere. There is no doubt but that concealing information from a tax assessor, disability fraud, and cheating one's employer on sick days are clear violations of duties with serious economic consequences for the public fisc. These characteristics alone do not make these actions "corrupt," however. Whatever their wrongfulness, they do not seem to involve the kind of loathsomeness that we ordinarily associate with corrupt acts.

Indeed, the wrongfulness that the breach-of-duty theory involves may not—in its extreme form—involve ethical or moral wrongs at all. A breach of a public duty is a breach of established laws, regulations, or other rules of conduct established by those who wield the powers of government. Although one might wish to anchor these duties in broader notions of "right" or moral conduct, there is nothing in the idea of corruption as breach-of-duty that requires that linkage. As many writers have noted, such moralistic notions are, in fact, an additional gloss that the breach-of-duty model does not, of itself, involve.[31]

The indiscriminate sweep of the breach-of-duty theory should not surprise us, since this is, after all, a shell theory of corruption—one that simply borrows its understanding of prohibited (corrupt) acts from other sources. As was true of corruption-as-illegality, examined above, this shell theory simply uses as its normative core those laws, regulations, organizational and social rules, and other standards independently adopted by government or other powerful elites. As a result, corruption is, under this theory, simply "a disintegration of the belief system upon which a particular political system rests."[32] In some situations, the existing norms or duties prescribed by government or other power brokers might be congruent with the "good"; but in other situations, those norms or duties might be distinctly harmful to out-of-power groups, general economic goals, or other important interests. Under the breach-of-duty theory, corruption is simply "an extra-legal institution used by individuals or groups to gain influence over the actions [of government; it] . . . tells us nothing about the contents and effects of the policies so determined."[33]

Indeed, in some cases, the norms or duties that are transgressed might, from an ethical or moral point of view, be more worthy of condemnation than their breach.[34] For instance, the possibility of "good corruption"—that is, the breach of duties that involve harmful red tape, unjust rules, or ethically or morally unjust actions—arises under the breach-of-duty theory.[35] Such acts may be "good," in their effects, even if the actor involved pursues them for purely self-seeking ends. Although one could certainly conceptualize corruption in this way—as an intentional, serious breach of duty, which may have (as its effects) the taking of the economic, political, or moral high ground—this is not, in common usage, what we understand the word to mean. It is not "corruption" in this sense that fuels popular outrage or undermines regimes. By "corruption" we mean, as was previously stated, something that is powerful, insidious, and destructive of human lives and institutions. Because the norm that the breach-of-duty theory imports is a simple, transactional one, this shell theory fails to capture what corruption, in the common understanding, means.

In short, the idea of corruption as the intentional and serious breach of duty by a public servant seems to describe some of what corrupt acts involve, but it is not enough alone. The idea of breach of public duty is both more and less than the core concept. It is more in that it includes behavior that we do not, in fact, believe to be corrupt. It is less in that it fails to capture (at the least) the moral opprobrium or loathsomeness that we believe corruption to involve.

TRADITIONAL SUBSTANTIVE THEORIES

The failure of shell theories to capture the idea of corruption suggests that we need something more—something *substantive*—to successfully identify what corruption involves. Consider, for instance, traditional substantive theories that are commonly used (alone, or in combination with shell theories) to define corrupt acts. These theories are more bold than shell theories, in that they directly address the normative questions that shell theories avoid. Substantive theories define corruption as involving particular, substantive evils—evils that these theories, themselves, identify.

Corruption as Betrayal and Secrecy

The first and most common of the substantive theories is one that builds upon the breach-of-duty theory in the following way. Numerous commentators have observed that the breach-of-duty model, with (what we have called) its "shell" character, is inadequate alone to capture the essence of the corrupt act. In an effort to try to capture the particular, opprobrious nature of corruption, these commentators move to the idea of a *betrayal* of those whom an official serves. This is a substantive theory that uses the breach of a particular, substantive norm to identify the nature of the corrupt act. Under this theory, it is not enough that a public official (intentionally) acts in a way that is contrary to her sworn duty; this breach must be of a type that excites particular social condemnation. The public official must not simply disappoint us; she must *betray* us.[36] The idea of corruption-as-betrayal is reflected in such formulations as corruption as the "perversion"[37] or "abuse"[38] of power, or as the "exploitation" of power or leverage that legitimately belongs to someone else.[39]

Under this theory, the breaches of duty that corruption involves are particularly condemnatory because of the position of trust that public officials necessarily enjoy. It is asserted that the existence of trust, and its betrayal, is the core of corrupt conduct.[40] It is the particular nature of the trust relationship between the citizen and her legislator, or the citizen and her judge, which makes these relationships particularly crucial and their betrayal particularly heinous. The legislator, or the judge, or the agency administrator, is not simply someone who is doing a job; she is someone who wields tremendous power, and who, therefore, stands in a special, almost fiduciary relationship to the members of the public whom she serves. As a result, her intentional violation of those sworn duties is particularly condemnatory; she has *betrayed* those whose relative weakness and trust she has exploited.[41]

The idea of betrayal of trust by public officials does seem to tap into the moral or emotional reservoir that corruption evokes. With the addition of this idea, have we succeeded in capturing what corruption involves?

First, it must be observed that corruption-as-betrayal suffers, as a general matter, from the same inadequacies as the breach-of-duty theory upon which it is based. For instance, betrayal of trust, like breach of duty, is something that we would ordinarily assume to be morally condemnatory, but this is not necessarily so. Strictly speaking, one who betrays a trust is simply one who acts differently from the way that others had reason to expect. The "expectations or order" that the public duties and the instillation of trust were to uphold may be congruent with broader moral values, or they may not. We can imagine situations in which the betrayal of trust (in this sense) is morally condemnatory, and situations in which it is not.[42] For the betrayal of trust to always be of an opprobrious nature, we must elevate the idea of the honoring of trust *itself* to a morally iconic status—something that (in view of the fallibility of government) betrayal-of-trust theories are loath to do.

Indeed, the problems that are involved in the use of simple betrayal-of-trust notions to identify corruption are easily illustrated. We (the public) are victimized by all breaches of duties by public officials, whether (for instance) the official leaves work early to play golf or expedites building permits for her friends. In both cases, the trust that we have placed in that official is betrayed. Yet we would most likely label the first "annoying" or "unethical," and only the latter "corrupt." There is something more to corruption than knowledge of our weakness or the betrayal of trust by those whom we empower. These elements are involved in corrupt conduct—but we reserve the "corrupt" judgment for only a subset of these acts. Corruption is, in short, a *particular kind* of breach of duty; it is a *particular kind* of betrayal of trust.

In an effort to capture this further, elusive character of corruption, some corruption-as-betrayal theorists have added the idea of *treachery* or *secrecy* as an integral part of the corrupt transaction. For instance, the sociologist H. A. Brasz defines corruption as "the *stealthy exercise* of derived power" to the detriment of the public, "*under the pretence* of a legitimate exercise of that power."[43] He explains how "[t]hose who as subordinates, agents, and the like handle the affairs of principals are presumed to be and to act in good faith. If they sever the connection and enter into the service of a competitor or enemy of the principal they may, it is true, be branded as turncoats, but they are not guilty of corruption." Corruption requires, in addition, *"the treacherous venom of deceit, the pretence* of being absolutely loyal to the principal whilst in actual fact being intent on benefitting oneself and/or third parties." "The most essential characteristic of corruption is . . . the *furtive* exercise of formal authority and power under the pretence of legality."[44]

Indeed, this element of secrecy seems to figure prominently in our images of corrupt acts. As one commentator observes, the practical difference between campaign contributions and bribes may be that in the former, "parties openly espouse the ends which . . . contributors hope to achieve as a result of their largesse."[45] In one informal study, participants were confronted with a situation in which an industry announces that its most important goal is the defeat of a pending bill, and that it will support legislators if and only if they vote against it. When asked if this would be a bribe, many opined that it would not—presumably, at least in part, because of the seeming incongruity in finding corruption in open, aboveboard acts.[46] Similarly, a public official who openly announces her intention to deviate from her sworn duties may be condemned as a renegade or lawbreaker, but it is unlikely that she will be called corrupt.

Thus, corruption and secrecy seem to be intuitively linked. Upon deeper reflection, however, it is obvious that secrecy cannot be the critical element that we are missing. On the one hand, an otherwise innocent transaction, done in secret for privacy or other reasons, is not transformed—by reason of its secrecy—into a "corrupt" one. Conversely, as Daniel Lowenstein observes, "It would be anomalous [indeed] to conclude that an official with enough chutzpah to take bribes openly should thereby [be] . . . exempt from prosecution."[47] A breach of duty or betrayal of trust, done in secret, is (perhaps) quite likely to be corrupt. But although that setting may increase the odds that we are looking at a corrupt transaction, it is not in the idea of secrecy that we locate its loathsomeness.

Corruption as Inequality

A more sophisticated take on the role of secrecy in public corruption is presented by theorists who see the problem of secrecy (and corruption generally) in democratic-governance terms. Under this substantive theory, it is not secrecy qua secrecy that is the problem with corrupt acts; it is that secrecy is incompatible with the way that we expect democratic government to be conducted. In this view, "[t]ransactions between citizens and politicians [for example] can be judged corrupt when they subvert or circumvent a democratic process and its associated values of openness, equality, equity and accountability."[48] Secrecy, in this understanding, is important as an instrumental matter: it is important because it allows the subversion of the ideals of democratic governance, particularly, the *equal treatment of all citizens*. In other words, the secrecy or openness of the transaction can be a useful indicator of the presence or absence of corruption, because it is in the darkness of secrecy that the violation of democratic principles—particularly, the equal treatment of all citizens—thrives. As one commentator observes, "[D]emocracy depends on the accountability of public officials to citizens. . . . [Secret, corrupt transactions] violate[] the rules and procedures that are supposed to govern political life, giving rise to perceptions that the political system is basically unfair."[49]

The idea that inequality lies at the heart of corrupt public conduct has become increasingly prominent in academic commentary[50] and judicial opinions[51] in recent years. Under this approach, a hallmark of a liberal democratic system is the idea that all citizens are equal before the law. Corruption—whether bribery, extortion, kickbacks on public contracts, nepotism, or other acts—quintessentially involves the denial of this principle. The unifying core of corrupt conduct is that some citizens are afforded special access, deals, processes, or contracts[52]—or, in the case of extortion, the justice or other civil benefit guaranteed by law—for a price. Whether the corrupt act enables the citizen to obtain better than fair treatment, or simply fair treatment,[53] the bottom line is that the principle of equality of all before the law has been deliberately violated. As Tina Rosenberg describes it, "The doors of the bureaucracy close in the face of the poor; judges never rule against the wealthy and powerful; new entrepreneurs find it almost impossible to navigate huge bureaucracies and compete in a world of crony-dominated commerce."[54]

The observation that corrupt acts often involve a denial of equality seems to be a true one. If an individual engages in bribery, or extortion, or kickbacks, or nepotism, the character of the act—indeed, the *objective* of the act—is to obtain what others, obeying the rules, do not. Does this, however, successfully identify what corruption, as an idea, involves?

Upon closer analysis, a fundamental question haunts this theory: equality of what? It is apparent that the idea of simple equality—or equal treatment of similarly situated persons—is inadequate, itself, to distinguish corrupt from noncorrupt decisions or acts. In the political sphere, for instance, similarly situated persons are often not treated equally, for reasons that we accept. We do not demand that a legislator weigh every constituent's interest equally, or that every hiring decision for public employment employ no discretionary elements. Although there are settings in which we maintain the ideal that all similarly situated individuals receive scrupulously equal treatment before the law (for instance, in the meting out of criminal punishments), in most areas of political or public life we are considerably more tolerant.

When we speak of equal sentences for equal crimes, the idea of equality might be fairly straightforward. However, when we consider the more complex settings for corruption in government decision making, the simplicity and clarity of this idea rapidly disintegrates. For instance, equality in the political process might mean:

- *equal opportunity* to make one's case at crucial times and places;[55]

- *equal voice*, in the sense of the ability to be heard or the ability to influence, in the making of public policy;[56] or

- *equal outcomes*, in the sense of equal benefit from official policies.

Let us consider these possibilities. The first—*equal opportunity* to make one's case at crucial times and places—is the least demanding. Under this idea, a kind of "equal process" is required: citizens must be able to present their arguments, objections, and desires to government decision makers on equal terms. It draws heavily on the idea of corruption-as-secrecy: secret avenues and channels, available to some and not to others, are corrupt. The ability to petition government and to be heard must be freely, openly, and (thus) equally available to all.

Superficially, the idea of equal opportunity to make one's case seems unassailable. Indeed, we often enshrine this right, in the form of a guaranteed right to petition government, in constitutional or other foundational documents.[57] Our inquiry here, however, is not about the robustness of this democratic idea but about whether it usefully distinguishes corrupt from noncorrupt conduct.

When we consider this question, we find that the idea of equal opportunity falls short. Despite the power of this ideal, we do not, in fact, expect legislators, mayors, or other officials to spend equal time listening (in person) to each citizen or considering equally each citizen's written request. Nor do we expect all conversations that officials have with citizens to be public events, with open access to all. This is true even if the official is motivated by favoritism, the receipt of campaign contributions, or other personal reasons. The denial of equal opportunity or equal access has not risen to this level, with regard to the executive or legislative branches of government. If an official has lunch with a particular constituent, or affords lobbyists special access, we might *suspect* that something corrupt is going on, but it is not the inequality in access or the secrecy of the communication that is, *itself*, the corruption. It is, perhaps, a fertile setting for a corrupt act; but that corrupt act is something else.

If we consider the judicial branch of government, the formal requirement of open and equal access is much stronger. Judicial rules generally prohibit ex parte contacts with judges, and the opportunities for presentation and response are elaborately orchestrated. A judge's violation of these rules would risk rebuke, or stronger sanctions. Violation of equal opportunity, in this context, seems unfair. However, a judgment of *corruption* from this violation is another question. A judge's engagement in an ex parte contact, or other violation of the rules of equal access, would clearly breach a duty—but would it be corrupt?

Although the question is a close one, I do not believe that— on the basis of that act alone—the appellation would apply. The question is close because the *ethical* obligations that such rules enforce are, in a sense, *moral* obligations, and it is with morality that corruption deals. However, the moral transgression that violation of such rules involves seems, of itself, to be far more trivial than the moral transgressions that are associated with corruption. Again, it would seem that such rules are more concerned with prevention of a setting in which corruption might occur, than with the direct proscription of corruption itself. The second possibility listed above—that of *equal voice*, in the sense of the ability to be heard or the ability to influence, in the making of public policy—is more demanding. Here we are saying that officials must not only afford citizens equal access: they must also afford citizens *equal influence*. This principle would seem to underlie the common belief (for instance) that disproportionate influence of "special interests" is corrupt.

Although equal voice might be an ideal that is defensible in certain circumstances (for instance, "one man—one vote"), it is quickly apparent that this cannot be a general test for acceptable political decision making or for distinguishing corrupt and noncorrupt conduct. For many reasons, citizens will have differing abilities to influence government policy—reasons that range from their personal stake in the matter, to the intelligence of their views, to the numbers of citizens who share their positions. Surely, the mere fact that Citizen A had more influence than Citizen B in the making of public policy is not, of itself, corrupt. More is required—some other theory of duties, politics, morality, or what have you—to identify the essence of the corrupt transaction.

The final possibility above—that of *equal outcomes*, in the sense of equal benefits from political policies—is an even more extreme demand, and suffers from similar objections. The achievement of equal outcomes for all citizens as the result of government policies is not something that government can possibly guarantee. Nor is its absence a reliable test for the presence of corruption. Just as we would hesitate to label a lawmaker's failure to give all parties equal influence "a corrupt act," we would clearly not label a political or judicial process that produces unequal benefit "a corrupt public policy."[58]

What is missing in all of these equality theories is an underlying understanding of what democratic or representative government *substantively* guarantees. As Robert Williams has written, determining corrupt conduct "forces us to say something about the character of politics"—something about "our general sense of what is politically legitimate."[59] Whether we view unequal opportunity, voice, or outcomes as corrupt or noncorrupt will depend upon complicated questions of political theory, such as whether we see legislators as simple implementers of constituents' desires or as trustees bound to exercise independent judgment for the broader public good.[60] Corruption, under equality theories, is the subversion of the political process. We must know what the political process guarantees before we can begin to determine what corrupt acts are. The simple notion of equality does not answer such questions.

The use of equality as the "corrupt" touchstone, in legislative and executive contests particularly, is troubled on another ground. Although we tend to endorse equality in the political process, we tolerate—indeed, celebrate—the existence of material inequality, which (in turn) exacerbates the political inequality that we condemn. Greater wealth means greater opportunities for financial support of candidates and causes, more social, political, and economic connections, and greater ability to broker power in the halls of government—leading inevitably to inequality in opportunity, voice, and outcomes. If equality is our test, why aren't influence and power obtained through wealth the products of corruption? "Equality" in opportunity, voice, and outcomes provides no answer.

Before we leave equality theories, we must consider one more argument in their favor. Although the idea of corruption-as-inequality might be hopelessly simplistic in policy-making contexts, perhaps it is more useful when simple, administrative acts by public officials are involved. If the official's duty is simply to administer or enforce an existing law, there is less room for deliberate, disparate treatment of similarly situated individuals. For instance, we might know, in the case of bureaucratic corruption, what the rules are and, as a consequence, when illegitimate, unequal treatment has certainly occurred.[61] In other words, when the ideal of equality is considered, favoritism by the import-duties collector must be distinguished from favoritism by national legislators.[62]

Before we become too enthusiastic about this proposition, we must first acknowledge that the distinction between administering the law and creating the law is a notoriously difficult one. Arguably, few bureaucratic acts involve the mechanical application of the law to facts, with no discretionary or interpretive elements. Although not "lawmaking" in a formal sense, the argument for citizen "input" and influence in many bureaucratic decisions might be every bit as strong as in the traditional legislative arena.

Still, we can surely identify *some* acts, in the administrative arena, to which individuals are entitled on an equal basis. For instance, the processing of a foreign visitor's visa should not depend upon political influence or the payment of "speed money" to the consular official involved. Our instinctive outrage at such corruption of the administrative process is illustrated by the scandal involving David Blunkett, Britain's former top law enforcement officer. Blunkett resigned after acknowledging that his department had fast-tracked a residence visa for a Filipina nanny employed by his former lover, American magazine publisher Kimberly Clark. Although his personal role in the administrative action was unclear, Blunkett resigned, stating that "any perception of this application being speeded up requires me to take responsibility."[63]

Press accounts of the affair were harsh. For example, one commentator wrote that "[u]ntil now, . . . most people in this country . . . believed the [visa] process was generally objective and fair. Now we know different." "[T]his is, or rather was, the Home Secretary speaking; the Home Secretary of a country which rightly prides itself on the low level of corruption in public life." "Think . . . of a Britain in which you had to place a £20 note in your passport before negotiating the green channel at customs, a Britain in which your neighbor could buy passports . . ., a Britain where every entitlement was actually a favour with a price."[64]

Thus, in the realm of visa processing, at least, the notion of equal treatment by government seems very straightforward. Consider, however, the following colloquy, as recently reported on National Public Radio:

Melissa Block, host: Heightened security since 2001 has made it harder for foreigners to visit the United States. Musicians are especially hard-hit because they have to get a new visa every time they tour the US. They say the visa bureaucracy has become burdensome and expensive. NPR's Martin Kaste reports from Rio de Janeiro.

Martin Kaste, reporting: Standing outside the Sao Paulo Airport, Brazilian artistic manager Ana Buono is in a panic.

. . . .

Kaste: Bad weather has delayed the flight of her 68-year-old client, internationally known jazz musician Hermeto Pasqual. Now that he's finally here, they have to race to get to the US consulate in time for their visa appointment.

. . . .

Kaste: As their cab breaks multiple traffic laws, Buono and Pasqual go over the paperwork one last time. If he and the other band members miss their appointment, they'll also miss their concert date at Lincoln Center in three days. Ana says that the visas often come through at the last possible minute. Her booking agent in California, Bill Smith, says he can never be sure the visas will be ready in time for a concert. . . .

. . . .

Kaste: The [Department of Homeland Security] refuses to take phone calls about visa petitions, even from a desperate booking agent. Smith says when he has a big concert planned, the only way to get some peace of mind is to write a check.

Smith: You're forced to use the defense mechanism of spending a thousand dollars to ensure that you'll get an answer within 15 days so that the tour can happen.

Kaste: The thousand dollars is the so-called premium processing fee which moves a visa into a special fast track. . . .

Back in Brazil, manager Ana Buono says she found this shocking.

Buono (through translator): I said, "Wow, I thought it was just here in Brazil where you have to pay people under the table to get things done."[65]

Indeed, if we dig more deeply, we find that "speed money" and immigration processing are routinely and publicly linked. During a recent trip to England, I noticed a "Fast Track" line for immigration at London's Heathrow Airport. Who was entitled to this, I asked? The answer: this preferred government service was reserved for those who arrived on first-class airline tickets. In the Raleigh-Durham Airport in the United States, a special security checkpoint for departing passengers (manned by Transportation Security Administration personnel) was reserved for "First Class, Business Class, and Advantage Gold and Platinum" passengers. The United States State Department advertises "expedited service" for obtaining a U.S. passport for an additional $60.00.

The payment of speed money for the performance of bureaucratic tasks is as roundly condemned as corrupt in the United States as it is in Britain. No one in the United States would expect to slip a $100 bill with court papers to be filed, or slip a $1,000 check with visa papers to speed up their processing. Yet, preferential treatment for those who pay more is not only tolerated, as noncorrupt—it is entrenched and formalized in law. The idea that unequal treatment of similarly situated individuals is corrupt is confounded by these cases.

One could attempt to rationalize the situation by refining one's idea of equality; perhaps the operative idea is not equality of *treatment* (outcome) but rather equality of *opportunity*. Because the option to pay speed money is provided by law, the democratic principle of equal treatment by government is preserved: anyone who seeks special treatment, and is willing to pay for it, is entitled to it.

Is this the kind of "equality" that the theory of corruption-as-inequality envisions? Is the concern with "inequality," which corruption evokes, assuaged if there is equal opportunity to seek special favors, pay speed money, and the like? It may be, if the special treatment is relatively easily obtainable by anyone—for instance, if anyone who asks is granted special dispensation, or if the amount of speed money required is small enough to be easily paid. If, however, the published criteria for special favors specify personal (otherwise irrelevant) characteristics, or the amount of speed money (such as $1,000 for an expedited visa) is clearly beyond a nominal gesture, it is difficult to see how equality, in any meaningful sense, is afforded. Indeed, if "equal opportunity" (regardless of individuals' available resources) is the criterion for noncorrupt conduct, there is no reason to condemn bribery, which is the most universally condemned corrupt act. Bribery is, after all, an "equal opportunity" crime. As one commentator has written, "In a strict sense, bribery is a *quid-pro-quo* on *comparatively* free and equal (if illicit) terms."[66] Presumably, all individuals are equally able to offer a bribe and to obtain the benefits that the bribee has to offer. If denial of equal opportunity is the core idea for corrupt conduct, there is no reason to indict the briberous system or the briberous act.

Thus, we are left with a conundrum. The idea of inequality seems to be associated clearly with the idea of corruption. It seems to be particularly important in the identification of the deficiencies in the governmental system—unequal treatment, access, influence—that corrupt acts by public servants so often involve. However, simple political inequality—whether in opportunity, voice, or outcomes—does not, by itself, identify corrupt conduct. We do not condemn, *as corrupt*, all unequal opportunities to make one's case, or all unequal voice in the making of public policy, or all unequal outcomes in the sense of benefits from official policies. Nor do we applaud, *as noncorrupt*, all situations in which equal opportunity to obtain bureaucratic services or influence government decision making is afforded. Although we might say that inequality is often *the result* of much of what we believe to be corrupt conduct, it is, of itself, of little help in identifying what corruption, as an idea, involves.

Public-Interest Theories

The problems with other substantive theories—particularly, the absence of adequate grappling with the normative ideas that associate betrayal, secrecy, or inequality with corruption—have led some theorists to advocate an understanding of corruption that is both substantive and boldly normative. This approach "explicit[ly] and simply assert[s] that corruption involves the subversion of the public interest."[67] For instance, Arnold Rogow and Harold Lasswell wrote that "[a] corrupt act violates responsibility toward at least one system of public or civic order and is in fact incompatible with (destructive of) any such system."[68]

The core notion here is that there is a public or citizenry which has distinct interests, and that those interests are damaged by private-regarding (corrupt) conduct. Self-seeking behavior, under this approach, may have personal or factional goals;[69] the important idea is that the public interest is sacrificed in favor of the personal interests of the corrupt actor or others of her choice.

A public-interest theory of corruption could be conceptualized as a shell theory or as a substantive one. If the former, a public-interest theory of corruption would simply assert that corruption "involves the subversion of the public interest," without advancing any particular idea of what that public interest is. Understood this way, a public-interest theory of corruption would offer little more than other shell theories, such as corruption-as-illegality and corruption-as-breach-of-duty, and would be subject to the same critiques. If, on the other hand, it is the latter—if the public-interest theory of corruption includes a substantive idea of the public interest, as an integral part of its understanding—then it is more interesting. It also promises to drive closer to the central issue: that corruption involves "bad conduct" in a deeply evaluative sense.

How effective is a substantive public-interest theory of corruption in capturing what we believe the idea of corruption to intrinsically involve? Put another way, does a public-interest theory of corruption of this type identify the deeper, normative ideal that corruption intuitively transgresses, and that the prior theories that we have discussed have failed, so far, to adequately identify?

To grapple with this question, we must examine, more closely, what this theory's substantive idea of the public interest is. If the public interest is simply viewed as *an interest*, "develop[ed] pragmatically from the conflict among contending . . . interests,"[70] then this public-interest theory has advanced us little. As so imagined, the public interest has no necessary grounding in or congruence with any moral notion, something that we have identified as important to articulating the corrupt core.

It is possible, however, to imagine the public interest in different terms—for instance, "as an ethical imperative . . ., some superior standard of rational and 'right' political wisdom."[71] If we understand "the public interest" to be some kind of transcendent notion, then the problem of moral invocation or moral grounding is solved. The precise nature of this transcendent notion may be problematic, since there is no guarantee that members of a governing elite, let alone all government actors or all citizens, will share a common view of what this public interest is, in any situation.[72] (Indeed, one could argue, the "public interest" is an essentially derivative normative idea, requiring resort to other theories—e.g., government, economics, morality, or equality.) It is perhaps because of this problem that analysts who utilize a public-interest theory of corruption rarely consider, in any depth, what that public interest is. However, it is certainly conceivable that one could adopt a particular, normative idea of what this is.

So, does a public-interest theory of this type solve our problem? Does it capture what corruption, as an idea, involves? In fact, we find that inadequacies remain. Like legally based theories, trust-based theories, and others discussed above, a public-interest theory of this type captures *more* than corrupt conduct in some cases, and *less* than corrupt conduct in others. As Scott observed, "[W]e can imagine many acts we would commonly call corruption—e.g., placing destitute immigrants illegally on the city payroll—that could be considered in the public interest, just as we can imagine acts against the public interest—e.g., the legislative creation of tax loopholes for the very rich—which, however much they smack of favoritism, are not commonly seen as corrupt."[73] Indeed, substantial arguments can be (and have been) made that the public interest may sometimes *require* practices that are generally believed to be corrupt. For instance, bribes and other payoffs might be the justified means for assimilating new groups into the existing political system,[74] or the way to circumvent bureaucracy in the service of economic entrepreneurs.[75] Although—once again—violation of the public interest often seems to be involved in corruption, it does not seem to be enough, alone, to identify its core.

Corruption as Abuse of Power

In a recent analysis, Franklin Zimring and David Johnson advance an understanding of corruption that uses elements previously discussed, but with a distinctive twist. The distinguishing feature of corruption, they argue, is the *abuse of institutional power*.[76] Corruption is not simply the violation of a norm (established by law), although a violation of that kind is required.[77] Nor is it the pursuit of such acts for personal gain or other personal objectives, although that is also required.[78] Rather, the distinguishing characteristic of corruption is its institutional context: it is the use of institutional power, in violation of law, for personal aims.[79]

In some ways this is a shell theory of corruption, since the bad (corrupt) nature of acts depends upon whether they are "unlawful as a matter of law of the place where the behaviour occurs."[80] This is the way that Zimring and Johnson "separate corrupt behaviour from permissible discretionary acts."[81] For instance, the authors specify that "the meanings of the key terms in the definition [of bribery]—inducement, improperly, duty, and so on—cannot be discerned independently of the law and norms of a particular place."[82] From this point of view, this theory is contentless: externally determined, "local" norms determine what is or is not corrupt.[83] Thus, in Zimring and Johnson's view, "an act is corrupt if it is prohibited by laws and if it is not prohibited, it is not corrupt, even if it is unethical or abusive."[84] "Only a legal standard can provide a definition of corruption that qualifies both analytically and morally as a crime."[85]

In another, deeper sense, however, this abuse-of-power theory is distinctively normative. There is a working conception, entwined with this theory, that "abuse of power" (as defined above) is bad, and identifiable for that reason. For instance, corrupt acts include those when a "government official charged with selecting the most qualified firm to provide trash collection to the city instead selects the firm that offers him the most money in a personal bribe . . .; [when] the schoolteacher with the power to assign grades on a merit basis . . . instead trades high grades for cash or personal favours . . .; . . . [when] the president of a nation grants public licenses . . . to his friends and family rather than auctioning them off and making the proceeds available to the common good"; and so on.[86] These acts are characterized as corrupt not only because they are unauthorized; they are corrupt because they are "socially wasteful."[87]

In addition, and most interestingly, there is a normative dimension to the idea of abuse of power that this theory introduces. There is an image, in the idea of an abuse of power, of "the strong . . . prey[ing] on the weak,"[88] with "power becom[ing] the instrument of criminality."[89] This theory's focus on an institutional setting, in which an inherently powerful individual abuses her power through "use[] of force,"[90] invokes substantive ideas of oppression, overreaching, and otherwise undesirable power arrangements.

This theory is useful and unique in its focus on institutional aspects of public corruption. When one is attempting to define public corruption, the institutional setting is perhaps obvious—a public official is someone who, after all, is acting in an institutional role. However, the abuse-of-power theory contributes more than this. It illuminates what this role may mean for the nature of the corrupt act. Corruption, in this setting, is likely more than an official acting in an unauthorized way—there is a cast of personal coercion and exploitative abuse of power that is often a part of corrupt acts.

Does this theory, therefore, identify the "essence" of corruption? Its insight that public corruption has deep, institutional roots is keen. It identifies useful elements that are in accordance with our intuitions of what corrupt acts often involve. As with the theories before it, however, something more is needed to complete the picture. A government actor can use her power to do something that is illegal, self-serving, and exploitative, and still not be involved in corrupt conduct. Consider, for instance, an official who unlawfully harasses or penalizes subordinates, or who whimsically refuses to serve particular members of the public for her own twisted, personal ends. Such an abuse of power would seem to be far from "objectively trivial,"[91] and thus within this theory's corrupt ambit; yet such acts, however undesirable or oppressive, would not likely be deemed "corrupt" under the common understanding of the term. Nor, in the other direction, are illegality and exploitative conduct necessarily a part of all corrupt transactions. As a bottom line, we might say that abuse of power (of some sort) is a part of all public corruption; but beyond this general statement, we have progressed only partially in our endeavor to identify the nature of the corrupt core.

ECONOMIC THEORIES

In recent years, some commentators have turned to the use of economic theories as a way to understand corruption. Economic theories generally fall into two categories, as described below.

Corruption as the Rectification of Market Failure, or as the Reallocation of Undesirable Power Arrangements

Under one set of economic theories, "corrupt acts" are identified in explicitly value-neutral and market-oriented terms. Under this model, public and private (including "corrupt") interests are simply conflicting claims that are mediated through legal and nonlegal market mechanisms. When legal schemes fail to reflect market pressures and realities, nonlegal ("corrupt") transactions serve to reestablish the appropriate market equilibrium.[92]

A classic example of this approach can be found in the work of Benson and Baden. Governments, they argue, operate by assigning, reassigning, modifying, or attenuating property rights.[93] Property rights are "'the sum of economic and social relations with respect to scarce resources in which individual members [of the community] stand to each other.'"[94] When individuals are confronted by the property-rights scheme that government has created, they can respond in one of four ways. They can "accept the given structure of rights as defined by the public sector and thereafter acquire and dispose of resources through voluntary transfers."[95] They can lobby government "in an effort to influence . . . [the alteration of] the rights."[96] They can "resort to theft."[97] Or they can "obtain[] a rights modification that, in a sense, combines theft and governmental influence: a rights modification can be purchased from a corrupt government official who is endowed with appropriate discretionary control."[98]

Thus corruption, under this model, is a kind of "underground" or "black" market that arises "when the institutional structure precludes private owners from allocating their resources in a competitive [way]."[99] As Robert Tilman observes, modern bureaucracies often implement what is, in effect, a form of the mandatory pricing model of market economics.[100] When there is a serious disequilibrium between the supply (of bureaucratic goods) and demand, the centralized allocative mechanism, which is the ideal of modern bureaucracy, may break down. That breakdown is corruption.[101]

Interestingly, the shell theory of corruption-as-illegality is crucial here: the acts that are deemed to be "corrupt" under this model are those that are not permitted by the governing legal order.[102] However, illegality is given no operational or normative significance beyond that simple statement. There is nothing that makes the legally sanctioned system of rights superior, in any moral or normative sense, to any other.[103] Corrupt acts, qua corrupt acts, are neither good nor bad; they are simply the manifestation of interests, which are equal—in any normative sense—to any other interests in the competitive sea. As Nathaniel Leff (a famous proponent of this view) writes, "Corruption is an extra-legal institution used by individuals or groups to gain influence over the . . . bureaucracy. As such, the existence of corruption *per se* indicates only that these groups participate in the decision-making process to a greater extent than would otherwise be the case."[104] Indeed, it is because of the undesirability of the legally sanctioned system—that is, its inefficiency—that a system of underground "rights modification" (corruption) has arisen.[105]

The fundamental theoretical contribution of this theory—that corruption may, in fact, have positive economic, social, or political outcomes—was a revolutionary insight in its time, even if controversial and now largely discredited.[106] From the point of view of understanding the *idea* of corruption, however, this theory adds little. The idea of corruption expressed in this theory is simply a restatement of the idea of corruption-as-illegality or corruption-as-breach-of-duty, theories whose inadequacies were exposed above. The uniqueness of this theory lies not in its unique definition of corruption but in its unique understandings of the consequences of corrupt acts. Indeed, this economic theory is—if anything—*less* congruent with the common understanding of corruption that we are exploring, since any notion of moral opprobrium (as the result of illegality or breach of duty) is, under these theories, disassociated from the corrupt act. As a matter of empirical fact, corruption might well be seen as simply "illegal" acts, which can positively rectify market failure and otherwise circumvent undesirable laws. This model, however, captures none of the essential moral outrage that we associate with corrupt acts.

Normative Economic Theories

Other theorists employ economic ideas to develop distinctly normative understandings of corruption. Under these theories, the first step is the identification of corruption with rent seeking. For instance, Jacob van Klaveren writes that "corruption means that a civil servant abuses his authority in order to obtain an extra income from the public." "Thus we will conceive of corruption in terms of a civil servant who regards his public office as a business, the income of which he will . . . seek to maximize. The office then becomes a 'maximizing unit.' "[107]

Corruption, thus, is defined as personal rent seeking by government officials in derogation of their duties to their principals (higher officials, the public) as established by law.[108] Such theorists acknowledge that rent seeking might be a positive or useful phenomenon in this context, since it may allow productive activities that existing laws or other public duties do not allow.[109] These theories, however, carry a distinctly normative imprint. From an economic point of view, rent seeking or corruption inevitably "introduce[s] costs and distortions. . . . [I]t encourages excessive public infrastructure investment . . . [and] discourages legitimate business investment."[110] In addition, proponents of these theories accept the idea that the rule of law is, itself, of great societal value, and that the delegitimation of government rules that corruption involves carries its own overwhelming costs.[111]

Do these normative economic theories capture the essence of corruption, in a way that other theories miss? They definitely recognize the opprobrious or loathsome nature of corruption, as it is generally understood. This brings them closer to the corrupt idea in a way that (for instance) corruption-as-rectification-of-market-failure does not. However, in what is this idea of the opprobrious or loathsome nature of corruption rooted? Do these theories successfully identify the nature of the corrupt core?

To the extent that these theories rely upon illegality—itself—as the idea of corruption, they add little that is new. When individuals disobey the law, there are clearly costs to those legal rules and to the government that implements them. We might even believe that disobedience is "bad," in a moral sense, if our moral scheme demands it. The "bad" that is associated with general lawbreaking, however, is not at all necessarily congruent with the "bad" associated with corruption. As we established above, not all lawbreaking is corrupt, and not all corruption involves lawbreaking. Although the idea of costs to government veers more closely to interests that are the essence of corruption, it is not *illegality* that identifies the corrupt core.

Let us consider, in the alternative, the economic bases on which these theories rest. The idea that individuals pursue their own interests—that they are driven by the desire to maximize their own interests—obviously does not distinguish corrupt from noncorrupt behavior. Under normative economic theories, self-interest motivates all human behavior, corrupt and noncorrupt alike. Not all self-interested actions are "bad" or "inefficient," let alone corrupt. Rather, theorists maintain that corrupt actions involve a failure to channel self-interest toward appropriate or "productive" ends.[112]

How, then, do we determine whether particular exercises of self-interest are appropriate or productive? Normative economic theorists suggest that it is the efficiency of those actions that is the crucial criterion. For instance, Susan Rose-Ackerman acknowledges that identifying corruption is difficult—"[o]ne person's bribe is another person's gift."[113] Her aim "is not to set a universal standard for where to draw the legal line between praiseworthy gifts and illegal and unethical bribes."[114] She does, however, aspire to identify, through the lens of economic efficiency, "the factors that should go into the choice."[115]

The idea that the efficiency of corrupt acts should be considered in policy making is an obviously useful one. We should be reluctant, for whatever reason, to ignore economic costs. However, is the efficiency or inefficiency of particular acts truly useful in identifying their corrupt or noncorrupt nature? After even cursory reflection, it is apparent that this idea falls short. Certainly all inefficient actions are not corrupt as "corruption" is generally understood.

Actions by government actors can be incompetent, wasteful, market thwarting, or otherwise inefficient, and not be necessarily corrupt. By the same token, corrupt actions are not *necessarily* undertaken for financial gain,[116] and are not *necessarily* inefficient.[117] An official could break the law and grant a special favor to his brother, with 1) no economic payoff for that official and 2) the achievement of greater "efficiency" for other, specified government ends. In short, although financial distortions and inefficiency may characterize many corrupt acts, and although they may be reasons why we condemn corrupt acts, we cannot capture the root idea of corruption in purely economic terms.

For those economic theories that retain the idea of corrupt acts as a meaningful one, something is needed beyond the ideas of self-interest and efficiency, ideas with which economic analysis is generally concerned. Neither self-interest nor inefficiency engenders the outrage or destructive power that corruption charges involve. There must be some other normative ideal that corrupt, self-interested, inefficient actions violate (and that noncorrupt, self-interested, and inefficient actions do not). For some economic-corruption theorists, this normative baseline is provided by "illegality";[118] for others, it is provided by "breach of duty."[119] In every case, however, "[t]o be able to point to those cases of interest/income maximising which are also politically corrupt, one has to appeal to constructions of public office and the public-interest which draw on norms and values which are external to the market model."[120]

Economics is, in short, a limited tool for the analysis of corruption. Economic theories may be a way to explain the incidence of and effects of corruption; but they do not—of themselves—provide any new or unique way to identify the corrupt act. To the extent that economic theories retain the idea of corruption as a distinct social, political, or moral phenomenon, they presume the existence of other, unrelated norms that corrupt acts transgress. As a result, economic theories—while interesting—do not get us closer to understanding what corruption, as an essential idea, is.

COMBINATION THEORIES

We have found that although traditional understandings often seem to capture particular elements of corruption, none succeeds in capturing the totality of the idea as it is commonly understood. Although violation of law, breach of duty, betrayal of trust, secrecy, inequality, and inefficiency are often characteristics of corrupt acts, none of these theories successfully distinguishes corrupt acts from noncorrupt ones. We have no basis, under these theories, to distinguish violations of law that are corrupt from ones that are not, or breaches of duty that are corrupt from ones that are not, and so on. Corruption, as a unitary concept, has some additional meaning that is at work in these cases. None of these theories captures that meaning.

Before we leave traditional theories, there is another possibility to be considered. Taken individually, these theories are inadequate; but perhaps if taken in combination rather than singly they might more successfully express what we believe corruption to mean.

Some theorists have actively embraced this idea. For instance, Mark Philp offers what might be called a "combination theory." He states:

> We can recognise political corruption where:
>
> 1. a public official ("A")
> 2. in violation of the *trust* placed in him by the public ("B")
> 3. and in a manner which harms the *public interest*,
> 4. knowingly engages in conduct which *exploits* the office for clear *personal and private gain* in a way which runs contrary to the *accepted rules and standards* for the conduct of public office within the political culture,
> 5. so as to benefit a third party ("C") by providing "C" with access to a good or service "C" would not otherwise obtain.[121]

Another, more elaborate combination theory is offered by Syed Hussein Alatas, who argues that corruption has the following characteristics:

(a) a *betrayal* of trust;

(b) *deception* of a public body, private institution, or society at large;

(c) deliberate *subordination of common interests* to *specific interests;*

(d) *secrecy* of execution . . .;

(e) the involvement of more than one person or party;

(f) the presence of mutual obligations and benefits, in pecuniary or other forms;

(g) the focusing of attention on those who want definite decisions and those who can *influence* them;

(h) the attempt to *camouflage* the corrupt act by some form of lawful justification; and

(i) the expression of a *contradictory dual function* by those committing the acts.[122]

These theories combine betrayal of trust, secrecy, subordination of the public interest, illegality, and breach of duty. All of these must be present before an act is "corrupt." Do these elements, in combination, successfully express what we believe corruption to involve?

When we consider the problem of the overinclusivity of traditional theories, the layering of requirements in this way is helpful. We do not mean—by "corruption"—the violation of any law, or the breach of any duty, or the subversion of any public interest; we mean only those violations, breaches, or subversions that involve (for instance) secrecy, betrayal, and self-dealing. Since all of these characteristics are associated with corrupt conduct, requiring their simultaneous fulfillment will obviously, and helpfully, narrow the identification of acts within our net.

However, do such combination theories eliminate the larger problem? Although we have presumably reduced the number of acts identified by these overlapping requirements, we still lack a way to distinguish—within that universe—corrupt from noncorrupt conduct. For instance (to use Philp's theory) there are certainly fewer acts that violate the law or other public "rules and standards," harm the public interest, and involve a breach of trust, for personal gain, than that simply have one of these characteristics alone. Yet not all acts that share these characteristics are corrupt. To paraphrase a previous example, a healthy government employee could call in sick or feign disability, and thereby violate applicable rules and standards, harm the public interest, and breach the public trust, all for personal gain—but we would not, in the absence of other conduct, consider the action to be "corrupt."

We could add other elements to this combination theory to make it more robust: for instance, we could additionally require that the act involve secrecy, inequality (of some kind), and/or inefficiency. However, for all of those cases where these elements will help to narrow the field, and target (what we believe to be) corrupt conduct, they will, in other cases, create problems of *under*inclusivity, by excluding acts (such as overt bribes, "equal" bribing opportunities, and "efficient" bribes) that we nonetheless believe to be corrupt.

The bottom line is this. Combination theories can be seen, in a sense, as kaleidoscopic presentations of traditional theories: the elements can be combined and recombined in complex combinations that are far richer or more exacting than those elements alone. The fundamental problem, however, remains. Corruption is more than illegality, breach of duty, betrayal, secrecy, inequality, the subversion of the public interest, and inefficiency, whether these elements are considered alone or together. Traditional theories, whether shell or substantive, alone or in combination, fail to account for significant and substantial aspects of prevailing beliefs and intuitions about what the idea of corruption is. Put another way, although all of these theories identify elements that are often important characteristics of corrupt acts, they are not *the essence* of corruption—they are not, alone or in combination, all that composes the corrupt core.

So far, the traditional theories that we have examined (whether shell theories, substantive theories, or economic theories) attempt to identify the acts—or characteristics of acts—that constitute corruption. They attempt, through the identification of these acts, to identify the necessary and sufficient conditions for a judgment that corruption has occurred. When these conditions are met, and *only* when these conditions are met—"if and only if"—corruption has occurred.

We have found that in this enterprise, the traditional theories fail. None of them specifies a consistent set of characteristics that corrupt acts (and only corrupt acts) share.

There are two responses that one could make to this situation. First, one could argue that the problem with these theories is not their substance but that they have, methodologically, set too high a bar. There is (perhaps) no particular set of characteristics that is a part of *all* behavior that we believe to be corrupt. Rather, it is possible that acts we deem to be corrupt are united only by a family resemblance—for instance, they share certain similar (but not identical) characteristics, or there are overlapping characteristics that are shared by some but not by all. For instance, we might conclude that kickbacks are corrupt because they are similar to bribery, whose status as "corrupt" is beyond question. Or we might believe that although secrecy is a common, identifying characteristic of some examples of corrupt conduct, personal gain is the common element for others.

This argument might well be true in a descriptive sense. For instance, we might imagine "illegal" and "corrupt" conduct in the schematic way shown in Figure 1.

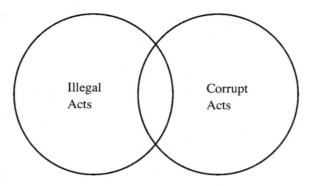

Figure 1

This would illustrate that some illegal conduct is corrupt, and vice versa, but that the overlap is partial at best.

Then, we could superimpose the idea of "breach of duty" as shown in Figure 2.

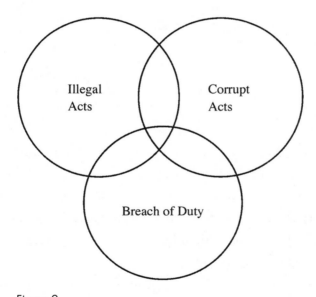

Figure 2

This would illustrate that some conduct that is a breach of duty is illegal, some is corrupt, and some is both illegal *and* corrupt; and some is neither illegal nor corrupt.

Then, we could attempt to superimpose the idea of betrayal as shown in Figure 3.

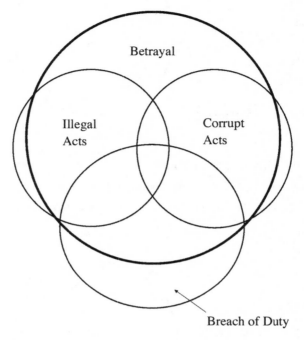

Figure 3

This would illustrate that some betrayals are illegal, some are corrupt, some are a breach of duty, and some are *all* of these; and some are none of these.

We could go on, adding more and more of the elements that the traditional theories identify, and generating more and more complex schematic drawings.

However, what would we accomplish? Making our aspirations for identified, required commonalities in corrupt acts less ambitious would undoubtedly increase the chances that those commonalities would be found. However, we have not, through this approach, advanced any farther in our understanding of what corruption—as an idea—is. To put it another way, these diagrams do not tell us what places particular behavior within the "corrupt" circle—an essential demarcation that exists apart from the other, particular characteristics (illegality, breach of duty, betrayal, and so on) that corrupt behavior might or might not also share. We are still, under these approaches, using *some additional, unarticulated* notion of corruption in our choices of acts for comparison, or in our choices of characteristics that signal the presence of corrupt acts. We do not know what deeper idea unifies these intuitions, or composes the corrupt core.

The second, more plausible reason for the failure of traditional theories is that *the idea of corruption involves additional substance that these theories simply do not capture*. It is this deeper reason that I believe to be the true one, as presented in the chapters that follow.

2 THE IDEA OF CORRUPTION

Toward a Deeper Understanding

In the prior chapter, we found that traditional theories of corruption—although useful as far as they go—fail to capture all that we mean by the concept of corruption. Although violation of law, breach of duty, inequality, abuse of power, and so on, seem to describe parts of this idea, they do not capture all that we commonly mean by this concept.

In this chapter, I establish why this is true. I argue that the common idea of corruption is, in fact, far deeper and more complex than traditional academic theories acknowledge. First, corruption is an explicitly moral notion—it describes a powerful, all-consuming evil. Furthermore, corruption is not, in our common understanding, simply an act or series of acts with particular, prescribed characteristics. Rather, it is envisioned as an external force, to which we (as human beings) are innately susceptible. It describes, in short, *the capture by evil* of one's soul.

This idea of corruption might seem, at first blush, quite improbable or even shocking. However, in this chapter we shall uncover the congruence of this idea with our deeper intuitions about this concept. We shall also see how this idea of corruption silently motivates and shapes our treatment of public corruption, as a matter of both popular culture and law.

This additional character of corruption, as an idea, can be established through a series of propositions. First:

- Corruption is an explicitly moral notion.

Most traditional theories, whether shell theories or substantive theories, labor to avoid the obvious: that corruption is an explicitly moral notion which serves, in its general understanding, to condemn conduct on moral grounds. Looking for the essence of corruption in the violation of law, breach of duty, betrayal of trust, poor economic outcomes, and the like, will always feel viscerally unsatisfactory if, in the end, the explicitly moral core of corruption is not recognized. Corruption is not simply the breach of some politically chosen standard; it expresses the transgression of some deeply held and assertedly universal moral norm.

Take, for instance, the bribery of public officials. Bribery is universally condemned. "Not a country in the world . . . does not treat bribery as criminal on its lawbooks."[1] No one admits to it; "[n]ot merely the criminal law—for the transaction could have happened long ago . . . —but an innate fear of being considered disgusting restrains briber and bribee from parading their exchange."[2] The shame associated with bribery is so strong that it goes beyond the merely illegal. Rather, it points to the deeply moral nature of the crime.[3] When Vice President Spiro T. Agnew resigned in 1973, he pleaded nolo contendere to tax evasion. "Agnew demonstrated that socially and politically[,] bribery was a far more damaging crime to be thought guilty of than tax evasion, felony though it was. As a tax evader he could try to hold his head up. As a bribetaker he was lost."[4]

Indeed, recognition of corruption's explicitly moral nature helps to explain a puzzle often observed in law. Federal and state bribery statutes almost always require that the briber "corruptly" give, or the bribee "corruptly" receive, something of value with the intention to influence an official act.[5] Yet, what does this add? Such statutes otherwise specify the required quid pro quo.[6] As Daniel Lowenstein has observed, such bribery statutes require proof that "a public official is offered, seeks or accepts an individual benefit that is intended to influence the recipient's official actions. What more is needed to make the offering, seeking, or accepting 'corrupt'?"[7]

Although some courts have struggled to interpret this requirement as a further indication of the explicit nature of the quid pro quo requirement,[8] others have interpreted this additional, undefined element to signal an additional element of "wrongfulness," or an open invitation to the fact finder to import some unspecified, raw moral norm.[9] For instance, a federal appellate court has stated that "'corruptly' [as used in criminal law] is the adverbial form of the adjective 'corrupt,' which means 'depraved, evil: perverted into a state of moral weakness or wickedness.'"[10] This invitation to invoke ideas of morality would seem odd, if we think of corruption as involving (only) particular, specified acts. It is not odd, if we understand corruption to involve, at its core, a deep (and unspecified) moral wrong.

The idea of bribery and other public corruption as morally depraved or "evil" has a long historical pedigree. As John Noonan has observed, "'[M]oral opprobrium toward bribery is nothing new. It goes back some 4,000 years, with prohibitions found on Babylonian tablets.'"[11] The idea of political or public corruption as a deeply moral notion can be found in both Platonic and Aristotelian notions of democratic government, its maintenance, and its decline.[12] Scholars of the medieval and early modern periods have found the fusion of ideas of corruption and evil throughout the writings of these periods in England and in France.[13] For instance, in *Le Dictionnaire de l'Académie Françoise, dedié au Roy*, published in 1694, corruption is described as "concerning all moral deprivations and especially those with regard to justice."[14] In his famous dictionary penned in the eighteenth century, Samuel Johnson defines corruption as "[w]ickedness; perversion of principles."[15] In this view, "[t]o say corruption is wrong is rather like saying that murder is wrong. Both statements express what is, in effect, a conceptual truth or grammatical necessity."[16]

The equation of corruption with moral evil has endured and thrived in contemporary accounts of the phenomenon. Arnold Heidenheimer observes that "[t]he present usage of the term *corruption* in political contexts has obviously been colored by the meanings [of corruption] in the 'moral' category," namely, as involving "depravity," "moral deterioration," and "decay."[17] Some analysts of political corruption embrace the idea of its moral content as an obvious truth. For instance, Wilmer Parker states that political corruption "is marked by immorality and perversion; [the corrupt person is] depraved; venal; dishonest."[18] Robert Brooks describes political corruption as an "evil," corrupt transactions as "sins," and the engaging in corruption as the manifestation of "moral weakness."[19] Ronald Wraith and Edgar Simpkins write that corruption "is above all a moral problem, immeasurable and imponderable."[20]

Indeed, the idea of corruption as a moral concept is so powerful that it seeps into the work of those who champion traditional academic theories, even as they take pains to exclude it from their definitions of the word. Although Robert Klitgaard describes his theory of corruption as a breach-of-duty model, he acknowledges that "'corrupt' invokes a range of images of evil. . . . There is a moral tone to the word."[21] Colin Leys, who criticizes what he calls a "moralising approach" to corruption,[22] nonetheless describes corruption in terms of the "strength of the rules of private morality" and assaults on "moral rules."[23] Bayless Manning, although not a "moralist" himself, acknowledges the explicitly moral nature of the idea of corruption as commonly understood. He states flatly that "the American looks upon his politics as a Morality Play," and "to his elected officials for moral affirmation[]."[24] This "elevated moral vision of [the United States] and its officials,"[25] he argues, has driven Americans to continually expand the range of corrupt offenses to new (and, to his mind, unnecessary) lengths.[26]

What is this moral evil that corruption is believed to represent? It is best described as *self-involvement, self-indulgence, the loosening and discarding of the restraint of social bonds.* As such, it is associated with public and personal luxuriousness, indolence, excess, and other forms of decadence.[27] For instance, Syed Hussein Alatas describes the case of Gaius Verres (115–43 B.C.), a Roman ruler who was notable for the "rapaciousness and the extent of his corruption"—including "extortion, plunder, bribery, rape, sexual exploitation of other men's wives, treachery, murder, looting works of art, selling public offices, money-lending at usurious rates, [and] embezzling [from the estates] . . . of the deceased."[28] The "lack of restraint" that characterized such corrupt rulers "manifested itself in . . . sexual relations, political intrigues, economic manipulations, and . . . social behavior."[29] Today's corruption, Alatas argues, is rooted in the same "materialism, impersonalism, status-seeking, greed for money and power, and an unwillingness to adhere to moral values."[30] Another contemporary writer observes that corruption involves "luxuriousness and indolence."[31]

The association of political corruption with explicit ideas of evil should not be surprising to us. As a general matter, the ideas of evil and corruption have long been associated in Western religious and philosophical thought. Early philosophers, who believed that evil involves a "weak" or "deficient" will, illustrated this conviction with copious references to "vice" and "corruption." For instance, in the fifth century St. Augustine wrote of "the corruption of the body," which is "the punishment of the first sin." "[I]t was not the corruptible flesh that made the soul sinful, but the sinful soul that made the flesh corruptible. And . . . from this corruption of the flesh there arise certain incitements to vice."[32] Anselm of Canterbury (1033–1109), the "father of scholasticism," wrote of evil as "the privation of the good," or "vice or corruption."[33] St. Thomas Aquinas (ca. 1225–1274) wrote in *Summa Theologica* of "corruptible beings" who "can fail in goodness"; "for corruption is itself an evil."[34]

The association of original sin, moral depravity, and corruption was pursued at length by John Calvin (1509–1564). Original sin, he wrote, "is the depravity and corruption of our nature, which first renders us liable to God's wrath. . . . As we are vitiated and corrupted in all parts of our nature, we are held rightly condemned on account of such corruption alone and convicted before God."[35] Two centuries later, Jonathan Edwards warned that "the heart of man is naturally of a corrupt and evil disposition." To the question of whether man's nature "is good or evil, pure or corrupt, sound or ruined," Edwards unequivocally answered that "all mankind have an infallibly effectual propensity to . . . moral evil"; indeed, "the nature of man may be said to be corrupt and evil."[36]

Later examples of the association of evil and corruption can be found in the work of figures as diverse as Immanuel Kant, Jean-Jacques Rousseau, and the Marquis de Sade.[37] For instance, Kant wrote extensively of "the wickedness (*vitiositas, pravitas*) or, if you like, the *corruption* (*corruptio*) of the human heart" in his explorations of the phenomenon of evil.[38] In his view, a man is evil when his "cast of mind is . . . corrupted at its root."[39] Rousseau wrote of social corruption as "the violence, the betrayals, [and] the treacheries" that cause suffering, poverty, and vice.[40] American political philosophers from the revolutionary and postrevolutionary periods drew heavily upon classical republican and civic humanist antitheses of tyranny and liberty, virtue and corruption.[41] As J. G. A. Pocock has written, "Americans . . . inherited rhetorical and conceptual structures which ensured that venality in public officials, the growth of a military-industrial complex in government, other-directedness and one-dimensionality in individuals, could all be identified in terms continuous with those used in the classical analysis of corruption."[42]

Given this long and entrenched religious and social history, we should not be surprised that contemporary accounts strongly associate political corruption with general moral decadence, degeneracy, and evil. Indeed, such associations can be found in virtually any major city newspaper's account of a recent corruption scandal. Some colorful examples include:

- The vice mayor of Beijing, Wang Baosen, committed suicide in 1996 after having been presented with evidence implicating him and his staff in "systemic corruption."[43] "Wang was guilty of squandering public funds, acquiring expensive real estate, and booking hotel suites for 'pleasure-seeking,' according to officials. 'He was morally degenerate and lived a rotten life,' the Xinhua news agency said." Of another implicated official, Chen Xitong, it was observed that he amassed a personal fortune, engaged in nepotism, and "kept a mistress for six years."[44]

• In a story about a New York City detective convicted on corruption charges, it is noted (as relevant) that on one occasion "one of his criminal friends orchestrated a bachelor party at a downtown hotel. The party became so raucous that everyone was thrown out, and the festivities resumed at a nearby brothel."[45]

• In the fall of former Brazilian president Fernando Collor de Mello to corruption charges, it is noted that "proceeds from the influence-trafficking ring had been spent on building an elaborate garden at his ranch house . . ., with eight artificial waterfalls and a swimming pool." He "drove around in a Mercedes convertible and maintained a luxury apartment in Paris, where it was rumored that he would live in exile." In the end, his downfall was brought about by his brother, because he (President Collor de Mello) "tried to seduce his [brother's] wife."[46]

• In an article about rampant public corruption in India, a former attorney general of the country was quoted as saying that " '[i]t's spread like a cancer. . . . It's reached a terminal state. There is a complete breakdown of [moral] values.' " The question, the story continued, is "whether the country's very soul has been irredeemably warped."[47]

• Discussing the fallout from the indictment of superlobbyist Jack Abramoff on corruption charges, a columnist wrote that "the scandal literally had Republicans, led by President

Bush, turning money Abramoff gave them [as campaign contributions] over to charity, as if casting away their sins."[48]

• A columnist describes Randy "Duke" Cunningham, congressman from California, as "engaged in 'unparalleled corruption.' The ordinary lawmaker can't be bought for the price of an antique armoire—or, in Cunningham's case, nine armoires, six Persian carpets, three antique oak doors, two candelabra and a China hutch. A fighter-pilot-turned-congressman-turned-felon, Cunningham took the gold in brazenness and gluttony. . . . In all, he raked in an astonishing $2.4 million in graft."[49]

• "On May 28, 1986, Joseph A. Bevilacqua, chief justice of the Rhode Island Supreme Court, resigned his position. The judge faced an impeachment hearing because of allegations involving his personal associations with reputed mob members . . . [and] free electrical work the judge reportedly accepted from a contractor. . . . In addition, the judge was accused of committing adultery in a motel that was owned by convicted felons."[50]

• A court described a witness to be "not just a corrupt lawyer, but an 'evil, corrupt lawyer,'" with a "*curriculum vitae* of gambling, bribery, and cavorting with underworld figures."[51]

• "An investigation into the sale of black-market kidneys and fake Gucci handbags evolved into a sweeping probe of political corruption in New Jersey, ensnaring more than forty people . . ., including three mayors, two state lawmakers and several rabbis. Even for a state with a rich history of graft, the scale of wrongdoing alleged was breathtaking. An FBI official called corruption 'a cancer that is destroying the core values of this state.'"[52]

- A Mississippi state court judge, who was a civil rights leader as a young prosecutor, was charged in a bribery case involving a $1 million bribe and a dangled federal judgeship. "'DeLaughter became a hero, and now he's fallen,'" a civil rights veteran stated.[53]

Similar associations can be found in academic writings. Thomas Burke writes that in "the classical sense[,] . . . corruption [is seen] as involving luxuriousness and indolence."[54] H. A. Brasz observes that "even corruption on a minor scale can easily suggest wide-spread decadence to the public."[55] "Besides business and politics," writes Robert Brooks, "other spheres of social activity are subject to corrupt influences. Indeed wherever and whenever there is a duty to be shirked or improperly performed for motives of more or less immediate advantage[,] evil of this sort may enter in. This is the case within the church, the family, with educational associations, clubs, and so on throughout the whole list of social organizations. . . . A large proportion of the cases of divorce, marital infidelity, and childless unions, reflect the operation of corrupt influences."[56]

In these portrayals, it is apparent that corruption is not simply something that is undesirable or "bad" in an ordinary sense; rather, it is seen as a powerful, all-consuming evil, with what often seem to be religious roots. The corrupt are described as "guilty as Satan."[57] One contemporary analysis of political corruption describes the "scarlet thread of bribery and corruption" in the "jungle of nepotism and temptation."[58] Another informs us that the statement that "all power corrupts, and absolute power corrupts absolutely" has "a religious root, [which] . . . is typically Western and Christian. It harks back to the notion of the two kingdoms . . ., the earthly and the heavenly city," and the susceptibility of humans to the power of moral depravity and moral decay.[59] Another commentator breezily observes, "Corruption is something that we have all had to live with since Eve took the first bite of the serpents' apple, and . . . that we will have to live with . . . to the end of time." "Lucifer, in his many names, was cast from the portals of Heaven for the corruption that he bred, at least according to Milton [and others]. . . . [T]he temptation to corrupt and to succumb to corruption is part of our estate."[60] In the same vein, a former prosecutor ends his commentary on a corrupt politician with a flourish: "[E]very person will at some point in [his life] . . . and at some level hear the seductive, siren song of the corrupt temptress summoning us to, in Dante's words, enter . . . the gates of Hell."[61]

The idea of corruption as involving a temptation toward decadence to which an individual succumbs, and which—in turn—destroys that individual,[62] has tremendous resonance in our understanding of this concept. Indeed, this brings us to our second proposition:

> • Corruption is an external force, to which we, as human beings, are innately susceptible.

In contemporary accounts of corruption and its causes, even those who resist the idea of corruption's moral or religious roots often lapse into these images when describing the corrupting process. Whether acknowledged or not, corruption is portrayed as an *external* evil,[63] which attacks and undermines better human impulses. It is, furthermore—because of our weakness— something to which we are all potentially susceptible, if the conditions are right.

The forms that this external evil takes are many. For some, this external force takes a human form: the victim falls to the "corruptor"[64] or "tempter"[65] whose influence he cannot resist. For instance, Joseph Borkin's study of corrupt judges[66] is one of the most searing indictments of judicial corruption to be found. Yet not all fault, in his view, lies with the judges themselves. "A judge," Borkin writes, "cannot be corrupt alone. For every judge studied, there were the inevitable *corruptors*. They consisted most frequently of lawyers and clients, trustees and receivers, clerks and assistants, *rapacious* 'finders' and *predatory* intermediaries."[67] In this picture, the individual who pays the bribe is not simply a participant in the scheme; rather, he is a "corruptor" who induces the (passive) "corrupted" person's downfall.

An example can be found in the press account of John Gaw, a New York City police detective who acknowledged that he had been on the payroll of organized crime for six years. An article in the *New York Times* explained, "John Gaw [was] a young single man who still lived with his parents. . . . [T]he courtship of Detective Gaw began shortly after he made one of his first arrests, breaking up a gambling parlor on East Broadway. Soon afterward, Detective Gaw bumped into one of the gambling house men on the street. . . . Law enforcement officials said that the man, whom they regard as a *professional corruptor*, entertained Detective Gaw for weeks. He escorted him to Atlantic City, slipped him tickets to shows and sporting events. Finally, Detective Gaw gave in and agreed to work for him."[68]

Similar accounts of "corruptors" or "tempters" can be found in the legislative arena. Recent press accounts of the corruption scandal involving Jack Abramoff, former Washington lobbyist and power broker, reflect this view. Abramoff and his employees are described in terms that are evocative of "dark angels" or figures of evil, who set out to corrupt weak, greedy, and naive lawmakers. Described as dressed in a black fedora and trench coat,[69] looking "like a film noir villain,"[70] "Mr. Abramoff pleaded guilty . . . to conspiring to corrupt members of Congress and other public officials."[71] Five months later, a former top aide to Republican Congressman Bob Ney who worked for Abramoff followed suit, "admitting he conspired to corrupt Ney, his staff and other members of Congress with trips, free tickets, jobs, meals and campaign events."[72] Their "efforts" apparently were successful. Congressman Ney, amid reports of the "stress on his family because of what he called the 'ordeal' of the scrutiny over his ties to Mr. Abramoff,"[73] and his admission to an inpatient alcohol treatment program, agreed to plead guilty to corruption charges four months after that.[74] In another contemporaneous case, Democratic Congressman William J. Jefferson was accused by the FBI "of taking hundreds of thousands of dollars in bribes from [Mr. Vernon Jackson,] a Kentucky businessman[,] and stashing $90,000 from the scheme in his home freezer in Washington."[75] The congressman, who was a member of the Congressional Caucus on Nigeria, is described as "*a logical target* for Mr. Jackson," who wanted to secure high-tech contracts with the Nigerian government.[76]

Other writers describe the external, corrupting force in pathogenic terms. Corruption, in this view, "is not only the absence of an element or principle; it . . . involve[s] the presence of some foreign element that debases or undermines the whole."[77] Discussions of corruption are rife with images of corruption as a "cancer,"[78] "virus,"[79] "disease,"[80] or "pathology."[81] It is "insatiable."[82] In a typical statement, a commentator opines that "[o]nce corruption finds its way into a certain place or sector, like a virus, it tends to spread out to other areas and sectors."[83] A

Boston police officer was described as "so thoroughly corrupt" that his "misdeeds spread like a cancer in the entire Boston Police Department."[84] The passage of the Foreign Corrupt Practices Act[85] is described by another commentator as having been "partially motivated by an endemic, expressed American fear that the contagion of corruption, . . . caught abroad, would emigrate to the United States, corrupting otherwise law-abiding domestic business." The Act "was conceived as a vigorous inoculation against this disease."[86] Yet another commentator observes that once the contagion of corruption is embedded, the only solution is to "cut away the diseased tissue."[87] As James D. Wolfensohn, then president of the World Bank, stated, "Let's not mince words. We need to deal with the cancer of corruption."[88]

Indeed, references to the organic nature of corruption—as warping, corroding, perverting, or degrading the afflicted individual or organization—can be found throughout the sociological and legal treatments of the subject. Corruption is described as a loss of purity and purpose,[89] or the "decomposition of the body politic through moral decay."[90] As one commentator has observed, "[T]he word corruption, used with reference to social phenomena, [is frequently juxtaposed] with such words as slime, filth, sewage, stench, tainted, rottenness, gangrene, [and] pollution."[91] Another states that "[c]orruption and nepotism rot good intentions and retard progressive policies."[92] In one account, corruption of human organizations is likened to infestation by insects: "[C]orruption has its own autonomy. The economic, political and social structures [that human beings create], independent of their type, are vulnerable to an infestation of corruption. Like termites, the corrupt attack any structure."[93] A court described a judge's corruption as "a 'cancer that destroys the very concept of democratic government.'"[94] "[C]orruption in one sector breeds malfeasance in another. . . . [Destroying corruption] is similar to destroying the Gordian knot."[95]

Under all of these accounts corruption is powerful, and human beings are weak. As the vice attorney general of Venezuela once told me, in what seemed—at the time—to be an enigmatic comment, those who engage in corruption "don't respect themselves."[96] They yield, to their detriment, to their own internal weaknesses. Susceptibility to corruption is believed to be "within us all, like the potential for violence, deceit, and no doubt lust."[97]

This view of the operation and power of corruption might explain what might otherwise be seen as a strange anomaly: the distinction between "active" and "passive" bribery that many legal systems employ.[98] Under this approach, the one who gives a bribe is guilty of "active corruption," while the recipient is guilty of "passive corruption" only.[99] It is difficult, at first blush, to imagine how an official who accepts a bribe could be seen as "passive," or indeed (as in some countries) less culpable than the one who pays it.[100] The payment of a bribe requires the active participation of both parties, and it is the public official, after all, who breaches the public trust. The passive/active model is explicable, however, when we imagine corruption as an external force to which the official (like all human beings) is vulnerable. The briber ("active corruptor") in this view preys upon the human weakness of the "victim." As a result, we condemn the tempter more than the one who succumbs.

The idea of corruption as involving an external evil, to which a human being succumbs and which—in turn—destroys that person, leads us to the third, final, and most fundamental proposition:

• Corruption does not simply describe an act or a series of acts. It describes the capture of a human being by evil.

All of the traditional theories of corruption that we considered above—corruption as illegality, breach of duty, betrayal, secrecy, inequality, subversion of the public interest, and so on—assume that corruption is *an act, or series of acts,* that we identify (through the chosen theory). In fact, this assumption is fundamentally misconceived. What we mean by corruption cannot be captured by *conduct* alone, no matter how identified. It is, as our first two propositions suggest, far more. It is an idea that describes an individual's deepest character. It is *the capture, by evil, of one's soul.*

Consider, again, the following statements:

- A has broken the law

and

- A is corrupt.

In our prior discussion of these statements, we noted that they may have little congruence: an act can violate the law but not be corrupt, and vice versa. Now we can make a deeper and bolder assertion of difference. Corruption is different from simple lawbreaking in the following fundamental way. In the case of lawbreaking, it is *an act* that we condemn. In the case of corruption, it is *a person* whom we condemn.

Corruption, in short, confers *a status.* A person, now corrupt, has changed. Evil has captured his being, his essence, his soul.

The extent to which contemporary accounts use this model and yet fail to recognize its usage is stunning. All of the following examples were taken from academic or judicial writings that assume that corruption is simply an act that we condemn on legal, public-duty, public-interest, or other grounds. Yet, consider the following images of "capture":

- Individuals who commit corrupt acts are described by status: "corrupt insiders," "corrupt bidders," "corrupt lobbyists," "corrupt officials," "corrupt leaders."[101]

- Corruption offenses are cumulatively described as "thorough going corruption,"[102] "corruption of character."[103] A "rogue Boston police officer who enlisted two fellow motorcycle patrolmen in a brazen scheme to escort and protect cocaine shipments into the city" is described as "so thoroughly corrupt that no crime was too small for him and literally no crime was too big for him."[104]

- It is observed that "[b]ribes *corrupt people*. Those who pay bribes are corrupted as well as those who receive them."[105]

- A corrupt judge is described in the following terms: "Once he embarked on the path of bribetaking, . . . [h]e had forsaken his judicial oath. . . . His deviation from the path of righteousness . . . was cold, calculated, and spanned a period of years. . . ." His bribe taking was not "just another 'bias' or 'influence,' something external to his personality, or at least some severable part of it." Rather, "the cancer of the judge's corruption . . . invaded [his] decisionmaking." It "remove[d] him from the category of the 'average' man."[106]

- The same judge is described by the United States Supreme Court as having led "a life of corruption," in which he "corrupt[ed] justice." He was "shown to be thoroughly steeped in corruption through his public trial and conviction."[107] In his sentencing recommendation, the prosecutor stated that the judge "surpassed the category of corrupt jurist to chart a new territory of defilement."[108]

- A commentator observed that when devoted to public service, the official's "whole personality is claimed"—a demand that is thwarted by corruption.[109]

• Another stated that "[w]hen the prospect or the receipt of campaign money influences the behavior of public officials, *they are corrupted*, whether or not a deal has been made."[110]

• Removing a trial judge from office after he took a single bribe was justified, the New Jersey Supreme Court declared, because he "sold [his] . . . power, he sold his judgments, he sold his independence."[111]

• In his closing argument, a prosecutor stated that "'Supreme Court Judge Gerald Garson became corrupt Supreme Court Judge Gerald Garson, disgraceful Supreme Court Judge Gerald Garson, disgraced Supreme Court Judge Gerald Garson.'"[112]

• A state court judge, describing the corrupt activities of a former police commissioner, stated that the defendant's attempts at "personal gain and aggrandizement" were "a dark place in the soul."[113]

Or consider the following account of the prosecutor's closing argument in the corruption trial of an attorney and part-time judge:

During the trial, Tokars' attorneys presented their client as a pillar of the society, a respected attorney, a family man, and a political supporter of respected elected officials. The government argued that he was "a wolf in sheep's clothing." [He was a] [m]an who had carefully cultivated an outward appearance of goodness, but who underneath was evil and corrupt. Government counsel . . . suggested to the jury that an analogy of Tokars' conduct may be found in the poetic masterpiece, the *Inferno*, [by] . . . Dante Alighieri, one of the greatest poets of all time. . . .

[In the *Inferno*,] [a]s the poets traveled through Hell's gates, . . . they visited many levels. In the Sixth Bolgia they came upon the Hypocrites. . . . Dante described the hypocrites' outward appearance as shining brightly, passing for holiness. But, underneath the gilded robes, each hypocrite carried the terrible weight of his deceit which his soul must bear throughout all eternity. . . . It was suggested to the jury that, while Frederic Tokars' outward appearance was of goodness, underneath he carried the weight of deceit. . . . Frederic W. Tokars lived a life of hypocrisy, a life of corruption.[114]

Such references to "corrupt officials," "corrupt leaders," "lives of corruption," judges "steeped in corruption," "corrupt hypocrites," and so on, do not seem strange or to be instances of overreaching to us. On a visceral level, they seem to be entirely appropriate characterizations of this evil. We are deeply convinced that corruption is not simply an act that may be forgiven, punished, or regretted, or an attitude that may prevail in someone's mind one day and be gone the next. We believe it to be far more powerful. It is a "virus," a "contamination," an external, destroying force that must be "purged" if ever it is to be eradicated.[115] It is the capture of a human being by evil. It is the purchase, by the devil, of one's soul.

Recognition of the influence of this idea of corruption explains why the traditional theories of corruption, described above, fail to capture the essence of this concept. However, much remains to be explored. What is involved in "capture by evil"? What does this status, as I have described it, distinctively mean? If someone is corrupt, in this sense, how is this different (for example) from status as "a felon" or "a thief"? Is there really anything *particularly damning* or *particularly threatening* about this concept?

We shall consider these questions in the chapters that follow.

3 CORRUPTION-AS-DISPOSITION

A Different Crime

So far, we have seen that corruption, as commonly understood, confers *a status* on the one who is accused. A person, when corrupt, has changed. Evil has captured her being, her essence, her soul.

The question that arises is how this status is different from the status that accusations or convictions of crime otherwise present. For instance, if someone is labeled a "burglar" or a "thief," or even—quite generically—a "criminal" or a "felon," those statements clearly confer a status as well. Is there something more essential or more damning about the status that corruption confers than there is about the status conferred by the commission of other crimes?

In this chapter, I argue that the status that corruption confers is, indeed, very different from that conferred by other crimes. Most crimes are statements about *acts*; corruption is a statement about *character*. To put it another way, corruption is a *dispositional concept*, which describes the deep, moral character of the accused. This affects—as we shall see—the way in which we conceptualize this crime, the way in which we prove this crime, and our attitudes toward individual responsibility for this crime.

NATURE

Let us begin our discussion with an understanding of *dispositional* properties, whether they be of objects or of persons. Without becoming too mired in the philosophical issues that surround this subject,[1] dispositions are generally understood to be properties of objects (such as solubility, fragility, or elasticity) or of persons (such as loyalty, honesty, or courage) which describe an object's or person's character, and which (as a result) describe how that object or person will behave under particular circumstances.[2] The important point is that *dispositions* must be distinguished from their *manifestations*; although a manifestation of a disposition might make us aware of that disposition, a disposition is a continuant that "predate[s], outlast[s], and may exist entirely without the existence of" its manifestation.[3] An object or person can have a disposition without its ever being manifest. Thus, to assign a disposition to an object or person is not simply to describe past, or future, manifestations; it is a statement about a deeper characteristic that independently exists. As U. T. Place has observed, "To say that the glass is brittle is not a mere ungrounded prediction of what is liable to happen in the future [or a statement of what happened in the past]. *It is to say something about the glass.*"[4]

In a similar way, when the disposition that is our focus is one involving human moral character, that disposition must be distinguished from specific actions that the person performs.[5] We may conclude that a person has a particular disposition or moral character because her acts exhibit a particular pattern of behavior, and we consider that pattern to be *evidence* of the underlying disposition of that person. A distinction must be drawn, however, between a person's disposition or overall moral character and the specific actions she adopts. Although there *may* be a correlation between dispositions and actions, that correlation is by no means guaranteed.[6]

What has this to do with corruption, and its comparison with other "status" crimes? The critical point is this. Corruption is a *dispositional concept*, in the sense just described. Like other dispositional concepts applied to human beings (such as loyalty, timidity, courageousness, generosity, profligacy, and others), the statement that someone "is corrupt" is a statement about that person's deeper character (in this case, moral character). This statement involves more than a report of acts. We may see *evidence* of this disposition in acts (by this person), but those acts are not, of themselves, the disposition with which we deal. It is, as I have just noted, entirely possible that a disposition may exist even if it is never manifest. A person may be corrupt or "captured by evil" and yet (because of incapacitation or infirmity) never commit a corrupt or evil act. Corruption is a more profound judgment about the character, or disposition, or nature of a human being. It is a condition that is beneath thoughts, or acts, or judgment. *It is deeper, more fundamental, a part of the individual herself.*

A judgment that someone is "corrupt" is thus quite different from a judgment that someone is "a burglar," "a felon," or "a thief." If someone is a thief or a felon, she is someone who has committed a prior (prohibited) act. Was this the manifestation of a "bad" or "evil" disposition, or simply aberrant behavior on this person's part? From this status alone, we do not know. If the person is labeled a murderer, perhaps we come closer to a statement of character, but still we do not know. Even murderers can be excused by the passage of time, necessity, or provocation. As the philosopher Sergio Pérez has written, "A bad action does not make a wicked man."[7] That someone "is corrupt," on the other hand, is a certain statement. It is a dispositional judgment—a statement about fundamental character—that establishes, beyond doubt, the moral deficiency or depravity of the accused. As the philosopher Maeve Cooke has observed, we make a "moral distinction between a basically good person who commits a single or occasional immoral acts, and one whose identity is fundamentally . . . corrupt."[8] Indeed, the idea of corruption as character—as a deep, dispositional property—is reinforced by the idea of corruption as physical or corporeal change induced by infection, contamination, or other adulteration. We are not saying simply that "a corrupt" person has done something wrong; we are saying that *the fiber of her being* is rotten to the core.

When we consider the journalistic, academic, and legal descriptions of corrupt actors, we find copious use of explicitly dispositional language in the descriptions of the offenders in these cases. As I noted above, offenders are described simply as "corrupt insiders," "corrupt officials," "corrupt leaders," and "corrupt jurists."[9] Courts describe how an official "is corrupted" and thereby "perfidiously fails to perform his public service and duty."[10] Corruption involves an official's "character" or "personality."[11] It is a state of "moral degeneration,"[12] "weakness," or "wickedness."[13] Although an attorney (accused of corruption) had "an outward appearance of goodness, . . . underneath [he] was evil and corrupt."[14] He (the offender) had "a corrupt mind."[15]

The identity of corruption as a profoundly dispositional concept, distinguishable—on that basis—from other crimes, provides another way to express the deficiency inherent in all of the traditional theories examined above. Corruption as illegality, breach of duty, betrayal and secrecy, and so on, attempts to express corruption in strictly behavioral terms. The problem is not that these acts or behaviors are unrelated to corruption; indeed, they are (quite often) important *evidence* of it. Corruption as an idea, however, is something deeper. It is a dispositional statement about the *moral fiber* of the accused. It is this dispositional character of corruption, together with other elements, that constitute the corrupt core.

If corruption is indeed a dispositional idea, this will have profound implications for the way that we imagine the problem of corruption and, if criminalized, the nature of the crime. The consequences of this idea for our treatment of public corruption are, as we shall see, of tremendous importance. As a précis of what is to come, I shall note several here.

First, and most centrally, corruption—as a dispositional idea—means that its essential focus will change from traditional theories' concern about a breach of duty or other act committed, to *concern about the very presence of the corrupt individual as a part of public life*.

To illustrate this, let us consider the famous (or infamous) case of Sir Francis Bacon. Bacon—scientist, philosopher, politician, and inventor of the idea of secular jurisprudence[16]—was also corrupt. In 1621, while Lord Chancellor of England, he was impeached by Parliament for accepting bribes. As alleged in the Articles of Impeachment, Bacon received a total of £12,230 in outright gifts, loans, and items in kind from litigants and others having business with his office.[17] When confronted, Bacon confessed to the receipt of these moneys and other gifts, and agreed that they were intended (by the givers) to be bribes.[18] At the time, taking bribes under such circumstances was apparently common; others who took bribes included every major officer of King James's court, and also the king himself.[19] However, Bacon's defense, as a public matter at least, did not rest upon bribery's widespread nature; the evil that it signaled was apparently too strong. Rather, he asserted that this bribe taking, although true, never influenced his decisions. He was unaffected by these gifts, he claimed, and often decided against a briber.[20] He was, in his own words, "the justest judge that was in England these fifty years," although he acknowledged the practical and political need for censure.[21]

Bacon's defense did not move Parliament. However, when the question of punishment reached a sympathetic king, Bacon escaped the most serious penalties. He spent three days in the Tower of London and was fined £40,000, a debt that was assigned to friendly commissioners who never insisted upon collection.[22] Only one significant punishment was exacted: he could never hold public office again.[23]

Whatever the mixed motives for Parliament's actions— scholars have suggested, for instance, that those motives were more political than legal[24]—the rejection of Bacon's defense on the "merits" was foreordained for other reasons. Whether a corrupt person's actions have harmed anyone subject to that person's trust—or, indeed, are even (on that basis) themselves "corrupt"—is not the issue. Rather, it is the *presence* of the corrupt person *in the public office that he holds* that is, itself, the crime. Bacon argued that the bribes that he received had no impact on his decision making, and, indeed, they may have had none. This does not, however, address the central evil that corruption, as a dispositional crime, identifies. It is not whether Bacon *executed* the bribed promises that is the focus of corruption's harm; it is the fact that he *would take* them. Having taken the bribes, he was corrupt, in a personal, dispositional sense—and the rest was simply irrelevant.

Indeed, if a public official were to announce "I am corrupt" yet perform (to our knowledge) no corrupt acts, her continued presence in office would present a difficult problem. This difficulty might be due, in part, to our fear that she might act upon her stated disposition in later overt or undetected ways. However, even if we knew that such acts were impossible (for lack of capacity, lack of opportunity, or other reasons), her continued presence as a public servant would offend the principles that public office demands. She would be, essentially, *the wrong kind of woman*. Such a declaration of character would not lead to her criminal prosecution, but it would most certainly lead to her removal. Acts are important in the proof of a person's corruption. But we would also take action, if we knew of that disposition without them.

In short, we are concerned not only with corrupt acts; we are concerned also with the disposition that drives them. When it is a disposition that we are trying to detect and prohibit, it is that disposition that (effectively) becomes the crime.

A second consequence of corruption as a dispositional idea is that it *is assumed to confer an irrevocable moral status*. A disposition, as a deep trait of character, has an aura of permanence; its pervasiveness and fundamental character belie the possibility of change. A physical object that is "corrupted"—that is, "warped," "corroded," "perverted," or "degraded"—is assumed to be permanently altered. There is little or no chance that a rotten apple will become fresh or that warped wood will spring back to the condition it once had.

Corruption, as a dispositional idea, reflects this quality. Just as the corruption of objects is assumed to be permanent, so is the corruption of individuals. Jack Abramoff, the former lobbyist, when sentenced to nearly six years in prison for fraud, may tell the judge that he is working to become "a new man";[25] but even in that statement, he admits the Herculean task, and our skepticism is palpable. Few officials, once deemed to be corrupt, recover from that statement.[26] Prominent officeholders in American history have survived allegations of corruption, and continued their public careers;[27] but they have almost never survived a formal finding of corruption by a court or other government body. Of ninety-seven governors, judges, senators, representatives, cabinet members, and other government officials found (by final official decree) to have engaged in corruption,[28] only three successfully resumed public careers.[29]

The irrevocable moral status that corruption confers also works to distinguish it from other crimes. A thief or other felon presumably could renounce her past actions and (albeit with a bit of tarnish) rejoin the civil society of which she had previously been a part. The "corrupt" man cannot. Although Immanuel Kant may have believed that a corrupt or evil disposition is mutable,[30] that is a belief which we generally do not share. As was noted about former Vice President Spiro Agnew, as a felon "he could try to hold his head up. As a bribetaker he was lost."[31]

A third consequence of corruption as a dispositional idea is that *the corrupt individual is completely and thoroughly consumed by this condition*. As Cooke has pointed out, moral disposition or character "refers to the enduring and organizing aspect of . . . identity. It is a matter of fundamental orientation as manifest in habits, actions, beliefs, relationships with others, [and] traits of personality."[32] If corruption is a matter of moral disposition, we assume that it consumes the individual who is the target of our judgment. A man, once corrupt, has lost any other positive identity or redeeming characteristic. Indeed, the idea that someone may be "somewhat" or "partially" corrupt is, in fact, a linguistic oxymoron. Corruption (we believe) captures its victims. Far more imaginable—indeed, far more assumed—is the idea of the "perfectly corrupt man."

This effect of a corruption charge or conviction can be illustrated, again, by Sir Francis Bacon. Despite his unquestioned contributions to science, philosophy, politics, and law, Bacon—in the popular mind—is remembered more often for his fall than for his achievements. Even for a man as brilliant as he, the maintenance of a positive legacy is extremely difficult. This is because we believe that corruption, with its dispositional nature, consumes its victims. Once it has "perver[ted] . . . the human heart,"[33] that man's life and works—for all practical purposes—are tainted to the core.

Finally, if corruption is a dispositional idea—if it destroys or corrodes that of which it is a part—this means that we must assign to public corruption a far greater and more important role than the simple destruction of those officials in whom it is detected. Like medieval heresy, whose existence was believed to threaten religious truth,[34] the crime of corruption threatens more than affected individuals. When a corrupt individual holds public office, *her corruption means systemic damage*. The corrupt politician, police officer, or judge does not simply threaten harm to particular individuals with whom she might come into contact; her existence threatens the entire governmental system of reliance, trust, and the rule of law of which she is a part. The insidious process of corruption, the importance of its targets, and our own fears of vulnerability to its powers combine to make its threat to us far more than the simple evil of individual transgression. Thus, it threatens us far more than the isolated con man, murderer, or thief.

EVIDENCE

The dispositional nature of corruption, thus, deeply influences our ideas about the nature of this affliction. It also influences our ideas about its proof.

The identification of corruption as a dispositional idea leads to an odd paradox. Although we deny that corruption (in this sense) is synonymous with "acts," our detection of the presence of corruption (in this sense) is dependent upon acts. As Gilbert Ryle observed, dispositions themselves "narrate no incidents." They do not, of themselves, "report[] . . . observed or observable states of affairs." They are, however, "intimately connected with narratives of incidents," for it is those incidents that we use, indirectly, to demonstrate those dispositions' presence or truth.[35]

This situation—that dispositions are not the same as acts, yet must be proven by acts—leads to obvious difficulties in the proof of corruption. Exacerbating this difficulty is our additional conviction that corruption is a very serious affliction, whose presence we must detect. When these elements are combined, the result is a conception of evidence in corruption cases that differs sharply in *meaning, scope, and sufficiency* from standards of evidence required for other crimes.

First, the ideas that we are directly detecting character, that there are difficulties in proof, and that the stakes are very high make us willing to do in corruption cases what we are generally reluctant to do in other settings: to draw a conclusion (about character) on the basis of a single act alone. In the usual criminal case, it is the identified (criminal) act that is our focus; it is that act which we use to assess the need for incapacitation, the chance for rehabilitation, or other routine criminal-justice goals. As a result, we generally require multiple acts of theft, robbery, embezzlement, or other crimes before we conclude that a felon's character is "hopeless," and that punishment is justified (under a "habitual offender," "three strikes," or similar law) on the basis of what is essentially character alone.

In corruption cases, our intuitions are different. After a single instance of bribery, we readily deem a judge, customs officer, or official to "be corrupt." We do not need other instances of corrupt conduct to demonstrate the extreme danger that she presents, or to justify the severe sanctions that we impose. This is because the single act's significance lies not in the particular criminality that it evinces *but in the disposition that it proves*. It does not matter, for instance, if the corrupt official truly regrets her actions, or if the chance of recidivism (for other reasons) is very low. In corruption cases, our concern is not with the offender's incapacitation or rehabilitation. It is with the detection of a cancer, a virus, a contagion—which, if found, must be immediately, unhesitatingly, and completely excised.

In addition, the dispositional character of corruption, our alarm at its presence, and the potential slimness of traditional, act-based evidence make us willing to broaden what we see as "evidence" of corruption beyond what we would consider fair game for other crimes. Corruption, as we have seen in the popular, journalistic, and academic accounts above, is not simply indicated by acts such as bribery, extortion, embezzlement, or kickbacks; its presence—indeed, its essence—is demonstrated by greed, gluttony, materialism, luxuriousness, sexual rapaciousness, and other kinds of personal vice.[36] Although these acts would seem to establish only that a person is (in addition) a lowlife, drunk, glutton, or libertine, the "evidence" that they provide in this context is believed by us to be much stronger. For instance, faced (perhaps) with a paucity of evidence consisting of a single act of bribery, this evidence of vice will enhance our conviction that our detection of the accused's underlying, corrupt character is correct. Such evidence, we believe, identifies those who reject the critical constraints of social bonds. Therefore, such evidence, we believe, works to prove a *disposition of corruption*.

The use of this kind of evidence to establish or bolster a finding of corrupt character is commonplace. Indeed, the association of personal vice with corrupt behavior is so strong that the presence or absence of this evidence has at times become a political litmus test for the fitness of candidates for public office. Consider, for instance, the notorious period in recent U.S. judicial and presidential history when evidence of marijuana smoking at any time in one's life was considered to be a fatal flaw in the character of judicial or presidential candidates (leading to presidential candidate Bill Clinton's famous remark that although he had smoked marijuana in college, he "didn't inhale").[37] Or consider the recent legislative action against corrupt civil servants (or *possibly* corrupt civil servants) in the Chinese city of Nanjing. Faced with evidence "that 95% of convicted corrupt officials in China have mistresses," Nanjing authorities "called on officials to declare any changes in their marriages" as a prophylaxis for the problem.[38] Whether Nanjing authorities believed that mistresses *cause* corruption, or simply that keeping them is *evidence* of corrupt character, is unclear. What *is* clear is that personal vice of this kind is believed to be reliable evidence in corruption prosecutions.

In summary, our treatment of evidence is quite different under a dispositional—as opposed to a behavioral—understanding of corruption. Although "the act" (the bribe, the kickback, and so on) is "evidence" in both cases, whether it is evidence simply of the act itself *or* is evidence of a deeper, profound, and malignant disposition will change our understandings of both its meaning and its sufficiency. If the act is evidence of a deeper (corrupt) disposition, we are much more willing to draw sweeping conclusions about character from that act. In addition, the evidence *beyond* that act that is deemed to be probative of corruption is much broader. General immorality, lawbreaking, and vice are all confirmatory (under this view) of the underlying, corrupt diagnosis.

RESPONSIBILITY

The idea that corruption is a dispositional idea has complex and contradictory implications for the question of whether a corrupt individual bears responsibility for her crime.

It is probably a safe assumption that each of us, at this moment, has a particular disposition or moral character that affects our acts. Is each of us, in fact, responsible for that disposition? Are we responsible for our courage, or timidity, or sympathetic leanings, or destructive tendencies?

The answers to such questions would depend upon profound psychological, physiological, philosophical, and theological issues that go far beyond the discussion that is possible here. Suffice it to say that when we speak of human dispositions, the question that is immediately raised is that there may be more involved than simple individual responsibility for individual choice.

It follows that because corruption is a dispositional idea, these questions are prominent and unavoidable when we think about it. In particular, corruption-as-disposition raises the distinct possibility that corrupt character or corrupt acts may be the product of more than individual volition alone. In particular,

- the acquisition of a corrupt disposition may be the result of influences (such as inborn, or innate, propensities or later external influences) over which the individual has no control; and

• once acquired, a corrupt disposition may be seen as irresistible in its influence. For instance, it is generally assumed that a disposition, by definition, must command causal powers.[39] This may mean that an individual, once afflicted with a corrupt disposition, is thereby released from responsibility for her acts.

Both possibilities are reinforced—unintentionally, perhaps—by the terms that we use to describe corrupt phenomena. As I discussed above, corruption is commonly portrayed as an external force which preys upon its victims and to which they, eventually, succumb. Whether this external force is portrayed in pathogenic terms (e.g., as a "virus" or "fungus") or in human terms (e.g., as a "corruptor" or "tempter"), its threat elicits at least a partial sympathy for its victims. It is implied that we are all, on some level, susceptible to this influence; that resisting it is difficult; and that once it is rooted in one's being, it commands causal powers. Recently, this view was vividly illustrated in the case of Larry Langford, former mayor of Birmingham, Alabama, who was sentenced to fifteen years in prison and fined $360,000 for accepting $230,000 in cash and gifts while chairman of the Jefferson County Commission, in exchange for steering business to a local businessman.[40] The press account states, "Some residents expressed sympathy . . . for the former mayor's predicament. . . . Charles Hicks [the owner of a local barbershop] said he was disappointed by Mr. Langford's recent behavior but believed the former mayor was well-intentioned and was corrupted by wealthy businessmen. . . . 'Larry had great ideas, but he got caught up in the trap,' [Mr. Hicks said]."[41]

There are often grounds for sympathy toward and forgiveness of the corrupt man. There are also reasons for condemnation and contempt. Along with ideas that the corrupt are victims (of either their own innate propensities or of malevolent, external influence) are ideological strains that corruption involves a human "weakness" or "defective nature" or "absence of character" that moral acts require. In this way of thinking, a disposition is, after all, simply descriptive in nature; an assessment that a man is brave, or timid, or corrupt says nothing in itself of how he came to be that way. A dispositional idea of corruption does not *require* that a corrupt man be freed of responsibility for his nature or actions; rather, it only allows for this possibility, which, if it is true, must rest on other grounds.

To put it succinctly, there is a tension in the idea of corruption—as involving dark innate, external, or other irresistible forces or as resulting from individual responsible choice—that corruption-as-disposition explicitly displays. All of us know (and fear) the power of the corruptor, the tempter, the seducer. Yet, there is also personal choice in that some succumb and others do not. Whether it is in the creation of the disposition or in its later manifestations, the choice—to be corrupt or not—is, we believe, at least to some extent our own.

Perhaps the best way to make sense of these competing views is this. Corruption is, in fact, a very predictable mixture of personal responsibility and unavoidable (even sympathetic) human weakness. We are, we believe—because of innate or acquired dispositional factors—all susceptible, to some degree, to corruption's allures. This belief, however, does not mean that we absolve the corrupt man of his actions. Rather, the opposite is true. We must, we believe, be charged with the duty to resist corruption's temptations. Indeed, our inner knowledge of our own, peculiar susceptibility to this crime demands that we redouble our efforts. *Because of* its dispositional nature, if we are to fight this phenomenon, if we are to resist this phenomenon, the descent into corruption, we believe—indeed, we *must* believe—requires acts and decisions of our own.

The struggle to reconcile dispositional ideas with volitional ideas in human conduct is, of course, not limited to this context. Perhaps most famously, this struggle pervades the foundational idea of evil, in which (as we have seen) corruption is thoroughly steeped. What the idea of evil adds to the mix is explored in the next chapter.

4 AN *EVIL* DISPOSITION

Further Explorations

As we have already established, the idea of corruption—as commonly understood—is a dispositional idea. It is not a statement, simply, about acts; it is a statement about character. It is about moral degradation and moral failure. To call someone corrupt is to make a statement about the fundamental character of the accused.

There are, of course, many possible shades of bad character. Those who are lazy, shirkers, boastful, liars, cheats, or exploitative of others might all be deemed persons of bad character, although some might be considerably more morally reprehensible than others. In the case of corruption, there is no such uncertainty in the nature of the dispositional crime. In the common understanding, those who are corrupt are not simply "bad" in some unspecified moral sense. They are *evil* to the core.

What does this idea of *evil* introduce? Why do we so readily associate corruption with evil, and nothing less? The idea of corruption as evil reinforces its core meaning, in political and legal contexts, as involving moral degradation and moral failure. Evil is an extreme term that musters our greatest powers of condemnation. It is also an incredibly freighted term, loaded with centuries of theological, philosophical, and sociological meanings. In this chapter, we shall explore some of those meanings and their implications for the idea of corruption.

THE NATURE OF EVIL

What is evil? This question has preoccupied human beings for centuries. The literature on this subject, even in the past hundred years, is rich and vast. It is impossible in this study of corruption to canvass all of the strains of thought that converge in our postmodern, Western conceptions of evil. We shall consider only the primary strains here.

Western conceptions of evil have changed with the evolution of religious, philosophical, epistemological, and other human cultural beliefs and understandings. The philosopher Amélie Oksenberg Rorty has observed that evil is "an umbrella concept that has undergone dramatic transformations, marked by a rich vocabulary of distinctions [including] . . . abomination, disobedience, vice, malevolence, willfulness, immorality, cruelty, aggression and crime. [The] sources and analysis, . . . instances and characteristic scenarios [of evil] have changed dramatically, in ways that indicate much larger changes in the conceptual worlds in which each of these notions function[ed]."[1]

In very early writings, such as those by Egyptian and Jewish scholars, evil was generally conceived as rooted in disobedience to divine commands.[2] The association of evil with God's disfavor had several conceptual outcomes. First, evil was generally understood to encompass both natural disasters ("physical evils") and human perpetration of human cruelties ("moral evil"), without any important distinction between them. The focus was on human suffering, of whatever kind, and the divinely grounded reasons for it; beyond this, it was not particularly material how that suffering occurred.[3] In addition, there was intense preoccupation with the problem of theodicy, or how the existence of evil could be reconciled with the existence of an all-good, all-powerful God. This problem, pursued by Greek philosophers, early Jewish and Christian writers, and skeptics alike, was discussed by the early Christian theologian Tertullian of Carthage. "If God is good . . . and has knowledge of the future, and also has power to avert evil, why did he suffer the man, deceived by the devil, to fall away from obedience to the law . . . ?" "So if, being good [God] . . . had wished a thing not to happen, and if, having fore-knowledge, he had been aware that it would happen, and if he had had power and strength to prevent it from happening, that thing would never have happened which under these three conditions of divine majesty it was impossible should happen. But . . . as that did happen, the very opposite is proved, that God must be assumed to be neither good nor prescient nor omnipotent."[4]

As Christian thought matured, conceptions of evil entered a new phase.[5] Focus shifted more strongly to moral evil, or evil perpetrated by human choice, and how this could—in view of Christian teachings—be explained. Evil was still seen as a falling away from the good, but with a new, more robust explanation. Human beings were believed to be endowed by God with free will and, at the same time, to be weak and vulnerable. As evidenced by Adam's actions in the Garden of Eden, human beings were characterized as knowing what is right and in accordance with God's law, yet choosing sin and evil.[6]

In the seventeenth and eighteenth centuries, philosophers such as Gottfried Leibniz and Immanuel Kant developed more substantive theories of moral evil and the role of responsible human agency in bringing evil about.[7] Ideas of human weakness and religiously rooted moral law continued; however, whether humans engage in evil became more clearly a function of free-standing moral choice. Human beings were more likely to be described dichotomously as morally good or morally evil,[8] with evil status equated with deficiency in overall moral character,[9] "self-love,"[10] "wickedness,"[11] and "corruption of the human heart."[12] This trend continued in the nineteenth and twentieth centuries, as evil—now something substantively and distinctly identifiable—came to be seen as a function of (aberrant) human psychology. "'[A]t this point,' . . . evil 'cease[d] to be a religious or metaphysical problem' and bec[ame] a subject of human agency and moral choice."[13] Today, moral evil is generally conceived as "a fundamental disorder of the self, whereby the self loses or abandons its orientation toward the universal moral imperative to treat human beings in a moral way."[14] It is "a loss of moral orientation [which] has disastrous consequences for the moral identity of the individual concerned."[15]

In contemporary understandings, "evil" is used to identify moral transgressions of the most serious and threatening kind. "Typically it is assumed that what counts as evil is relatively clear, for example, gratuitous cruelty, intentional humiliation, the extreme suffering of innocents."[16] In the criminal context, for instance, evil is reserved for those persons whose "deliberate, habitual savagery defies any psychological explanation or attempt at treatment."[17] Evil actions are those that are "abominable" or "inhuman."[18] When it comes to vice, evil is used to describe those character traits—such as greed, disloyalty, squandering, envy, and self-indulgence—that serve, under the circumstances, to threaten the social order.[19] Evil excites feelings of both disgust and fear. It revolts us; it is something that we abhor.

Postmodern conceptions of evil have attempted to break the link between evil and religion that played a pivotal role in most earlier conceptions.[20] The goal of postmodernists has been to conceptualize evil in a way "'that does not depend on cognitive claims about the existence or attributes of a supreme being.'"[21] Whatever the success of these efforts in philosophical, psychological, and sociological circles, their impact on common conceptions of evil has been mixed. On the one hand, we are deeply invested in psychological and other nondeistic explanations for the phenomenon of evil in postmodern life. On the other hand, we fear that grounding the idea of evil in issues of purely human agency and secular moral principles will fail to capture the extreme, absolute, trust-shattering nature of evil, and will fall victim to arguments of ethical and cultural relativism.[22] The academic arguments that track these conflicting impulses are well expressed by Jennifer Geddes:

> [There] are two opposing views of the relationship between evil and postmodernism. According to one view, there has been so much violence associated with the word "evil," particularly as it has been used by political and religious fundamentalists to justify their aggression against others, that we would do better to be rid of the term. According to this view, the word "evil" is seen as a holdover from metaphysical and religious vocabularies that have been revealed by postmodern thought to be oppressive, binary, totalizing, and exclusionary. . . . The word has been used so often to justify cruelty and violence, is so laden with its historical abuses, so outdated, so metaphysically and theologically burdened, and inextricably linked with the very

atrocities it describes, it is argued, that we would do well to jettison it from our vocabulary. . . .

According to the other view, articulated by those who focus on the moral relativism that is widespread in our postmodern world, it is not the case that postmodernism reveals the dangers and baggage associated with using the word "evil," but rather the opposite: that the reality of evil reveals the shortcomings of postmodern thought. Postmodernism, it is argued, has few resources with which to respond to the occurrence of evil, few resources which might guide one in making moral judgments. . . . Evil after postmodernism, it is argued, becomes aestheticized as transgression, as excess, as sublime. . . . [W]e need to be able to identify evil and judge it, and postmodern thought is powerless to do so.[23]

Whatever confusion these conflicting strains in current thought might create, the claims of some commentators that we have lost the language for describing evil[24] are clearly premature. Evil, as an idea, retains its power in identifying extreme and threatening moral depravity in academic, theological, political, journalistic, and all other kinds of common discourse. Whatever our uncertainty about moral relativism in some contexts, there are examples of evil—such as the Holocaust, torture, gratuitous cruelty, and genocide—that no one would dispute. As one philosopher has written, "*Auschwitz* . . . stands for all that is meant when we use the word *evil* today: absolute wrongdoing that leaves no room for account or expiation."[25]

Moreover, in our contemporary understandings of evil, certain historical elements persist. The idea of evil as reflecting human weakness—whether of a psychological, religious, or constitutively "moral" character—strongly colors current understandings. We are not only appalled by evil people—we are also disgusted by them. In addition, "[the idea of] [e]vil carries theological resonance even when explicit theological foundations are rejected."[26] The nature of evil, as an absolute concept, seems to require the involvement of transcendent (religious) moral ideas. As Peter Dews has written, "[T]he notion of evil cannot be . . . readily detached from its previous theological and metaphysical contexts. . . . For it is hard to see how evil can be thought of as both relational and radical (or absolute), contrastive and noncontrastive, without drawing on [religious or other transcendent] conceptual resources. . . . Not to think of evil in this way would deprive it of the quality that Paul Ricoeur . . . describes as an 'absolute character of irruption.' . . . [T]his quality is crucial to our sense of evil. . . . In general, it is far from clear that the concept of evil can be entirely naturalized and secularized."[27] Evil has been called "as antique an item as any in the well-stocked museums of ideology, a relic freighted with moralistic lumber carved biblically from that one-of-a-kind species Tree of the Knowledge of Good and Evil."[28]

Perhaps our approach to evil in contemporary thought and discourse might be best summed up this way. We are leery of evil's claim to exemption from examinations for postmodern moral relativity, and we are uncomfortable with its long religious legacy and religious roots. At the same time, however, we find evil both conceptually and linguistically indispensable in the meaning it conveys. For instance, in a recent newspaper article on serial killers, a psychiatrist argues that it is " 'better to avoid the term evil . . . in the courtroom, [because] . . . for many it evokes a personalized Satan [or] the idea that there is a supernatural causation' " for crime.[29] However, Dr. Angela Hegarty, a leading psychiatrist in the study and diagnosis of violent criminals, found that although she "was skeptical of using the concept of evil[, she] . . . realized that in her work she [was] . . . thinking and talking about it all the time. [For instance,] [i]n eleven years as a forensic examiner in [the United States] . . . and in Europe, . . . she count[ed] four violent criminals who were so vicious, sadistic and selfish that no other word could describe them."[30] Dr. Michael Stone, a psychiatrist at Columbia University who has examined several hundred murderers, supports the use of "evil" in this context. " 'We know from experience who these people are, and how they behave.' . . . [I]t is time . . . to give their behavior 'the proper appellation.' "[31]

CORRUPTION AS EVIL: IMPLICATIONS

Just as evil and religion have long been intertwined, so have the ideas of evil and political corruption. For instance, ancient Greek and early Christian scholars wrote of corruption in describing the moral failures of politics,[32] and of general corruption of flesh and incitements to vice.[33] The association of corruption in the political arena with luxury, vice, and other forms of moral evil was robust in fifteenth- and sixteenth-century Italian political thought, in which republican and civic humanist thinkers contrasted civic *virtù* with corruption, decay, and the ruin of cooperative social structures and government.[34] English opposition thought and American revolutionary thought continued the use of these models in the seventeenth and eighteenth centuries.[35]

The deep association of political corruption and evil remains in popular, legal, and academic discourse today. This association is both explicit, as described above,[36] and of a deeper, conceptual nature. Consider, for instance, the following passage from an essay on evil in contemporary thought, written by the sociologist Jeffrey Alexander:

> The social sciences have not given evil its due. Social evil has not been sufficiently respected; it has been deprived of the intellectual attention it deserves. Evil is a powerful and sui generis social force. It must be studied in a direct and systematic way.
>
> . . . .
>
> [In the political context, the idea of democracy] is taken to sum up "the best" in a civil community, and its tenets are considered sacred. . . . The negative [or antidemocratic] side of this symbolic [dichotomy] . . . is viewed as profane. Representing the "worst" in the national community, it embodies evil. The objects it identifies threaten the core community from somewhere outside of it. From this marginal position, they present a powerful source of pollution. To be close to these polluted objects is dangerous. Not only can one's reputation be sullied and one's status endangered, but one's security as well. To have one's self . . . identified in terms of these objects causes anguish, disgust, and alarm. This code is taken to be a threat to the center of civil society itself.[37]

If one were to substitute "corruption" for "evil" or "antidemocratic" concepts in this passage, one would have a perfect conceptual match.

What does this association mean for corruption as a contemporary political and legal concept? There are several implications.

- Corruption, as evil, invites broad association with crimes of "immorality" and vice.

As observed above, evil involves a rich vocabulary of transgressions—abominations, vice, malevolence, cruelty, wickedness, savagery, greed, sin, self-indulgence, and more. The rootedness of the idea of corruption in evil means that corruption, or evidence of corruption, involves this broad range as well. We may believe that corruption itself has these qualities—for instance, that it is malevolent, or wicked, or sinful—or, at least, that these qualities are evidence of the individual's corrupt core.

Corruption's rootedness in evil encourages corruption prosecutions to sweep in broad evidence of other immorality and vice. As described above,[38] allegations of corruption in popular, journalistic, and academic accounts are bolstered by evidence of the target's materialism, gluttony, deviation from sexual mores, and general greed. Since it is evil that we are detecting, through evidence of corruption of character, all of evil's many faces are possibly forms of the malady we have found.

- Corruption, like evil, leaves room for no account and no expiation.

As the philosopher Susan Neiman has observed, whether one considers physical evils (such as the philosophically famous Lisbon earthquake of 1755) or moral evils (such as Auschwitz), the meaning of "evil" in human suffering is clear: it involves "absolute wrongdoing" for which there is "no account and no expiation."[39] Evil is so wrong that no account of a benevolent God or a rational human being can explain it. Furthermore, when it is perpetrated by human hands, there can be no expiation. If an act is truly evil, no passage of time, no remorse, no attempts to rectify the wrong can erase the evil done or justify forgiveness. This belief is attributable (we might surmise) both to the nature of the transgression of evil itself and to our belief that evil acts have revealed the character of the perpetrator to be beyond the pale of human volitional efforts at change or redemption.

Corruption, rooted in the idea of evil, shares this character. Corruption, as commonly understood (and as explained above),[40] is generally believed to confer an irrevocable moral status. Once corrupt character has been diagnosed, we are reluctant to accept any exculpatory, mitigating, or explanatory words or actions by the accused. If a man is corrupt, we do not care if he is remorseful, or was driven to it by perceived financial hardship, or has subsequently performed good works in an effort to clear his name. A corrupt man is . . . a corrupt man. He is warped, perverted, and degraded in the eyes of others. Whatever he may say or do, however long the passage of time, that condition—that *character*—remains unchanged. Something more than human effort, forgiveness, or absolution is needed to change the corrupt man's character or clear his name.[41]

In many ways this may seem curious. As Robert Brooks has posed the question, we can "[forgive] statesmen who have given most distinguished service to their countries [and who] have been, for example, intemperate in the use of liquor or unfaithful in the marriage relation. If in such cases we excuse and forget, why not also excuse and forget corrupt transactions that have been more than repaid by general brilliant conduct of affairs of state?"[42] The answer that Brooks suggests is that while drunkenness or philandering might be seen as unrelated to senatorial or executive duties, corrupt actions affect the same sphere of human conduct—performance as a public servant—as the proffered virtues.[43] This is undoubtedly true, and an explanation to some extent. However, it cannot be all that there is to it. We rather easily forgive and forget other errors or transgressions in public office that relate to performance, but almost never corrupt ones. There must be more behind this universal and unyielding condemnation. The "more," I would suggest, is the belief that corruption involves capture by evil, or a fundamental warping or transformation of an individual's social and moral personality. This is not simply a bad person, or a morally degenerate person; this is a *corrupt* person, who—by his very presence—threatens the governmental order of which he is a part.

- Corruption, rooted in evil, is a moral concept that evokes religious explanations and religious condemnations.

Evil, as we have seen, is steeped in religious histories, inquiries, conceptions, and images. Even if one jettisons the ideas of biblical evil, original sin, and other explicitly religious ideas, the association of evil with belief in transcendent norms and transcendent harms persists. Indeed, it is the very extreme and absolute nature of evil that seems to call out for unquestioned ("god-given") assessments of right and wrong. Corruption, although (perhaps) a more ostensibly secularized idea today, retains, in fact, this deep religious resonance. The common conception of corruption is rooted in religious and biblical ideas of evil, change, possession by the devil, and redemption. As we have seen, discussions of corruption by journalists, commentators, judges, and others easily slip into the language of "Eve and the apple," the guilt of "Satan," temptation by "Lucifer," and so on.[44] Corruption involves "the price of a soul."[45] Just as the idea of evil—by its very nature—seems to thrive in the absoluteness and certainty of religious notions, so does the idea of corruption.

  • Corruption (like evil generally) can ultimately be defeated only through moral suasion.

When we think of the phenomenon of evil in human history, the need to utilize the law to control or punish evildoers is apparent. If we are to deal effectively with murder, genocide, human exploitation, and other acts of depravity, we must respond with coercive societal measures in the form of immediate and severe criminal sanctions. Legal sanctions are necessary to incapacitate offenders, express societal outrage and frustration, deter others, and achieve collective reinforcement of violated norms.

Important as criminal sanctions are, however, they cannot be the only or the most profound response to the threat that evil poses in the world. Criminal sanctions may incapacitate some and deter others, but the impulse toward evil is (we believe) far more widespread than post hoc punishment or threat of punishment can effectively address. As Robert Simon famously put it, "[B]ad men do what good men dream."[46] In the end, we believe that *moral* restraints are the only effective way to combat the threat of widespread *moral* evil in the world.

This conviction can be found even in the work of those who attempt to avoid metaethical, religious, or other philosophical "solutions" to the problem of evil. Consider, for instance, the work of psychologist Carl Goldberg, whose work exploring the potential for malevolence in the development of human personality is well known.[47] In the preface to his book *Speaking with the Devil*, he carefully explains that his subject is "malevolence," not "evil"—the latter being too steeped in metaphysics, religion, and philosophy to be appropriate in a psychoanalytic study of radically deviant human behavior.[48] At the same time, he acknowledges that the "psychological sanitation" of evil fails to capture the vicious quality of these immoral acts.[49] For instance, to give Hitler "diagnostic labels like 'paranoid schizophrenic,' 'manic depressive,' 'borderline personality,' and 'criminal psychopath'" is to fail dismally in understanding.[50] "To speak of the Hitlers, Stalins, Idi Amins, and Pol Pots of the world so glibly is to assume that their heinous crimes are readily explainable by standard, well understood diagnostic concepts. They are not."[51] Malevolence, Goldberg writes, "is a serious moral problem, not just the result of inexplicable psychological causes."[52] As a result, when formulating "constructive responses to malevolence" we must return to ideas that individuals ultimately choose between good and evil, and that social institutions, through their promotion of values, must foster or hinder the malevolent response.[53]

In short, just as early Greek and Judeo-Christian philosophers saw evil as the absence of goodness,[54] we continue to believe that moral suasion is critical to the prevention and containment of evil in the world. We acknowledge the possible validity of neuroscientific work that associates psychopathic tendencies with biological abnormalities[55] and other physiological explanations for the conduct of serial killers and others who occupy the top rungs of the hierarchy of evil. However, we also believe that evil involves moral choice and, as such, is vulnerable—in the ultimate sense—only to moral suasion.

Institutionally, this means (we believe) that although structured strategies for combating political corruption may have some impact, they will ultimately accomplish little if moral attitudes are not changed. For instance, Robert Klitgaard suggests reducing the discretion in bureaucratic decision making, changing systems of rewards and penalties, and better monitoring civil servants' performance as primary strategies for the fight against bureaucratic corruption.[56] Beyond this, however, he acknowledges the need to change ethical standards and bolster underlying moral values.[57] Others are even more direct in their moral pitch. For instance, Syed Hussein Alatas criticizes those whom he calls "structuralists," who attribute the existence of corruption to external causes, such as the legacy of colonial rule, the rise of bureaucratic government, cultural practices of gift giving and nepotism, and other conditions.[58] He writes that "[t]he structuralist explanation of corruption shifts the locus of responsibility from the human actor to factors external to the actor. [In fact,] [t]hese external factors are significant in understanding the extent and manifestation of the phenomenon, but they are not the terminal point of explanation. They are the starting point. The terminal point is the nature of man."[59] Combating corruption is, most deeply, a question of morality and the right foundational values.[60] Indeed, in Alatas's view, disregarding the need for moral regeneration in the fight against corruption "is itself an immoral act."[61]

In summary, the association of corruption with evil has many important implications for our contemporary notions of the idea of corruption. Through this association, corruption involves broad ideas of immorality and sin. It evokes, as a part of its moral nature, religious explanations and religious condemnations. Because of this nature, it not only involves acts such as bribery, extortion, kickbacks, and the like, but also involves association with general immorality of all kinds, including vice. Furthermore, corruption, rooted in evil, has no account and no expiation. Like evil generally, it can ultimately be defeated only through moral suasion.

All of these characteristics of corruption as capture-by-evil, together with its dispositional nature, pose both benefits and costs for its use in law. It is to these complex and difficult issues that we now turn.

5 CORRUPTION AS CAPTURE-BY-EVIL

Desirable or Not?

The idea of corruption as capture-by-evil captures many of our intuitions. Its use in law, however, is fraught with problems. As a dispositional concept, the idea of corruption as capture-by-evil potentially contravenes the idea that we should punish *acts*, not *persons*. In addition, invitations to decision makers to implement subjective ideas of evil are arguably invitations toward standardlessness, emotionally driven prosecutions, and other violations of basic guarantees of the rule of law. As Robert Brooks so well stated, "Public anger at some exposed villainy of this sort is apt to be both blind and exacting."[1] This idea of corruption might capture the essence of the concept that traditional theories miss; but the costs of the use of this idea are high.

Are the costs of the use of this idea sufficiently offset by benefits, such that its use is justified? In this chapter, I sketch the general costs and benefits that the use of corruption as capture-by-evil involves, in popular discourse and in law. In the next chapter, I apply these considerations to three settings: the corrupt politician, the corrupt judge, and the problem of campaign finance reform.

CORRUPTION AS CAPTURE-BY-EVIL: SOCIAL DANGERS AND LEGAL COSTS

The Dangers of Entwining Emotion and Law

Corruption as capture-by-evil has great emotional power. The profoundly moral, religiously steeped, and absolute nature of evil undergirds what is, as a result, essentially an emotionally evocative idea. Evil is not something of which we simply—or even seriously—disapprove. Our response to evil is stronger. It is *emotional*. When we are confronted with evil, we feel anger, revulsion, fear, and disgust.[2] Whether such emotions are wise or unwise, we believe that they are fully justified. We feel viscerally threatened. We feel retributive urges. We want *to take action* against the accused.

Emotions of this sort pervade the idea of corruption. Indeed, if—as I discussed in Chapter 1—the traditional ideas of corruption are often emotionally evocative ideas (with hints of secrecy, betrayal, and underhanded dealing), the idea of corruption as capture-by-evil is even more so. We do not regard corruption, rooted in evil, in dispassionate or coolly intellectual terms. When corruption is described by courtroom lawyers, trial and appellate judges, and popular and academic commentators as "depravity," "defilement," "evil," and "perversion," the situation—we are told—cries out for these emotions and for the condemnation of the accused. Whether such emotions are *justified* in such cases is not a serious question.

Furthermore, if "evil" is a part of a legal concept, its emotional content will be an integral part of the resulting principles of criminal law. If, for instance, we are to segregate for the harshest punishment those acts or offenders considered to be "evil," "depraved," "especially heinous," "atrocious," or "outrageously vile,"[3] or if we are invited by courts and commentators to think of corruption as "depravity,"[4] "defilement,"[5] "perversion,"[6] "sin,"[7] sensual or sexual excess,[8] or possession of "an evil heart,"[9] the invitation is more than an intellectual one. We are invited to indulge our disgust, to express our outrage, to feel our anger and desire for retribution against the accused. When corruption is described by courts and government officials as "a disease,"[10] "a cancer,"[11] "a virus,"[12] and so on, the revulsion and fear that we associate with these are explicitly evoked and implicitly (legitimately) transferred to the legal treatment of corrupt persons and corrupt acts. Corruption is not simply the transgression of some legal norm; we are reminded that it is also a threatening, externally induced evil, which—if not contained by the most extreme legal efforts—will destroy the government and the society of which we are a part.

The question of whether emotion of this sort has a legitimate legal role has been extensively debated. Some theorists have defended emotion of this sort as a part of law's constraining and prohibitive functions. For instance, in *The Anatomy of Disgust*,[13] William Miller argues that disgust and similar emotions have an important and legitimate role in the social orders that are identified and protected by law. Disgust, he writes, "helps mark [the] boundaries of culture"[14] and provides a voice for moral assertions.[15] Emotions such as this "signal[] seriousness, commitment, indisputability, presentness, and reality."[16] "They . . . convey a strong sense of aversion to something perceived as dangerous because of its powers to contaminate, infect, or pollute."[17] They play "a motivating and confirming role in moral judgment."[18]

With all of these functions, the emotions evoked by corruption as capture-by-evil seem to be perfectly aligned. Corruption as slime, ooze, rottenness, and pollution[19] causes us to recoil both intellectually and emotionally. The serious moral boundaries that are transgressed by corruption are identified and reinforced by the emotions of revulsion and fear that evil represents.

This reinforcement of moral boundaries is perhaps particularly critical, since corruption—as the object of opprobrium—is something that otherwise elicits strong temptation and desire.[20] Corruption as capture-by-evil recognizes the power of corrupt temptation in human lives by casting corruption as an external force to which we (as human beings) may succumb.[21] Indeed, ill-gotten riches, power, and the thrill of illicit betrayal are things about which almost all of us have fantasized,[22] if not acted upon. Aware of the razor-thin edge that separates the corrupt from the noncorrupt,[23] one might argue that it is all the more critical that the power of negative emotion be harnessed for the task.

Those who urge emotion's utility generally recognize that there are costs in letting emotions of this sort police our moral and social boundaries. For instance, Miller concedes that "[w]e fear that disgust and contempt may violate norms of fairness and justice, [and that] . . . they may maintain brutal and indefensible regimes."[24] However, he argues that emotions "do much salutary work,"[25] and that their excesses can be inhibited through "recourse to other norms [that] we accept."[26]

Are such emotions, when a part of law, so easily constrained? Whether this is in fact possible is a subject of extensive controversy. Martha Nussbaum has argued persuasively that the emotion of disgust, for instance, has "specific cognitive content [that] . . . makes it always of dubious reliability in social life . . . [and] especially in the life of the law."[27] When employed in the criminal context, it can generate reactions and dispositions that are problematic and unjust. Because of the rootedness of disgust in deep (and subconscious) fears of contamination and the animal, it can promote "magical thinking" rather than an assessment of real danger.[28] It carries the danger of extreme overreaction, as we attempt "to cordon ourselves off from something about ourselves" that the group or individual represents.[29] In other words, emotions may *themselves* promote some sort of different normative basis for the condemnation of persons and their acts—a result that may be unauthorized at best, and dangerous at worst.[30]

When emotions are extreme, and rooted in deep (and unconscious) psychological needs of decision makers, it is difficult to see how it can be assumed that these emotions will be controlled, channeled, and rationally applied through the mechanism of law. If the law invokes and legitimates the idea that an official who has taken a bribe is "despicable," a "monster," "contaminated" by the virus of evil, and riddled with subhuman qualities, it is extraordinarily difficult to imagine how that decision maker will simultaneously regard her as a human being entitled to equal status, worth, and the "mutual respect [due to] . . . all citizens."[31] In corruption prosecutions, tension between the emotions of the populace and the human rights of defendants is well known.[32] Emotion "makes very severe punishments seem rational[,] and suggests no limitation on . . . punishment other than its capacity to degrade offenders."[33] As Jeffrie Murphy has warned, "[W]e should be very cautious about overdramatizing and overmoralizing" the punishment of crime "by portraying it as some righteous cosmic drama . . . [or some] holy war."[34]

It is true, of course, that such raw emotions are always a part of all social institutions to some degree, including law. Emotion and cognition act in concert in the generation of human perceptions and reactions.[35] As a result, the idea of a "dispassionate" rule of law "greatly overstates both the demarcation between reason and emotion, and the possibility of keeping reasoning processes free of emotional [taint]."[36] As long as human beings with their conscious and unconscious motivations and prejudices are in the business of evaluating their fellows, emotion will be a part of law.

The inevitability of the influence of emotion in judging and punishing human deviance does not mean, however, that the law should enthusiastically embrace and fan the flames of emotional, impulsive, atavistic reactions to offenders and their deeds. As Toni Massaro has stated it,

> We surely do need our emotions—all of them—to inform our judgments about right and wrong, good and evil, retribution and mercy. And our anger, love, outrage, disgust, shame, guilt, compassion, empathy, fear, pride, envy, and jealousy all play some role in why we punish, what we punish, how we punish, whom we punish, and whom we excuse. Nevertheless, while we should try to isolate and attempt to understand these emotions, and to relate them to laws and social norms, we also should be extremely wary of . . . an assumption that legal rules or public officials can and should manipulate particular emotions in order to produce . . . behavioral responses.[37]

Indeed, to coolly maintain that emotion is simply a part of law, and that we should simply accept its influence, is to forget the lessons of emotional excess and popular hysteria in criminal prosecutions and punishment that mar every epoch of human history.[38] As Massaro has observed, "The well-documented ways in which group dynamics can quickly transform even fairly cool, moderate feelings into extreme and highly dangerous ones is a sobering caution against official celebration of, or ritualized release of, the already hot emotions of hatred or disgust."[39]

Historically, corruption prosecutions have not been immune to these dangers. Excesses of this type have been a common part of corruption prosecutions in the United States. They are particularly likely when emotional tinder is high for other reasons, such as race. During one notorious period, black politicians elected from the South after the Civil War were often the victims of toxic suggestions of corruption and the assumptions of race. John Adams Hyman, one of the first black politicians elected to the U.S. House of Representatives—from North Carolina in 1874— was a continual target for corruption allegations, although never charged with a crime.[40] The *Georgia Weekly Telegraph*, a white-owned newspaper, opined that Hyman was " 'seized with a desire to get possession of other people's wealth' " while in office and would " 'become a candidate for the North Carolina penitentiary.' "[41] Robert Smalls, a black U.S. representative from South Carolina, was charged and convicted of accepting a bribe. "The evidence in his trial was a check for $5,000 . . ., made out to cash. [It was alleged that] [i]t was intended to buy a vote from the congressman, according to a single witness."[42] That witness, a local printer, relied upon notes that were "encrypted so that only he" could read them.[43] Smalls won on appeal, "not so much because of the trumped-up charges, but as a result of a political deal with state Democrats, who in return were absolved of their involvement with [election] fraud."[44]

Finally, and paradoxically, the entwining of criminal prosecutions with emotions of this sort may actually work to *undermine* the enforcement of criminal laws in some cases. When an offender does not seem to fit the extreme, "monstrous" image that emotion demands, there may be a reluctance to cast her into the category that the law requires. For instance, when corruption charges involve middle-class personages, with families and other upstanding trappings, we may be reluctant to deem them "monsters," "possessed by evil," who are "beyond the human pale." Effectively, we have—through the evocation of an "extreme crime"—backed ourselves into an extreme corner. This problem may explain, in part, the notorious reluctance of juries to convict some blatantly corrupt characters,[45] and the lack of contemporary public consensus about the corrupt nature of campaign finance crimes.

Thus, the idea of corruption as capture-by-evil presents a powerful but disturbing picture. The emotion that this idea implicitly legitimates as a part of law marshals powerful forces of outrage against those who violate their positions of public trust and confidence. At the same time, that emotion implicitly authorizes an extreme view of corrupt acts and corrupt offenders that can undermine other important objectives of the criminal justice system. Whether the idea of corruption as capture-by-evil is desirable or justified, when considered on this ground, is a very difficult call.

The Problem of Character and Acts

Western notions of crime and justice are deeply rooted in ideas of voluntarism. As a general proposition, the criminal law assumes that individuals are voluntary actors who choose to engage in crime. (Indeed, if the crime is found to have been committed under less than voluntary circumstances—such as duress, self-defense, mental incapacity, and so on—either the act is not "criminal" or punishment is excused.) The avowed purpose of the criminal law—whether seen in the classic terms of deterrence, retribution, incapacitation, or rehabilitation—is to deter or punish voluntary acts.[46]

The criminally accused might, coincidentally, have bad character as well. This bad character might be deemed relevant to the kind of punishment that is meted out (particularly in gauging whether we need to worry that the convicted individual will commit a crime again). It might even (more controversially) be cited, directly or indirectly, in the proof of essential elements of particular crimes, such as intent or motive, or proving that the crime (e.g., murder) evinces a "depraved mind" or "depraved heart."[47] Even when indulging in these practices, however, we reaffirm that the criminal law is concerned with decision-based "acting," not "being."[48] Bad character is not what we punish. It is not, *in itself*, the reason for invoking the power of the state or the reason for the execution of punishment. Acts are the fulcrum on which the criminal process rests.

This focus on acts by the criminal law has many purposes. It reaffirms our conviction that human beings are generally voluntary actors, whose behavior can be guided by criminal sanctions, and who should be held responsible for what they do. It also protects individuals from the dangers that criminal prosecution for simple bad character would pose. If we were to implement the belief that the character of the accused is the true focus of criminal inquiry, we would flirt with the oppressive and whimsical application of state criminal powers. Standards, or criteria for prosecution, would be next to impossible to formulate. Citizens who successfully resist the temptations of character would nonetheless live in fear of prosecution for a victimless and responsibility-less crime.

When we consider corruption as capture-by-evil in light of these principles, we find a decidedly mixed picture. Corruption as capture-by-evil is a dispositional concept; it describes the character of the accused. As a legal concept, however, it is not *purely* a question of character; it involves both voluntarism and acts. Acts are a necessary part of this idea of corruption, since it is those acts, and only those acts, that trigger criminal prosecution and raise character concerns. By requiring acts—such as bribery, extortion, kickbacks, and so on—as the dispositional proof, we implicitly reaffirm the idea of responsibility for corrupt actions, and that the creation of corrupt character (or, at least, its detection) is the result of a series of choices by the accused. It is only those who make bad choices—who turn from good to evil—who will be ensnared in our criminal net. Absent such choices, there will be no criminal prosecution of the accused.

It is true, of course, that the idea of corruption as capture-by-evil contains other strains that are not quite so neatly tied to volitional ideas and acts. For instance, corruption as capture-by-evil contains the competing idea that corruption is induced by external forces,[49] which might undermine the idea of its voluntary nature. And we would undoubtedly clamor to remove an official who declares herself to be corrupt even if there is no proof of this through acts.[50] Neither of these observations, however, undermines the rootedness of corruption prosecutions in ideas of intentionality, responsibility, and demonstrated harm. However much we might pity the corrupt official who succumbs to her tempter, we do not (for that reason) absolve her of responsibility for her predicament. And although an official who declares herself to be corrupt should be promptly removed from office, she would not, by reason of this declaration alone, be subject to criminal prosecution.

From what we have considered so far, we might conclude that the dispositional character of corruption as capture-by-evil poses few problems. Although it is present in corruption prosecutions, they might be seen as sufficiently grounded in acts that any involvement of character can—as a practical matter—be ignored.

Before we blithely dismiss this issue, however, let us consider more deeply the effects of dispositional ideas on how we think about offenders and crime. To illustrate the dangers that dispositional ideas create, it is useful to consider another context in which dispositional ideas have been powerful, and their dangers familiar: the treatment of homosexuality as a general societal matter, and by law.

Homosexuality is not, of course, an inherently dispositional idea. As David Halperin has observed in his study of the history of the idea of homosexuality in Western cultures, before the late nineteenth century homosexuality was simply used to describe persons who engaged in certain sexual acts.[51] "[S]exual preference for a person of one's own sex was not clearly distinguished from other sorts of non-conformity to one's culturally defined sex-role";[52] it was simply used to mean an observation of one kind of personal nonconformity, among many others. Beyond the general fact of nonconformity, it carried no particular dispositional baggage about individual tastes, dispositions, or other aspects of human character.

In the late nineteenth century, a cultural shift occurred. A "new sexual taxonomy" was developed, which "was enshrined as a working concept in the social and physical sciences."[53] In this taxonomy, homosexuality was transformed from a general term that described human acts to a far more particular term that was pregnant with psychological and sociological meaning.[54] By

1891, for instance, homosexuality was described as a "persistent feature of human psychology."[55] Focus shifted from simple observations of the acts themselves to a "certain type of specifically sexual subjectivity which [was believed to] incline[] a person to commit those acts."[56] In other words, "the person"—not the acts—became the scientific category, based upon detected psychological (dispositional) characteristics.[57]

With this new, psychological approach, sexuality generally—and homosexuality particularly—became a "constitutive principle of the self."[58] In this view, homosexuality was "not a purely descriptive term, a neutral representation of some objective state of affairs. Rather, it serve[d] to interpret and to organize human experience."[59] Sexuality became, in the view of certain nineteenth-century theorists, "a singular 'instinct' or 'drive,' a force that shapes our conscious life according to its own unassailable logic and thereby determines, at least in part, the character and personality of each one of us."[60] It became "something more than an endogenous principle of motivation outwardly expressed by the performance of . . . acts; it [became] . . . a mute power subtly and deviously at work throughout a wide range of human behaviors, attitudes, tastes, choices, gestures, styles, pursuits, judgments, and utterances."[61] The notion became "that human beings are individuated at the level of their sexuality, [and] that they . . . belong to different types of being by virtue of their sexuality."[62] Sexuality was believed to "hold[] the key to unlocking the deepest mysteries of the human personality"; it was believed to lie "at the center of the hermeneutics of the self."[63]

As the result of the ascendency of this model of sexuality, which has persisted into the twenty-first century, difference became taxonomy and "acts" became "orientation."[64] "[N]ew sexual types [emerged]—namely, the homosexual and the heterosexual, [which were] defined not as persons who perform certain acts, or who adhere to one sex-role or another, or who are characterized by strong or weak desires, or who violate or obscure gender-boundaries, but as persons who possess two distinct kinds of subjectivity, who are inwardly oriented in a specific direction, and who therefore belong to separate and determinate human species."[65] To put it simply, sexuality generally—and homosexuality particularly—became an "innate, characterological disposition."[66]

When one stands back from this model, parallels between "the homosexual" and "the corrupt" are striking. In both cases, we progress from an initial observation about an individual's acts to a purportedly deeper, more profound diagnosis of underlying character. In both cases, acts are deemed to be important in the detection of that character, but "homosexual" or "corrupt" character is presumed to exist, hidden, without them. This can be seen in the trope that homosexuality's "highest expression is the 'straight-acting and -appearing gay male,' a man distinct from other men in absolutely no other respect [than] . . . his 'sexuality'";[67] and in the trope that the corrupt are "hypocrites," "shining brightly" outwardly but inwardly full of deceit.[68] In both cases, the diagnosed character is posed to be globally consumptive of the individual's behaviors, attitudes, tastes, styles, and judgments. For instance, homosexuals are described as a distinct "human species";[69] the corrupt are described as driven by depravity, gluttony, materialism, and greed.[70] In both cases, the underlying disposition is posed as powerful, "a mute power subtly and deviously at work."[71] It is an inexorable, permanent part "of the hermeneutics of the self."[72]

When supposed underlying dispositions are portrayed in these terms, it is but a short step to the conclusion that the *persons* who harbor these dispositions are indistinguishable from the dispositions themselves. Casual reference is made to "the homosexual" and "the corrupt." Furthermore, because of negative portrayal of these dispositions, the person who *is* the disposition is envisioned as having no redeeming characteristics. The "homosexual" is a "pervert"; the "corrupt man" a "monster." As a result of this:

- these dispositions are seen as polarizing and separating;
- the offender is branded with deviance; and
- the humanity of the offender is denied and disregarded.

We (the judging culture) see the individual in question "not as a person who has [engaged in deviance] . . . but as someone who is possessed [by deviance]." We "break the tie of kinship." We "create a chasm between [the offender] . . . and ourselves."[73]

Of course, there are important differences in the contemporary treatment of homosexuality and corruption, particularly in law. For instance, most liberal Western democracies today regard homosexuality as a "condition," not a crime.[74] However, the decriminalization of homosexual conduct does not address the odiousness and collateral effects of belief in the disposition itself. Few would deny that the view of homosexuality as an all-encompassing and profoundly negative dispositional characteristic has had devastating consequences for those labeled "homosexuals" in every sphere of social and legal interaction.[75] When homosexuals are considered to be a different, "deviant" species, implicitly less human than others, the moral constraints that generally inhibit social victimization and legal exploitation are brusquely shoved aside. With stigmatization of this sort comes judgment that the object is disgusting, threatening, and deserving of persecution.[76] "Shaming, humiliating, and degrading [an individual] . . . seems supremely logical and warranted" when his humanity is denied.[77]

The "corrupt," although similarly branded, are perhaps more difficult to imagine as victims of this process in view of their clearly criminal acts. On a certain level, the fact that the corrupt are branded and dehumanized seems to be a case of just deserts. Even in this context, however, the objectification and dehumanization of human beings in this way is troubling. Even the most heinous offender is entitled to individual consideration and intelligent prosecution. If a person is pronounced "to be corrupt," the signaled disposition works to deny the possibility of any explanation, excuse, remorse, or rehabilitation. Judgments of this type—"if left unqualified by other norms, such as decency and proportionality—offer[] little reason to oppose maximally stigmatic penalties or to contain our outrage and disgust."[78] In contemporary American society, we have rejected the idea of "corruption of the blood," which decreed that those convicted of crimes (and their offspring) were irrevocably tainted and stripped of their rights.[79] However, corruption as capture-by-evil veers toward such ideas. From a particular act, this idea confers sweeping and irrevocable status on the actor as a moral outsider, consumed by evil, whom we—as a society—should shun.

There is, in addition, a systemic cost that the dehumanization and "psychological separation" of the corrupt offender suggests. If—as has been observed with evil generally—those who commit an act are deemed to be "dispositionally different," "nonhuman," and "apart from us," then we—as a society—feel little responsibility for their acts.[80] As a result, we are less likely to recognize any role played by a corrupt social or governmental *culture*, and less likely to engage in real self-scrutiny or reform.[81]

In sum, an idea of corruption—such as capture-by-evil—that employs deep, dispositional convictions presents serious dangers. By branding an individual as dispositionally different, or "corrupt" to the core, we flirt with dehumanization and stigmatization. As a result, ideals central to our legal system—such as act-based prosecution and punishment, individualized consideration, and a view of the offender in systemic context—may be undermined or lost.

The Denial of Variable Criminal Culpability

Central to contemporary Western notions of criminal liability is the belief that criminal culpability, within a particular crime category, is variable. Particular facts about the act committed may make it more or less criminally culpable. For instance, a homicide might be committed with recklessness, or intent, or malice aforethought, and the degree of criminal culpability of the actor will depend upon the presence or absence of those elements. An unauthorized entry might be made of a commercial building, or an unoccupied dwelling, or an occupied dwelling, and the degree of criminal culpability of the actor will depend upon those elements. The reason is that we believe that some killings of fellow human beings, and some unauthorized entries, are—by their nature—more reprehensible than others. We do not invoke an image of uniform, predetermined moral outrage to these broad categories of criminal acts.

Compare, now, the crime of corruption. The idea of variable criminal culpability, within particular corrupt-crime categories, is largely absent regarding these acts. Although there are particular elements that are necessary to prove the crime of bribery, or the crime of extortion, or other crimes of corruption, these differences go more toward the identification *of the kinds* of corrupt conduct involved than toward the creation of a hierarchy of greater or lesser criminal culpability. We do not, for instance, think of different acts of bribery as inherently involving different criminal (or moral) culpability. Consider, for instance, the general federal bribery statute. If someone "corruptly gives, offers or promises *anything of value* to any public official . . . with intent . . . to influence any official act," it is bribery—under this federal law—and corrupt conduct.[82] There is no distinction made for the amount of the bribe, or the importance of the matter influenced, or other factors. The only distinction is between giving with intent to influence and giving without proof of that intent—in other words, between corrupt and noncorrupt conduct.[83] Once an act is deemed "corrupt," no further variation in criminal culpability is envisioned. Other federal bribery statutes follow the same pattern.[84] We do not have statutes that provide greater or lesser penalties for acts that are "excessively corrupt," or "excusably corrupt," or "corrupt but of minimal moral reprehensibility." Corruption is all of a piece. All corrupt acts are equally culpable.

This disinclination to assign variable assessments of criminal culpability to corrupt acts is plausibly explained by the idea of corruption as capture-by-evil. If an act is "evil," it is "evil." Although there are undoubtedly different degrees of evil— Hitler's acts in the extermination of millions of human beings were undoubtedly of greater evil than the taking of a bribe by a legislator or judge—the belief that an act is "evil" discourages use of ideas of excusability or lesser moral or criminal culpability. It is almost oxymoronic to think of "excusable evil," or "trivial evil," or "evil that raises lesser fears." On a deep level, "evil is evil." Corruption as capture-by-evil is, by its nature, threatening, inexcusable, and something to be harshly and completely eradicated from the body politic. It denies that corruption can be petty, or the transgression slight.

As a result, corruption definitions, prosecutions, and punishments often lack recognition of basic ideas of variable criminal culpability and the fairness that they should arguably allow. The idea that the giving of *anything* of value to any public official . . . with the intent . . . to influence any official act"[85] enjoys (at least by statutory definition) the same degree of culpability—whether, for instance, it is a pair of football tickets or $100,000 in cash— collides with other notions of fairness and just desert. There are persuasive arguments that corruption is always bad; but to view it as all of a piece in this way, when it comes to individual criminal prosecution and punishment, seems unfair. Knowledge that relatively minor transgressions can trigger the harshest legal sanctions might also make decision makers loath to initiate prosecution or reach conviction.

Indeed, the all-or-nothing consequences of corrupt or noncorrupt character may well contribute to the prevailing uncertainty in public attitudes about what corrupt conduct is. For instance, in a study conducted by John Peters and Susan Welch in 2002, the respondents were asked whether they believed certain acts by public officials would be corrupt.[86] When asked whether a legislator's acceptance of a large campaign contribution in return for voting "the right way" on a legislative bill would be corrupt, 91.9 percent answered yes, and 8.1 percent answered no. When asked whether the promise of a presidential candidate of an ambassadorship in exchange for a campaign contribution would be corrupt, 71.1 percent answered yes, and

28.9 percent answered no. When asked whether a defense secretary's large ownership of stock in a company to which the department of defense awarded a million-dollar contract would be corrupt, 58.3 percent answered yes, and 41.7 percent answered no.[87] It is interesting how—even when faced with what is clearly corrupt conduct, as in the first and third examples—there is no unanimity of opinion. It is of course impossible to know all of the factors that influenced the respondents' answers. However, it is quite possible that some of the discord in these answers is due to a reluctance to label "corrupt" what seem to be ordinary acts.

The failure of the corrupt/noncorrupt dichotomy to reflect the moral complexities of targeted acts has been noted by scholars, and has motivated attempts to introduce more complex models into our understanding of corruption. For instance, Peters and Welch discuss "gradients" of corruption,[88] and Arnold Heidenheimer has suggested that the corruptness of political acts should be evaluated as "black" (universally condemned corruption), "white" (often overlooked or petty corruption), and "gray" (corruption that draws varying assessments of opprobrium).[89] Such ideas, however, have not penetrated the core notion of corruption, as popularly or legally understood. Corruption is simply evil, and threatening. There is no variable criminal culpability for this crime.

The Problem of Standardlessness in Law

The interjection of notions of evil into legal understandings of corruption presents another difficult problem. It permits— indeed, invites—standardless decision making in this area of criminal law.

Criminal law must be implemented in a way that affords individuals notice of prohibited conduct and punishments. We do not (as a society) issue vague guidelines as to what criminal conduct is, and allow individuals to guess at their peril. Rather, we pride ourselves on the notice and fairness that law—in particular, criminal law—affords to the accused.

When, as the law frequently indicates, "corrupt" behavior is required for conviction,[90] and "corrupt" behavior is described as that which is "depraved," "evil," or "wicked," or exhibits "perverted moral weakness,"[91] there is hardly a legal standard here that can be announced or appreciated with any particularity. When does conduct exhibit "depraved" characteristics? What is "evil"? What kind of "wickedness" is the focus of these crimes? As one appellate court noted, " '[I]mmoral,' and its synonyms 'corrupt, indecent, depraved, [and] dissolute' . . . afford 'an almost boundless area for individual assessment of the morality of another's behavior.' "[92] To the extent that definitions of corruption are founded on such shifting and uncertain norms, those definitions are in danger of violating basic principles of notice and fairness that undergird the rule of law.

In addition, and more generally, standardlessness notions of evil permit—indeed, invite—highly dubious approaches to legal decision making in these cases. Ordinarily, in law, we assume the use of an *agentic* model by judges, juries, and others:[93] decision makers are seen as agents, guided and constrained by the societal rules and standards that are given to them. Under this model, "law consists of societally established principles and the use of rational processes to interpret or supplement those principles. [L]aw is [viewed as] a consensual enterprise, with its legitimacy rooted in societal acceptance of its norms. . . . The principles and processes that this model of law uses are ones that are societally articulated and societally understood; they are the principles and processes to which we (as a society) have collectively agreed.

[Accordingly,] [t]hose who interpret and enforce law—such as judges, juries, and executive branch officials—are our agents: they interpret and enforce the law as we (as a society) have established it."[94]

In certain rare instances, the law—as understood by legislators, commentators, and courts—appears to reject this model and to implement another. Under this latter, *conscientic* model, "the legal decisonmaker determines not what the law (as societally established) *is* but what the law (as a matter of conscience) *should be*."[95] In some cases, "this model [is] . . . used by judges, juries, and others charged with the enforcement and interpretation of law . . . when one or more premises of the agentic model of law fail and decisionmakers are forced, as a practical matter, to use this kind of decisionmaking."[96] Far more rare—and far more theoretically problematic—"are [those] cases in which conscientic decisionmaking is not a default rule, to which we reluctantly make limited recourse when the agentic model fails, but is itself the model of law that judges, jurors, and others are specifically commanded to enforce."[97] The theoretical problems with this approach are obvious. "In these cases, legal decisionmakers are commanded by the law to determine what the result, as a matter of personal conscience [or belief], *should be*—a command and a process that are completely inconsistent with otherwise entrenched ideas about the [societally dictated] content of law and the rule of law."[98]

When we instruct juries that a defendant is guilty of bribery or obstruction of justice or other crime if she acted "corruptly," and whether she acted "corruptly" depends upon the ideas of "evil," or "depravity," or "wickedness," and so on, we are clearly inviting decision makers to consult their own ideas of these and, on that basis, decide what this element of criminal law shall be.

The prospect "that those who interpret and enforce the law [will] . . . consult other, more 'personal' sources" of legal meaning leaves us, necessarily, with a sense of profound disquiet.[99] If law's legitimacy is "rooted in societal acceptance of its processes and norms, the idea that those who enforce the law will rely on judgments whose bases have not been accepted by others—indeed, whose bases *have not even been articulated to others*—is deeply and inherently troubling."[100] With decision making of this type "comes the danger of arbitrariness, the use of prohibited factors, and the violation of the very values that the law (as a consensual matter) has established."[101]

All attempts to define important concepts are, of course, imprecise to some degree; even legal understandings often contain uncertainties, leaving—of necessity—questions of interpretation to those who must enforce them. This is quite different, however, from the deliberate invocation of decision makers' personal beliefs about depravity, evil, wickedness, and perversion. To found notions of corruption on ideas that are as purposely broad, emotional, and nonlegal as these is clearly problematic. Such legal understandings of corruption might be potent political phenomena; they might satisfy the public's need for expression of its outrage; but they are fundamentally deficient as delineated elements of criminal prosecutions.

The Problem of Collateral Punishment

As noted above, the dispositional nature of corruption as capture-by-evil lends itself to "evidence" of corruption that ranges far beyond what we would consider fair game for other crimes. Greed, gluttony, materialism, luxuriousness, sexual rapaciousness, and other kinds of personal vice are routinely cited by journalists, academic commentators, and courtroom participants as confirmatory evidence that the accused's character is indeed corrupt.[102]

When evidence of this type is part and parcel of ideas of "corrupt character," it is inevitable that such evidence will influence decisions to convict and the punishments imposed. Recitations of crimes that include accusations of "moral degeneracy,"[103] "raucous" libertinism,[104] "brazenness and gluttony,"[105] "hypocrisy,"[106] and "defilement"[107] imply that these observations are relevant to corruption prosecutions and punishments. This is true even though, as a formal legal matter, the propriety of conviction or punishment on the basis of completely collateral matters such as these undoubtedly would be denied.

In summary, corruption as capture-by-evil presents many serious problems. The question that remains is whether there are offsetting benefits that might nonetheless justify the use of this idea.

CORRUPTION AS CAPTURE-BY-EVIL: THE POSITIVE CASE

Assertion of Corruption's Costs

The negative economic effects or "costs" of corruption have been extensively analyzed. Most directly, corruption often involves the diversion of public money or other government assets to private individuals. Accordingly, it involves the direct or indirect waste or theft of public resources.[108] Even if it does not directly involve the theft of public money, it involves the waste of government resources in other ways. For instance, government efficiency is ruined when officials wait for bribes to perform their duties or tolerate the inefficiencies of others as part of a corrupt, bribe-taking network. As Robert Klitgaard has written,

"[W]hen corruption becomes a decided possibility, the incentives of both officials and citizens are twisted toward socially unproductive, though personally lucrative, activities. Officials spend an increasing amount of their time looking for ways to secure bribes and extort payments, rather than exerting themselves in fulfillment of their public duties. Citizens, too, invest their energies in the pursuit of illicit favors, augmenting their incomes not through productive activity but through bribery, dishonesty, and collusion."[109] A study of corruption in the Philippines concluded that corruption "leads to the favoring of inefficient producers, the unfair and inequitable distribution of scarce public resources, and the leakage of revenue from government coffers to private hands."[110] Corruption in public employment cripples the implementation of merit systems in promotion and hiring, and destroys the efficiencies and productive capacities that merit systems would introduce.[111] Corruption has also been shown to have, in gross, undesirable distributional effects. As Klitgaard observes, "Most studies show that the rich and privileged benefit from corrupt schemes at the expense of the poor, the rural, and the disadvantaged."[112]

In recent decades, the assumption of corruption's economic negativity has been challenged by some economists and others who claim that there is, in fact, "good" economic corruption. Under this theory, corruption achieves efficiencies that government rules (such as unnecessary bureaucratic requirements or red tape) impede. Corruption, it is argued, "greases the wheels";[113] it permits entrepreneurs and other productive people to circumvent impediments that have been erected by political authorities who do not understand efficient procedures or have other agendas that impede economic development.[114] Essentially, in this view, it must be acknowledged that some existing rules and laws are bad—they impede people whose activities would increase economic productivity. Therefore, the disregard of these rules or laws is an economically desirable phenomenon.

Are such arguments convincing? There is no doubt that red tape and other rules can seriously impede economic productivity. However, the idea that corruption is a net positive economic phenomenon has little empirical backing. In recent years, world institutions—including those concerned with economic development—have well-nigh universally condemned the idea of "good" economic corruption.[115] The most penetrating academic analyses, including those of economists, have arrived at the same overall conclusion.[116]

What the advocates of "good" economic corruption fail to consider are the effects of nonlegal payoffs, nepotism, bribes, and other corruption on the underlying social fabric and the basic idea of the rule of law. In a society riddled with corruption, the social and political cohesion necessary for collective life are undermined; there is an atmosphere of distrust, in which each person grabs for herself, or for a small family group or clan to whom she owes loyalty.[117] For instance, in a study of a corrupt society in Italy, researchers concluded that it was governed by the ethic of the "amoral familist," in which "no one will further the interest of the group or community except as it is to his private advantage to do so."[118] Conditions of trust in others and willingness to sacrifice short-term gain for long-term goals are missing. In such a society, "the hope of material gain in the short-run will be the only motive for concern with public affairs."[119] For instance, "[i]t is taken for granted that all those who can cheat on taxes will do so."[120] The inducements that generally lead people to sacrifice for an organization's goals—such as identification with the purposes of the organization and trust in other members—are absent.[121] Under these conditions, organization—particularly public organization—is very difficult to achieve.[122]

The governance costs of corruption can be predicted from the social and political costs already described. Fundamental to the idea of government by law is the principle of public enactment of rules and regulations that are followed by all. The essence of corruption, as I have described it, is the reaping of benefits in a manner that is contrary to announced rules. Persistent and widespread violation of official rules leads to cynicism, distrust, and the conviction that the rule of law has no meaning.[123] When government policy is one thing and actual practice is another, corrosion of respect for government is an endemic problem.

Indeed, the psychological effects of corruption are so powerful that a few instances of corruption may generate popular conclusions about the prevalence of corruption that are complete distortions of reality. As H. A. Brasz has observed, "[E]ven corruption on a minor scale can easily suggest widespread decadence to the public."[124] Once such beliefs take hold—unjustified as they may be—popular outrage and political instability often follow.[125] Studies have linked corruption with regime change and the rise of totalitarian government. If citizens believe that they are victims of a government that is rife with corruption, instability, and special privileges for those in power, the promise of the "efficiency" and "equal treatment" of a totalitarian regime may appear to be highly desirable.[126] As Gunnar Myrdal puts it, "[T]he habitual practice of bribery and dishonesty tends to pave the way for an authoritarian regime, whose disclosures of corrupt practices in the preceding government and whose punitive action against offenders provide a basis for its . . . acceptance by the articulate strata of the population."[127] Corruption can become a scapegoat for other social and economic ills, leaving those problems unaddressed.[128]

Just as there are those who argue that there are economic benefits from corruption, there are those who reply that corruption has social and political benefits as well. These alleged benefits include the fostering of the integration of out-of-power groups,[129] the building of political parties,[130] and the achievement of general "bureaucratic responsibility."[131] Indeed, it has been argued that "[there are] places in the world today where corruption is progress."[132] (This last assertion may be a more powerful statement about the deteriorated conditions in those countries than it is about the desirability of corruption.)

Whatever the merits of corruption in isolated situations may be, there is little doubt that corruption in gross undermines societies and governments. The de facto establishment of government rules, policies, and norms by the individual, capricious, and unreviewable decisions of corrupt officials is destructive not only of the governmental order but also of the maintenance of the interpersonal trust necessary for the social fabric itself. Discussing corruption in the Asia-Pacific region, C. Raj Kumar has observed that "[l]aws are constantly violated, creating a vicious cycle of bribery and influence-peddling that has resulted in a cynical public attitude toward law enforcement. Even when anti-corruption laws are occasionally enforced, they become political ploys on the part of politicians to settle scores against the opposition. This has further accentuated the twin problems of the 'criminalization of politics' and the 'politicization of crime.'"[133] Describing—for example—the situation in Cambodia, a report prepared in 2004 for USAID/Cambodia, and set forth at length by Kumar, stated that because of corruption, "[o]rdinary Cambodians distrust the legal system, including the formal courts. The police and other enforcement bodies are also seen as corrupt. Impunity is the norm. No one with the patronage of the state is punished, whether for massive pillaging or petty theft. In fact, those most at risk are individuals and organizations that dare to resist corruption. Most Cambodians regard resistance as a futile act."[134] Corruption involves a compendium of human rights violations, including denial of access to justice, equal treatment before the law, and the economic development necessary to sustain life.[135]

Perhaps the most pithy response to those who argue for corruption's benefits was made by Sinnathamby Rajaratnam, former minister of foreign affairs and labor of Singapore. In a speech entitled "Bureaucracy versus Kleptocracy," Rajaratnam observed that among those who argue for corruption's "benefits," none (incidentally) wants it for his own country.[136] Discussing what he calls the "ideological justification for a kleptocracy [that] has in recent years been provided by certain scholarly gentlemen from the West," Rajaratnam argued that "a society that is indulgent toward corruption . . . is not . . . a liberal sophisticated society inspired with a shrewd understanding of human nature. . . . [I]t is what one sociologist has aptly termed a 'kleptocracy'—a society of the corrupt, for the corrupt, by the corrupt."[137] Experience proves, he writes, that "[i]n most developing countries, a few years of this kind of freebooting affluence [leads] . . . to economic anarchy, political instability, and the eventual replacement of democracy by civilian or military autocracies."[138] As the sociologist Hartmut Schweitzer states it, "[On] the question . . . [of whether] there are positive social functions of corruption, a question to which many authors have devoted their arguments, . . . corruption has no positive function except as an indicator that something is seriously wrong."[139]

Contemporary news accounts reinforce these realities. For instance, an article written in 2005 described the effects of corruption charges in Brazil and elsewhere in Latin America:

As he campaigned for the presidency in 2002, Luiz Inácio Lula da Silva boldly pledged to clean up the sordid politics of Brazil. His, he vowed, would be an ethical, honest and moral government the likes of which Brazil had never seen.

That pledge helped him win the votes of more than 50 million Brazilians and a sweeping mandate. But now, in a gloomy echo of what has happened time and again across Latin America, Mr. Da Silva's government is mired in the biggest, most audacious corruption scandal in his country's history.

A congressional inquiry has heard testimony that the governing Workers' Party paid dozens of deputies from other parties a $12,500 monthly stipend for their support. This month, a party functionary was detained at an airport with $100,000—stashed in his underwear—which he claimed to have earned selling vegetables.

Mr. da Silva's chief aide has been forced to resign, as have the president, secretary general and treasurer of the Workers' Party. . . .

Brazil's scandal is just the latest reminder of the unremitting corruption that has marked Latin American politics. . . .

. . . Opinion polls routinely cite corruption as a top cause for a dangerous disillusionment sweeping the region. The disaffection has led to violent popular outbursts, including the lynching of public officials in Peru, and has helped force out eight heads of state in five years.

. . . .

Latin Americans regard corruption as their most serious problem after the region's economic crisis, according to a survey of 18 countries taken in 2004.[140]

Gains against corruption and in favor of political stability have subsequently been made by a number of Latin American countries. In none of these countries, however, is it fair to say that the populace regards corruption as a necessary or benignly tolerable phenomenon.

In addition, corruption is increasingly recognized as a phenomenon with profound international consequences. Corruption is no longer something that is evaluated solely in terms of its effects on the citizens subject to the corrupt government; it is also recognized as something that poses a direct threat to the larger world order.[141] As Robert Legvold has recently noted, corruption influences "crucial facets of the international security agenda; issues of war and peace, including regional conflict; global terrorism; and the proliferation of weapons of mass destruction" controlled by corrupt states.[142] Corruption also risks the creation of failed states, international threats to human health, illicit trade, money laundering, and transnational crime.[143] Indeed, the connection between corrupt governments and world ills is so obvious that the only real surprise is the length of time that it has taken observers to focus on these risks.

The idea of corruption as capture-by-evil reinforces, in ringing terms, that corruption is far more scourge than benefit. It identifies—through its harsh imagery—what most would consider corruption's true social and governmental costs. Corruption is not something that can be minimized, or rationalized, or set aside; it is an evil, a cancer, whose very existence threatens societies and governments. Corruption as capture-by-evil asserts the true costs of corruption in a way that more detached, less condemnatory images do not.

When this idea of corruption is a part of legal proceedings and legal discourse, the costs of corruption are communicated in a powerful way. When—in the course of highly publicized criminal proceedings—corruption is described by advocates, judges, or the press as a "cancer," "virus," or "pathology" that "warps" the country's "very soul," there is no question about the speaker's view of corruption's costs. Corruption, through this portrayal and its adoption by the political and legal machinery of the state, is unequivocally seen for what it is: a phenomenon destructive of societies and governments.

Affirming the Need for Moral Injunction

The idea of corruption as capture-by-evil is rooted in the deep conviction that corruption is a scourge. It is, in addition, a *moral* issue. It demands a *moral* response.

The reasons for this moral grounding are multifaceted. First, the popular idea of corruption, as described above, involves self-involvement, self-indulgence, the loosening and discarding of the restraint of social bonds.[144] Since social bonds are generally viewed as *moral* bonds, it is but a small step to the idea that political corruption involves not only illegality but also deep moral transgression. We believe that a congresswoman who accepts bribes is not only worthy of criminal punishment; she is also a loathsome creature who has transgressed deeply entrenched and unquestioned moral norms. If an individual *is corrupt*, as indicated by her actions, we believe that one can fairly conclude that she is self-involved, self-indulgent, and generally contemptuous of moral injunctions that we believe are critical to social and political life.

The idea of corruption as capture-by-evil serves an important social function because it expresses this sentiment. It is the most powerful statement possible of the moral decay that we believe corruption to involve. It is an essential—indeed, necessary— expression of what deeply held cultural beliefs demand. If government is to be responsive to public sentiments, and if law is to perform its norm-enforcing function, then corruption as a deeply moral notion is an important part of corruption's condemnation and its punishment.

Indeed, the need for recognition of a contravening moral imperative is perhaps even greater in this criminal context than in others. First, there is the particular temptation that corruption presents. Whatever we may think of burglars, bank robbers, or murderers, we generally do not feel tempted to commit their crimes. They are, to our minds, "aberrational" persons whose acts we find to be far beyond our general range of considered conduct. For instance, as much as we might desire riches, we do not seriously consider breaking into someone's house to steal them.

Corruption is very different. The lure of possibly corrupt acts is something known to all of us. In dozens of ways in our daily lives we are faced with the temptation to breach minor duties and minor laws. Shall I, as a legislator, accept some unreported gift? Shall I, as a taxpayer, exaggerate my charitable deductions or "forget" to report some income (paid in cash) that I know will not otherwise be traced? To bolster our resistance, and reinforce legal norms, corruption as capture-by-evil adds religious and moral injunction with the demonization of those who "fall." Combating corruption, we believe, requires more than legal threats; it requires *moral* accountability, *moral* judgment, *moral* laws.

In addition, there is the problem of corruption's seemingly unique norm-changing powers. Generally, the fact that a particular kind of lawbreaking is common does not result in the erosion of that norm. For instance, when burglary is widespread, we do not generally find that burglary becomes more acceptable. However, it is precisely that response that corruption, whether petty or serious, often engenders. If everyone cheats on taxes, it becomes acceptable to do so. If most officials accept gifts or speed money, it becomes acceptable to do so. When we speak of a "culture of corruption," we speak of more than simply widespread lawbreaking; we imagine a society in which the underlying fabric of previously accepted social and legal norms has decayed.[145] As one observer described it, in a culture of corruption "official corruption is so brazen[] that it is almost taken for granted."[146] In extreme cases, there is a "fusion between the licit and the illicit,"[147] and the erasure of the distinction between private and public actors and power.[148]

In sum, the inherent appeal of corrupt acts, combined with the psychological effects of widespread violation, render anticorruption norms uniquely vulnerable. In a gradual process of erosion, the morally reprehensible nature of corrupt acts may become more and more remote, and committing them more and more acceptable. Corruption not only violates norms; it slowly and insistently *challenges the wisdom and validity of norms.* Thus, it can be argued, when we fight corruption, we must fight fire with fire. Corruption must be fought on the same ground on which it makes its challenge. Whether as a social or a legal matter, corruption must be seen as contravening a moral imperative that sharply contradicts temptation and bolsters anticorruption norms.

Recognition of Systemic Harm

The potential of corrupt acts to destabilize other individuals (through temptation) and to challenge the validity of norms leads us to the final—arguably the most powerful—positive function of the idea of corruption as capture-by-evil. This is the expression, through this idea, of corruption's unique ability to cause *systemic harm*.

Corruption, we have seen, involves the breach of duties, illegality, and other traditional notions, but it is more. It is a dispositional notion. It involves the conviction that an individual has changed, become morally degenerate, through the effects (somehow) of an external force.

In addition, when we consider the corrupt individual in society with others, we find effects that we do not ordinarily associate with crimes. Corruption, under this understanding, carries more than the threat of some individual transgression; it presents a vital threat to the larger societal fabric of which it is a part. The popular visualization of corruption as a "cancer" or "virus" is not incidental; it is a critical part of what the idea of corruption, under the common conception, attempts to convey. Corruption, in this view, is not simply an official's poor choice or bad act; it has *institutional effects and institutional dangers* that distinguish it from acts that are simply evil, or dangerous, or morally depraved. A terrorist's acts are evil or dangerous, but they are not corrupt. If an individual lies, cheats, or steals, we would not—simply on that basis—label her corrupt. Corruption involves more; it involves a threat to the fabric of shared values that is necessary to sustain societies and governments. A corrupt official does not simply threaten harm to particular individuals with whom she might come into contact; her existence threatens the entire governmental system of reliance, trust, and shared values of which she is a part.

The association of corruption with institutional capture and degradation is set forth by Dennis Thompson in striking terms. "In the tradition of political theory," he writes, "corruption is a disease of the body politic. Like a virus invading the physical body, hostile forces spread through the political body, enfeebling the spirit of the laws and undermining the principles of the regime." In democracies, "the virus shows itself as private interests. . . . The essence of corruption in this conception is the pollution of the public by the private." Furthermore, "[t]he modern conception of corruption, which includes both the individual and institutional kind, preserves this essence."[149]

Corruption, in short, involves not only the capture of the individual by evil—*it involves the potential capture of the system by evil*. Corruption involves power, and the threat of the misuse of power. We rarely think of a very poor person, or a powerless person, as corrupt. Corruption involves institutional power, effects, threats, and dangers. It threatens to pervert the apparatus of government. Corruption as capture-by-evil threatens "the actual and apparent integrity of public life."[150]

The idea of corruption as capture-by-evil involves many potential costs and benefits. In the following chapters we shall consider several settings in which this idea has great power. The question that we shall address is whether—or when—the use of this idea of corruption is justified in particular, concrete contexts, as a superior conceptualization of the vital interests that are at stake.

6 COSTS AND BENEFITS EXAMINED

Three Settings for Corruption

THE CORRUPT POLITICIAN

There is no shortage of recent tales of corrupt politicians who were claimed to be captured by evil. We shall examine the cases of four individuals whose actions cover a spectrum of allegedly corrupt conduct: Diane M. Gordon, former state assemblywoman from Brooklyn, New York; Rod R. Blagojevich, former governor of the state of Illinois; Don Siegelman, former governor of the state of Alabama; and Eliot Spitzer, former governor of the state of New York.

The Case of Diane M. Gordon

In the spring of 2008, Diane M. Gordon—a former state assemblywoman from Brooklyn, New York—was tried on corruption charges in state court. After a four-week trial, Gordon was convicted of eight of nine criminal charges brought against her, including the receipt of bribes and other corruption felonies.[1] The genesis of the charges was Gordon's offer to help a developer acquire city land if he would, in turn, provide her a house for free. The critical evidence at trial were video and audio recordings made by the developer, Ranjan Batheja, who cooperated with authorities after he was caught trying to bribe a building inspector in another case.[2] As a *New York Times* reporter put it, "Mr. Batheja sought to win the right to develop a $2 million parcel of vacant city land . . . in Brooklyn. And Ms. Gordon told Mr. Batheja, whom she called 'Raj,' what she wanted in return."[3] " 'Raj, . . . since I am an assemblywoman, I definitely need a detached home. I don't need to be attached to anybody. Private. . . . Detached. You can make it happen. Raj, you can make it happen.' "[4]

The house Gordon described was to cost about $500,000 and to be built in a gated community developed by Batheja.[5] Gordon asked for jacuzzis, cherry cabinets, a "nice-sized livingroom," and granite countertops.[6] Under the original terms of the deal, Gordon was to pay $1 for the house. Later she suggested a selling price of $200,000, which would be secured by a mortgage held by Batheja. Batheja would cancel the mortgage after the city contract was secured. Under the final form of the plan, she suggested putting the transaction in the name of her mother.[7] In the end, the scheme fell apart, and the house was not built. All that Gordon received was a pair of French doors, valued at $600, for her office. And Batheja was denied the contract to develop the city land.[8]

At her sentencing, Gordon's lawyer argued that she was not a bad person, only " 'a good person who stands convicted of doing a bad thing.' "[9] The prosecution argued that a long sentence was justified, because "not only had . . . Gordon tried to get a free house, . . . but . . . after her indictment, she had the gall to run for re-election, which she won. 'The defendant held on to the seat she defiled,' . . . the lead prosecutor [argued]."[10] The trial judge expressed regret at Gordon's fall but remarked that "the case represented an 'outrageous breach of trust.' "[11] Sentenced to prison for two to six years, Gordon was eligible for parole after twenty months.[12]

This case, in many ways, is a routine example of the corrupt politician. In such cases, the idea of corruption as capture-by-evil is routinely employed in both the description of the case and its disposition. Accounts of such cases describe not only bribery, or other corrupt conduct; they describe individuals who are "sinners," who are "morally degenerate," and whose personalities are characterized by self-indulgence and the disregard of the restraints of social rules. In Gordon's case, not only is the illegal quid pro quo transaction described; we are also told (in express and implied terms) of Gordon's hubris, excess, and apparent decadence. Gordon, we are told, "needed" a detached home costing some $500,000, signaling her hubris and greed. Not only was this to be an expensive house, in the usual sense; it was to be fitted with over-the-top luxuries such as jacuzzis, cherry cabinets, fine finishings, and granite countertops. When her lawyer urged at sentencing that she was not a bad person, only "a good person who stands convicted of doing a bad thing," the words ring hollow. The far stronger conclusion, from the facts presented, is that her character—her being—had degenerated into one of arrogance, indolence, rank materialism, and greed.

The benefits of the idea of corruption as capture-by-evil are obvious in this context. It is undeniable that the betrayal of the public trust by elected officials in cases such as this causes incalculable harm to the achievement of the goals of government and fosters public attitudes of lawlessness and contempt. The uncompromising idea of corruption as capture-by-evil reinforces the dangers of implicit claims of impunity by such figures, and reinforces awareness of their actions' true societal and governmental costs. The imagery and assumptions of the idea of capture-by-evil remind citizens, in no uncertain terms, that corruption is a moral issue. In this case, Gordon's removal and punishment were arguably very necessary to make a clear stand against this kind of venal scourge.

What about the costs of this conception of corruption? The greatest dangers in the use of capture-by-evil in routine cases of this type are the punishment of character (not crimes) and unjustified harshness in the treatment of the accused. In Gordon's case, it could be argued that the emotion that this idea aroused, and the character that it attributed to her, were extreme for what the acts, themselves, were. It could also be argued that evil's resistance to the notion of variable criminal culpability in such cases is unfair. This was (as far as we know) Gordon's first and only substantial criminal transgression, and—on a corrupt scale—certainly far from the worst of its type. One could question whether the prosecutorial zeal in this case was fueled in fact by the desire to punish character or to punish collateral acts. There is doubt (in the margins) whether Gordon would have been punished as harshly had the house she requested been simple, rather than luxurious, and whether the prosecutor was as outraged by her "gall to run for re-election" as by her allegedly corrupt act.

On balance, however, concerns about the costs or excesses of corruption as capture-by-evil do not gain much traction in cases of this type. Although the transaction was venal, the conduct was carefully orchestrated and required a strong, moral condemnation in response. Whatever dangers of corruption as capture-by-evil might carry in such cases, they seem to be ordinarily outweighed by the societal and governmental costs of such graft. When dealing with political corruption of this type, corruption as capture-by-evil seems to have substantially greater practical utility than demonstrable costs.

The Case of Rod Blagojevich

On December 9, 2008, Rod Blagojevich—then governor of Illinois—was arrested on federal corruption charges. Federal prosecutors alleged that Blagojevich and his chief of staff, John Harris, engaged in "a 'staggering' level of corruption involving pay-to-play politics in Illinois' top office."[13] In particular, "[f]ederal prosecutors, reinforced by testimony by Blagojevich insiders and hours of secretly recorded FBI audiotapes, . . . [alleged] that the two-term governor shook down businessmen and pressured enemies in a 'public corruption crime spree.' "[14]

Most damning was the allegation that Blagojevich sought money from the exercise of his power to appoint a replacement for Barack Obama in the United States Senate. Upon Obama's election as president of the United States, Blagojevich—as the governor of the state that Obama had represented in Congress—had the power to appoint his successor. According to press accounts, the charges alleged that Blagojevich "brazenly put [his power of appointment] up for sale." "In recorded conversations, . . . Blagojevich seemed alternately boastful, flip and spiteful about the Senate choice, which he crassly likened at one point to that of a sports agent shopping around a free agent for the steepest price. . . . At times, he even weighed aloud [the prospect of] appointing himself for the job."[15] " 'I've got this thing,' Mr. Blagojevich said on one recording, according to [the federal] affidavit, 'and it's [expletive] golden. . . . I'm just not giving it up for [expletive] nothing. I'm not gonna do it. And, I can always use it. I can parachute me [in] there."[16]

A Blagojevich aide told government investigators that "even a month before . . . Obama was elected president[,] . . . Blagojevich had begun searching for ways to make money or to gain a cabinet-level job, ambassadorship or private foundation job through his duty as governor to appoint a new senator."[17] The witness said that "he had ignored and never carried out some of the Governor's more extreme requests, including one that [he] . . . 'reach out' to a member of Congress . . . to suggest that a nonprofit group be created to benefit . . . Blagojevich in exchange for picking a particular Senate candidate."[18] Other alternatives were that "Blagojevich wished to be given the left-over campaign money from one unnamed Senate hopeful, or a $1.5 million donation from another." At one point, Blagojevich considered a private foundation job as the payoff, although when an aide suggested the salary might be between $200,000 and $300,000, Blagojevich's response was " '[I]s that all?' "[19]

After the corruption charges were filed, Blagojevich was arrested and released on bail. On December 30, 2008, he appointed Roland W. Burris, a former Illinois state attorney general, to the vacant Senate seat. This was over the objection of a "host of Illinois lawmakers . . . [who argued] that any choice would be tainted."[20] Senate Majority Leader Harry Reid immediately issued a statement, rejecting the appointment on the ground that "Illinois Gov. Rod Blagojevich is 'corrupt' " and that the Senate could not seat his appointee.[21] Reid asserted that "Blagojevich obviously is a corrupt individual. . . . We're talking about a cloud over the State of Illinois coming with anyone appointed by Blagojevich.' "[22] When Burris arrived in Washington, Senate officials rejected his paperwork.[23] Burris's seating was stalled for weeks, while Senate officials tried to decide whether there were legal grounds to exclude him.

On January 14, 2009, Blagojevich was impeached by the Illinois House of Representatives on a 117–1 vote. The Illinois State Senate voted 59–0 for conviction fifteen days later, and he was removed from office.

Three months later, Blagojevich was indicted on sixteen federal felony charges, including racketeering conspiracy, wire fraud, extortion, and the making of false statements to federal agents. The indictment charged that Blagojevich "used his official position . . . to seek financial gain in nearly every element of government work, from picking members of state commissions to signing legislation."[24] In addition to Blagojevich, others charged included Lon Monk, Blagojevich's former chief of staff; Christopher Kelly, a Blagojevich fund-raiser; and William Cellini, a Springfield power broker.[25] "Among . . . new allegations [were] . . . [t]hat Blagojevich, Monk, Kelly, and convicted businessman Tony Rezko 'agreed to direct lucrative state business' regarding a $10 billion pension bond deal in 2003 'to a company whose lobbyist agreed to provide hundreds of thousands of dollars'" to the four men.[26] According to the indictment, "[t]he tentacles of corruption . . . reached Blagojevich's household."[27] It was charged that Patti Blagojevich, a real estate agent and the ex-governor's wife, "received thousands of dollars in payments on deals for which she had done little or nothing."[28] After the indictment was issued, the press tracked Blagojevich and his family to a pool-side location in Disney World, where they were taking a family vacation.[29]

Blagojevich was arraigned on April 14, 2009, in federal court in Chicago. A reporter for the *Chicago Tribune* described the scene:

> Former Gov. Rod Blagojevich was inching toward a black SUV that would take him from federal court, declaring his innocence as he tried to shuffle through a thick ring of pushing and shoving TV cameramen and news reporters

who shouted questions while holding recorders an inch from his chin.

"I want to say this to the people of Illinois: I have not let them down," offered Blagojevich, sometimes jerking his head back to avoid an elbow or camera lens.

. . . .

The closer he came to Dearborn Street and his escape, the more cameramen piled in front of him, unwilling to give ground and miss a shot.

"Your colleagues are going to get hurt here," Blagojevich warned. "They're going to get knocked into cars."

One cameraman swore when he was shoved, then noticed Blagojevich nearby and apologized for the foul language.

"It's all right, man. I heard it before," Blagojevich said as he was jostled. "Listen to some of those tapes."

Excerpts of undercover government recordings—released at the time of Blagojevich's arrest—infamously caught him and his wife, Patricia, cursing.

. . . .

[At his arraignment, his attorney told the judge] that the former governor will soon ask [that restrictions on his travel be lifted]. . . . Blagojevich was ordered to surrender his passport at the time of his arrest. Sources familiar with the matter said he is looking to be allowed to travel to Costa Rica for the filming of a reality television show. An NBC representative confirmed that the show is called, perhaps fittingly enough, "I'm a Celebrity—Get Me Out of Here!"[30]

. . . .

Blagojevich was asked what his legal strategy will be to deal with what looks like the daunting task of defending himself. Aside from the tapes, a close group of former aides and fundraisers is lining up to testify against him in bids for leniency for themselves.

Blagojevich said he would be relying on the whole truth and nothing but the truth.

. . . .

Blagojevich did stop to greet a few . . . citizens as he left the courthouse . . ., seemingly gravitating toward anyone watching him who wasn't a reporter. He hugged one woman before making it to a revolving door, softly telling her, "God bless you."

Tony Stevens, 34, of Chicago was waiting for him on the sidewalk. He wound up in the center of the media herd when Blagojevich stopped answering questions and turned to Stevens for a photo-op.

Blagojevich stood patiently for a few minutes as a reporter tried, unsuccessfully at first, to operate Stevens' aqua blue Walgreens camera.

"Here we go. Smile, Governor," the reporter finally said. "Can I get a copy of that?"

But moments chatting with everyday bystanders were few and far between. . . .

What about his lawyers? What about Costa Rica? What about the tapes?

"My bigger concern is getting in the car," he said.[31]

On July 8, 2009, Harris pleaded guilty to wire fraud as part of a deal with prosecutors in which he agreed to testify against Blagojevich.[32] On September 12, 2009, Kelly died of a drug overdose, an apparent suicide.[33]

As he awaited trial, Blagojevich "never dropped out of the public eye. He [did] dozens of interviews and [was] back on the TV circuit."[34] When he appeared on the street, he was "immediately surrounded by tourists and locals who want[ed] to shake his hand, pose for photos or shout encouragement."[35] He published a memoir[36] in which he described "his childhood in a working-class, immigrant family; compar[ed] . . . himself to numerous Shakespearean characters; and [reflected] . . . on finding himself briefly inside a federal cell, where he did push-ups, he [said], to pass the time."[37] He compared himself in the book to Icarus, the character in Greek mythology who flew too close to the sun.

In October 2009, prosecutors complained in federal court that Blagojevich's planned appearance with Donald Trump on the NBC reality television show "The Celebrity Apprentice" might prejudice the potential pool of jurors for his later trial on corruption charges.[38] As one news account stated, "The show's premise is that celebrities who are often teased as being less than A-list stars compete in business challenges to raise millions of dollars for charities while trying to avoid being 'fired' by Mr. Trump."[39] Federal Judge James B. Zagel "agreed with prosecutors that . . . Blagojevich's comments on the show could complicate the trial. 'There are significant confessional elements,' Zagel said, noting that he had seen two earlier episodes."[40] A defense attorney responded that "[t]his is the first time I've ever heard of a law enforcement official saying, 'Please shut the defendant up.' "[41] Ultimately, the judge allowed Blagojevich's participation but ordered the parties to reach an agreement regarding his conduct.[42]

Professional observers were mystified by the apparent public revelry in Blagojevich's pretrial antics. One columnist quoted

Kent Redfield, a political science professor at the University of Illinois—Springfield, for the opinion that it should be "too late for Blagojevich to resuscitate his reputation. . . . [H]e was a complete disaster (as governor) in addition to being completely corrupt. . . . He's become a sideshow.' "[43]

On June 8, 2010, trial in federal district court in Chicago began. Blagojevich faced twenty-four felony counts carrying 415 years in prison and fines totaling $6 million. Commentators noted that "[i]nterest in the trial was high. The main courtroom and another overflow courtroom were filled to capacity."[44] Blagojevich was portrayed by his lawyers as "an insecure man, a serial telephone dialer (of friends who often stop answering), and a C student who surrounded himself with people he should not have trusted."[45] He was a good-hearted buffoon, whose judgment was " 'horrible. Just horrible.' "[46] During the trial, a parade of prosecution witnesses took the stand and testified about the money-making schemes of the ex-governor and his advisers. One claimed that "Blagojevich had a personal tailor and sometimes bought as many as nine suits at a time."[47] When asked about Blagojevich's taste in clothes, the witness reported it was " 'good,' " provoking laughter in the courtroom, "by Blagojevich as much as anybody."[48]

The trial lasted eight weeks, and more than two dozen witnesses testified. In his closing arguments, Blagojevich's attorney "portrayed Blagojevich as a foolish, ineffective governor who could not plan [the] . . . complicated scheme" that the government prosecutors alleged.[49] "Calling the ex-governor 'silly,' [the attorney] . . . mocked his client for asking about running routes in India as he considered an imagined ambassadorship. 'As much as I like him, and as much as he's loved around the world, this is a man who considered appointing Oprah

Winfrey [to the U.S. Senate],' [he] . . . said. 'No one's going to say that he's the sharpest knife in the drawer, but he's not corrupt.'"[50] A commentator noted that "[t]he prosecution made 25 objections during the roughly 100-minute oration in which [the attorney] . . . played comedian and brimstone preacher."[51] Another commentator reported that Blagojevich's lawyer "used every weapon in his rhetorical arsenal to end Rod Blagojevich's corruption trial with enough drama to try to cancel out dozens of damning secret FBI tapes that jurors heard in the last eight weeks."[52]

Ultimately, the jury convicted Blagojevich of one count of lying to the FBI, the least serious of the twenty-four felony counts against him. The jury was hung on counts alleging racketeering, conspiracy, wire fraud, extortion, kickbacks, and other crimes. The *Wall Street Journal*, which termed the trial a "fiasco," noted in an editorial that the government's "legal team failed to persuade a jury that Blagojevich was guilty [of corruption], . . . despite five weeks of argument and testimony that included selections from thousands of wiretapped phone calls. The defense did not call a single witness."[53] The government vowed to retry him on the deadlocked counts.

Facing retrial, Blagojevich was hired by Roll International Corporation to promote its product, Wonderful Pistachios. The company's president for advertising explained he was looking for the "buzz factor" in hiring the former governor.[54] In the advertising spot, Blagojevich was handed a black briefcase, he opened it, and hundreds of pistachios poured out. In a news release, Blagojevich stated that "'[t]he contents in the suitcase are like the accusations against me—they're nuts.'"[55]

The retrial of Blagojevich began on April 20, 2011—ten months after the first. The trial lasted six weeks. On June 27,

2011, after ten days of deliberation, the jury found him guilty of seventeen of twenty corruption charges. As the *New York Times* expressed it, "The verdict appeared to be the conclusion, at last, to the spectacle of Mr. Blagojevich's political career."[56] The Blagojevich ability to charm apparently came to its end. As the *Times* story put it, "[R]esidents [of Chicago] . . . seem to have grown inured by the Blagojevich story over more than two years."[57]

In many ways, the idea of corruption as capture-by-evil dominated attitudes toward this case. The sheer scope and completeness of Blagojevich's self-indulgence, massive betrayal of the public trust, and unabashed greed made a diagnosis of his thoroughly corrupt character a seemingly foregone conclusion. His alleged "staggering level of corruption"—in which, if the government's evidence was to be believed, virtually every power of the governor's office was used to extort bribes and kickbacks— made the image of "tentacles of corruption" reaching into all corners of the Blagojevich regime seem more than apt. Even before his trial, descriptions of Blagojevich as a "thoroughly corrupt individual" appeared to be undoubtedly true. To the casual observer, and from the media coverage available, there was little doubt but that Blagojevich, his associates, and his actions were tainted, and on the basis of this evidence, one would have expected no hesitancy whatsoever in the moral condemnation of the Blagojevich regime.

Indeed, confronted with such pervasive and brazen corruption, the benefits of the idea of corruption as capture-by-evil would seem to far outweigh its costs. Under such circumstances, we presumably should feel no hesitancy in invoking extreme moral sanction, or—for that matter—in harnessing the power of emotion with law. If Blagojevich's humanity was disregarded in this process, or if we were goaded by our emotions in our demands for punishment, the dangers of such excesses pale when compared to the need to condemn and terminate such damaging conduct. There is little resonance in such a case with concerns that the accused will be demonized, or that we should recognize variable criminal culpability, or prevent collateral punishment, or avoid the standardless use of emotion in law. The bottom line is that there *was* corruption here—*serious* corruption—and its complete eradication and punishment would seem to be the overwhelming priority.

Yet, there was another cost to the use of the idea of corruption as capture-by-evil in this case with which we must grapple. There were important ways in which this idea, and the image of the accused that it presented, did not fit. Just as the idea of capture-by-evil so powerfully indicted the alleged actions of the Blagojevich regime, it was also at odds with what this case presented. The idea of corruption as capture-by-evil diagnoses someone with corrupt *character*, depraved and defiled, who lives a life that exhibits hypocrisy and an "evil heart." When looked at this way, the Blagojevich case presented a more complex picture, one that he exploited. Blagojevich and his antics seemed almost too good-natured, too good-hearted, *too ordinary*, to signal the kind of dangerous and evil hypocrite that this idea of corruption assumes. He seemed to be more the misguided jokester, or the cluelessly naive wannabe, than the evil character that this idea describes. For instance, it seems incongruous that someone of evil character would worry (seemingly genuinely) about the physical safety of pursuing cameramen or the lives of ordinary citizens, or lampoon himself on a reality television show. There was, in addition, the apparent absence of the confirmatory vice that we expect in such cases.

Blagojevich was, as far as we can tell, the genuine family man; there was no evidence of gluttony, luxuriousness, sexual excess, or other such sins.

As a result, the idea of corruption as capture-by-evil was of decidedly mixed utility in this case, from a prosecutorial point of view. Its aptness (in some ways) served to inflame the just condemnation of Blagojevich, but, at the same time, its *inaptness* (in other ways) helps to explain Blagojevich's continued popularity and the reluctance of large segments of the public to believe that Blagojevich was as bad as prosecutors insisted. In cases such as this—where the accused *defies* the character-driven stereotypes that capture-by-evil assumes—it has diametrically opposed, and ironic, influences. It reinforces the idea of the accused's corruption, but simultaneously casts doubt. If the condemnation of Blagojevich and similar actors is the societal goal in such cases, the verdict on the idea of corruption as capture-by-evil is a mixed one. It *advances* that goal with its powerful moral critique of the individual's actions, but it *undermines* that goal with its implicit requirement that the individual meet the "monstrous" image that this idea demands.

The Case of Don Siegelman

On May 1, 2006, the federal bribery and racketeering trial of former governor Don Siegelman began in Montgomery, Alabama. Tried with him was Richard M. Scrushy, former CEO of the HealthSouth corporation, a chain of private hospitals. Prosecutors charged that seven years before, Scrushy gave $500,000 to Siegelman, who was then governor, to help retire a debt personally incurred by Siegelman in connection with his campaign for a statewide lottery to fund Alabama's schools. In exchange, prosecutors alleged, Scrushy was appointed by Siegelman to the

Alabama Certificate of Need (CON) Board, a state agency that approves hospital construction.[58]

At the time trial began, Siegelman was attempting a political comeback. He was elected governor in 1998 but had lost reelection in a close race in 2002.[59] In May and June of 2006, he was locked in a close race for the Democratic Party's nomination for the fall election.

This was not the first criminal prosecution of either man. Scrushy—who founded HealthSouth in 1984—was fired as the company's CEO after a criminal investigation uncovered an accounting fraud of some $2.7 billion. Criminally charged, Scrushy was acquitted in 2005 by a federal court jury in Birmingham, Alabama—a result deemed by commentators to be "astonishing,"[60] given that five former HealthSouth CEOs testified at trial that Scrushy had personally directed the scheme.[61] Experts opined that his conviction "should have been a slam dunk," and that his acquittal was nothing short of "a miracle."[62] In fact, the religious allusions were perhaps not all that far off the mark. As his trial had approached, Scrushy gave more than $1,700,000 to local churches and religious groups, many of whose leaders then supported the Scrushy team. During trial, these religious leaders attended each day and became known as "the Amen Corner."[63] The evidence, which jurors cited for acquittal, was thin. For instance, "jurors quoted in the papers said they were bothered by things like the lack of Scrushy's fingerprints on copies of the crucial documents."[64]

Siegelman, for his part, had been charged with federal conspiracy and bribery in 2002, in the heat of a prior (unsuccessful) gubernatorial campaign. These charges were later dismissed by a federal judge on the ground that there was no credible evidence to support them.

The trial of Siegelman and Scrushy began on May 1, 2006, and lasted for six weeks. After eleven days of deliberation, the jury acquitted Siegelman of twenty-two counts and convicted him of seven. He was convicted of conspiracy, bribery, "honest services" mail fraud, and obstruction of justice. Scrushy was convicted of bribery, conspiracy, and mail fraud.[65] After the verdict, Siegelman bitterly remarked: "'If I am really guilty of this, then every other person in public office had better look out. Because everybody is raising money and putting people on boards and in [other] positions.'"[66]

Siegelman lost the Democratic primary on June 6, 2006, while his trial was ongoing. He blamed the prosecution for his defeat, on the basis that it "was driven by politically motivated, Republican-appointed U.S. Attorneys."[67]

On September 14, 2007—more than a year after Siegelman's trial—Dana Jill Simpson, a lawyer and longtime Republican strategist in Alabama, testified before Congress about what she claimed to be illegal and unethical conduct by prosecutors in the Siegelman prosecution.[68] Under oath, Simpson testified that she worked on the campaign of Republican Bob Riley, who defeated Siegelman in his bid for reelection as governor in the fall of 2002. In that contest, Siegelman and Riley were neck-and-neck, until Riley pulled ahead at the last minute. Faced with the abrupt turnaround, Siegelman sought a recount.[69]

Simpson testified that while the recount proceeded, she participated in a conference call involving the Republican candidate's son, Rob Riley. Also participating was Bill Canary, a Republican political operative. In this call, Canary assured the group that they need "not . . . worry about Don Siegelman" because Canary's "girls" would "take care of him."[70] By "his girls"

Canary meant his wife, Leura, who was U.S. attorney for the Middle District of Alabama, and Alice Martin, a close friend who was U.S. attorney for the Northern District of Alabama.[71] When pressed for details, Canary said that "[h]e had already got it taken care of" and that the Justice Department in Washington "was already pursuing" Siegelman.[72] Simpson testified that Siegelman was deemed to be "a thorn" in the side of Republicans and that the Justice Department was enlisted for his prosecution.[73] Siegelman was later charged with federal conspiracy and bribery, but (as noted above) these 2002 charges were later dismissed by the federal trial judge.

Simpson testified that she had another conversation with Rob Riley about two years later, in early 2005. The topic of conversation "rolled around" to the next gubernatorial election, which was slated for the fall of 2006.[74] They talked about possible competitors to Governor Riley, who was running for reelection. They agreed that Don Siegelman was "the biggest threat" they had. They discussed how Siegelman was a "kind of . . . golden child for the Democratic Party" and "an incredible fund-raiser."[75] They lamented how one of Canary's "girls," Birmingham U.S. Attorney Martin, had botched Siegelman's 2002 prosecution.[76] Riley stated that "a decision [had been] made that they would bring a new case against . . . Siegelman" in the Middle District of Alabama, in Montgomery.[77] This was the office where Leura Canary was U.S. attorney. The idea, Riley told her, was "to prosecute [Siegelman] . . . with Richard Scrushy." "Because nobody like[d] . . . Scrushy," it was believed that this would assure Siegelman's conviction.[78] The federal indictments of Siegelman and Scrushy (containing the charges on which they were ultimately convicted) were issued three months later.

Simpson testified that she came forward with this information because several individuals had advised her that her knowledge of wrongdoing—and subsequent inaction—could jeopardize her bar license.[79] After her testimony was made public, her allegations were called "outrageous" and a "story . . . created by a drunk fiction writer" by those whom she named as part of the conspiracy.[80]

After his conviction, Siegelman was sentenced to seven years and four months in prison, three years of supervised release, and five hundred hours of community service. He was also ordered to pay a $700 special assessment, a $50,000 fine, and $181,325 in restitution. The district court judge "took judicial notice of the 'plethora of media attention' to the case by the local and national media, and relied on this in finding that the case had severely undermined public confidence in Alabama state government." He engaged in an "upward departure" from the sentencing guidelines to " 'preserve the integrity of the judiciary and the confidence of the people of the state of Alabama.'"[81] After Siegelman argued that an order for restitution was legally improper, the judge revoked that portion of his order.[82] Scrushy, for his part, was sentenced to just under seven years in prison.

The case and its resolution aroused outrage by commentators and court observers. In an editorial entitled "Selective Prosecution," the *New York Times* warned of "growing evidence that the [Justice Department] may have singled out people for criminal prosecution to help Republicans win elections. . . . Putting political opponents in jail is the sort of thing that happens in third-world dictatorships. In the United States, prosecutions are supposed to be scrupulously nonpartisan."[83] The editorial continued:

Individual Democrats may be paying a personal price. Don Siegelman, a former Alabama governor, was the state's most prominent Democrat and had a decent chance of retaking the governorship from the Republican incumbent. He was aggressively prosecuted by both the Birmingham and Montgomery United States attorneys' offices. Birmingham prosecutors dropped their case after a judge harshly questioned it. When the Montgomery office prosecuted, a jury acquitted Mr. Siegelman of 25 counts, but convicted him of 7, which appear to be disturbingly weak.

The prosecution may have been a political hit. A Republican lawyer, Dana Jill Simpson, has said in a sworn statement that she heard Bill Canary, a Republican operative and a Karl Rove protégé, say that his "girls"—his wife, the United States attorney in Montgomery, and Alice Martin, the United States attorney in Birmingham—would "take care" of Mr. Siegelman.[84]

A few days later, an editorial observer for the *Times* noted: "There are other red flags, besides Ms. Simpson's testimony. Mr. Siegelman was convicted of appointing the businessman Richard Scrushy to a state hospital board in exchange for a contribution to a campaign for a state lottery to fund education. Elected officials, from the president down, appoint people who contribute directly to their campaigns without facing criminal charges."[85]

Subsequently, several dozen former attorneys general issued a public statement calling for a probe of the Siegelman prosecution. The group included prominent members of both the Democratic Party and the Republican Party.[86] In a CBS television broadcast, a member of this group—former Republican

Arizona attorney general Grant Woods—criticized Siegelman's prosecution:

> [Woods]: "I personally believe that what happened here is that they targeted Don Siegelman because they couldn't beat him fair and square. This was a Republican state and he was the one Democrat they could never get rid of."
>
> . . . .
>
> [Woods]: "You do a bribery [prosecution] when someone has a real personal benefit. It's that you're exchanging an official act for a personal benefit. Not, 'Hey, I would like for you to help out on this project which I think is good for my state.' If [you] . . . start indicting people and putting them in prison for that, then you might as well just build nine or ten new federal prisons because that happens every day in every courthouse, in every city council, and in the Congress of the United States.
>
> [Interviewer]: "What you seem to be saying . . . is that this is analogous to giving a great deal of money to a presidential campaign. And as a result, you become Ambassador to Paris."
>
> [Woods]: "Exactly. That's exactly right."[87]

A commentator continues, "Indeed, Karl Rove pursued financing for the Bush-Cheney campaign in 2000 and again in 2004 by organizing a special elite status—called 'Pioneers' and 'Rangers'—for persons who donated or raised $100,000 or more for the campaign. These donors understood that if they wanted to be appointed to a government office, like an ambassadorship, they only had to ask for it."[88]

On March 6, 2009, the Eleventh Circuit Court of Appeals reversed two of Siegelman's convictions for lack of evidence and affirmed the remaining five. His sentence was vacated, and the case remanded for resentencing.[89] Upon remand, the U.S. Attorney's Office argued that Siegelman's prison sentence should be *increased* from seven to twenty years, even though two of his convictions had been vacated.[90] In a subsequent appeal to the United States Supreme Court, the case was remanded for reconsideration in light of *Skilling v. United States*,[91] which narrowed the grounds for conviction for "honest services" mail fraud.[92] Three of Siegelman's remaining convictions were on this ground. Under the new Supreme Court interpretation, "honest services" statutes require proof of bribery or kickbacks.[93] On remand, the Eleventh Circuit held that Siegelman's convictions met this test.[94] On August 3, 2012, Siegelman was sentenced to six and one-half years in prison.

The idea of corruption as capture-by-evil seems inapt in this case. Although Siegelman's acts might meet the technical requirements for a corrupt act, there are, at core, serious doubts about the "evil" nature of the alleged quid pro quo transaction. Unquestionably, Siegelman stood to gain from Scrushy's "contribution," in the sense that a debt for which he was otherwise personally responsible was canceled. However, this transaction—although formally "corrupt" in its exchange of financial gain for official appointment—lacks essential capture-by-evil qualities. The debt that was forgiven was not incurred in pursuit of personal material gain or other personal vice; it was a campaign donation made by Siegelman in an effort to secure a funding source for Alabama's public schools. In addition, the kind of quid pro quo involved—the appointment of an individual to a government board, in exchange for a campaign contribution—is, as Siegelman and others argued, a routine occurrence in American politics. There was nothing apparently inherently wrong about Scrushy's appointment to the CON Board; Scrushy had served on the board under the three previous governors of Alabama.[95] Rather, Siegelman's mistake was his explicit offer of a quid pro quo; had he simply solicited Scrushy's donation and then—in a "separate" exercise of judgment—appointed Scrushy to the board, his actions would have been no different from the kinds of rewards given to supporters that are the daily grist of American politics.

Moreover, if bad character is the issue, there is little in Siegelman's case that supports the charge. Siegelman's association with Scrushy (a man for whom there is ample evidence of hypocrisy and greed) creates suspicion about Siegelman's character. However, there is little else in Siegelman's lifestyle or history that supports the charge. It is true that Siegelman was a politician, with the suspicion of corruption which that presents (i.e., a hunger for power and the possible willingness to sell one's soul to get it). But, despite the innuendos of the prosecutors in this case, there is no independent evidence of bad character to make the charge convincing. Indeed, the secrecy and hypocrisy of those who sought Siegelman's prosecution tend to make them (if the evidence is believed) of equally questionable character.

Despite these weaknesses, the idea of corruption as capture-by-evil appears to have permeated the treatment of this case. The trial of Siegelman with Scrushy, who was (if Simpson's testimony is to be believed) of known "evil" character, was intended to paint Siegelman with the same brush. The "plethora of media attention" and the conclusion that "the case had severely undermined public confidence in Alabama state government," cited by the federal trial judge in sentencing Siegelman to an enhanced sentence of more than seven years in prison, a $50,000 fine, and

$181,325 in restitution, seemed to be plausible in light of the emotional testimonials of "evil" that accompanied the prosecution of this case. There was no serious consideration of corruption as a crime of varying culpability, or the calibrating of the sentence to that end. Indeed, the position of the federal prosecutor—that Siegelman's sentence should be *increased* from more than seven years to twenty years, after two of his convictions were reversed—is ample testimony, itself, to that fact.

In short, the dangers of the use of the idea of corruption as capture-by-evil for the administration of justice, in this case, appear to substantially outweigh its benefits. If "evil" is the standard that corruption demands, neither Siegelman's conduct nor his character presents a convincing case. If the function of the idea of capture-by-evil is the assertion of corruption's public costs, and the identification of the morally derelict, its usefulness in this case is marginal. In addition, and critically, the dangers of this idea in cases of marginal criminality and marginally questionable character are profound. As evidenced by the protests of seasoned prosecutors of such crimes, there are serious questions whether Siegelman's prosecution—to the extent it succeeded— was driven more by ideas of corruption's "taint" (e.g., association with Scrushy) and the emotion of vengeance by prosecutors than by any legitimate assessment of the public interest.

The Case of Eliot Spitzer

In February 2008, federal law enforcement authorities—who were monitoring wiretaps of a prostitution ring—heard "details . . . [of a planned encounter] between a prostitute named Kristen and a man described as 'Client 9,' whom law enforcement officials identified as Mr. [Eliot] Spitzer," then governor of New York.[96] The prostitution ring, named the Emperor's Club, provided high-priced prostitutes (costing between $1,000 and $5,500 per hour) to wealthy clients in New York, London, Paris, and other cities.[97] On the evening of February 13, 2008, Spitzer took a train from New York to Washington, and met the prostitute at the Mayflower Hotel.[98]

Later describing their investigation, law enforcement sources stated that "investigators conducting a routine examination of suspicious financial transactions reported to them by banks found several unusual movements of cash involving the governor of New York." There were "transactions by . . . [the] governor, who appeared to be trying to conceal the source, destination or purpose of the movements of thousands of dollars in cash. . . . The money ended up in the bank accounts of what appeared to be shell companies, corporations that essentially had no real business. The transactions . . . suggested possible financial crimes—maybe bribery, political corruption, or something inappropriate involving campaign finance."[99] Instead, investigators discovered that the money was being moved to pay for sex, and that the transactions were being manipulated to avoid detection.[100] Thousands of dollars were involved over a period of eight months, funding trysts in various cities.[101] Apart from the obvious illegality of buying prostitutes, officials stated that Spitzer's actions potentially involved financial reporting violations and violations of the federal Mann Act, which prohibits the conduct of prostitution activities across state lines.[102]

The revelations were startling, since Spitzer, a Democrat, had "ris[en] to political power as a fierce enforcer of ethics in public life."[103] As New York's attorney general, he made his name prosecuting corrupt financiers on Wall Street. He also prosecuted at least two prostitution rings through the use of the state's organized crime task force. In one such case, "Spitzer spoke with revulsion and anger after announcing the arrest of 16 people for operating a high-end prostitution ring out of Staten Island."[104]

The day that the news broke, Spitzer, who was forty-eight years old and married with three daughters, appeared briefly with his wife at his Manhattan office to apologize. " 'I have acted in a way that violates my obligations to my family and violates my, or any, sense of right and wrong,' the governor said. . . . 'I apologize to the public to whom I promised better.' "[105]

In the State Capitol, "[t]he news was met with disbelief and shock. . . . Some legislative assistants said they were too stunned to speak, and lawmakers gathered around television sets in hushed offices, trying to make sense of what had happened."[106] One lobbyist confided, " 'It's a shame. It's awful. This is why people lose faith in government. But I guess it shows that he's human like everybody else.' "[107]

Less than forty-eight hours after the news broke, Spitzer resigned—the first New York governor to be driven from office by scandal in nearly a hundred years.[108] In his resignation speech, he spoke of his "fall" and having "to atone for my private failings."[109] He also speculated about redemption, how "as human beings, our greatest glory consists not in never falling, but in rising every time we fall."[110] He pledged that "I will try once again, outside of politics, to serve the common good and to move toward the ideals . . . of hope and opportunity."[111]

Public response was swift. In a column entitled "Lessons from the Fall of Spitzer," the *New York Times* printed letters to the editor that decried Spitzer's "hypocritical arrogance" and the idea that prostitution is a victimless crime.[112] Supporters "grappled with a sense of . . . hurt, confusion, and even betrayal. 'I feel like someone died,' said [one supporter] . . ., whose husband . . .

joined Mr. Spitzer's administration as the insurance superintendent. . . . The sense of betrayal was deeper, those who had supported Mr. Spitzer said, because the governor had cast himself as a moral crusader."[113] One commented, "He was a guy of absolute honor and high moral fiber. It makes me wonder if there was some kind of disconnect in his brain."[114]

Commentators speculated about whether, in retrospect, the depravity lurking in Spitzer should have been detected. Anthropologist Helen Fisher, on the "Today" television show, opined that Spitzer's "very high cheekbones and a very heavy brow" were signs of extremely high testosterone, with all of the dangers of character that portends.[115] Psychologists speculated that Spitzer was haunted by a subconscious desire to self-destruct.[116] Some condemned him "not for his sin, but for his excess"[117]—the payment of thousands of dollars to prostitutes revealing his "hypocrisy, egomania, sophomoric impulsiveness and self-indulgence."[118] Women speculated that their male partners, whom they had thought they knew, might in fact (like Spitzer) be goodness on the outside, evil within. One reporter wrote, "Many wives in long marriages, presuming [Spitzer's wife] . . . was blown sideways by the news, were unnerved by the possibility that the person one has known since forever— that familiar, safe, pre-caffeinated face—could, in fact, be Dorian Gray. 'Your husband's sleeping, and you look across the bed and think, "Do I really know this person?"' said Regina Brab, a human resources consultant from Montclair, N.J., who has been married for 17 years."[119]

A woman who was married for more than twelve years to a Wall Street executive compared Spitzer's acts with her response when she learned that her husband had been visiting prostitutes. "[S]he came to see in him an angry, toxic arrogance. 'He believed he could do whatever he wanted and not get caught,' she said. 'Once you feed that dark side, the monster grows.'"[120]

After his resignation, Spitzer dropped abruptly from public life. He was not prosecuted, presumably due to prosecutors' belief that his legal transgressions were not worth the costs of prosecution. Later, he occupied himself writing commentaries and walking the family dogs. A political writer, interviewing him a year after his resignation, ruminated: "[H]is wife appears to have forgiven him; why can't we? . . . The public forgets but does not forgive."[121] In more recent times he made some attempts to mend his image, serving for a period of months as a commentator on the Cable News Network and giving occasional lectures about ethics and the financial crisis.[122]

In Spitzer's case, the idea of corruption as capture-by-evil seems to fit precisely. All of the elements of that idea—moral depravity, perversion, dishonesty, sin, sexual excess, greed, self-indulgence, a weak or deficient will—are present in ringing terms. Spitzer succumbed to his darker side; he is "fallen," corroded by the powers of testosterone and lust. In him, the "corruptor" or "tempter" of sexual hedonism found its mark. He exhibited the classic hypocrisy of the corrupt: he appeared to be good, but was evil within. He appeared to be a man of "absolute honor and high moral fiber," when in fact he was a corrupt, degenerate, sexually greedy man, whose true public and personal character was shot through with luxuriousness, indolence, weakness, and excess. There is little doubt, in this image, that Spitzer was a monster; indeed, his story was so powerful that it inspired "wives in long marriages" to wonder whether their husbands, like Spitzer, "could, in fact, be Dorian Gray." The fact that he has not been criminally prosecuted makes little difference; there is no doubt, in light of this evidence, about the nature of his character.

Indeed, the idea that Spitzer is captured by evil is so powerful that it works to swamp the power of rational consideration of his case. We (the public) feel deep, emotional revulsion from Spitzer's hypocrisy, betrayal, and moneyed sexual greed. The fact that he has not been criminally prosecuted might indicate that those in positions of power reject the emotion-laden response of the populace (or it might indicate that those in positions of power simply do not want to prosecute one of their own). Either way, however, Spitzer's character as a public figure is all but dead.

The question is whether, in this context, the invocation of the idea of corruption as capture-by-evil is a positive one. There is no doubt that secret vice—particularly while prosecuting others for that vice—is unacceptable in an official sworn to uphold the law. Lying and lawbreaking in pursuit of vice are undesirable characteristics—indeed, disqualifying characteristics—in many areas of public and private life. Yet, marital betrayal and the visiting of prostitutes are certainly not rare, nor deemed to be permanently character-destroying qualities in most men. No public money was converted by Spitzer, no bribe was taken, no acts of patronage or other political corruption occurred. Spitzer may not be a man whose word we can believe, when it comes to sexual morals, or whose political leadership we want or need. But is he the "monster" that is portrayed? The power of the idea of capture-by-evil in Spitzer's case illustrated the emotionally driven powers, and dangers, that this idea conveys.

THE CORRUPT JUDGE

Of all settings for public corruption, the notion of a corrupt judge is perhaps the most deeply and viscerally offensive. We might expect politicians to engage in political horse trading; but there are no gray lines or doubts when it comes to the standards to which the judiciary is held. Judges must be beholden to no one, and be completely impartial toward all who come before them, as required by law.

The Conviction of William Bracy

In February 1981, William Bracy,[123] Roger Collins, and Murray Hooper were indicted in Cook County Court, Chicago, Illinois, for the armed robbery, aggravated kidnapping, and murder of Frederick Lacey, R. C. Pettigrew, and Richard Holliman.[124] On July 29, 1981, Bracy and Collins were convicted by a jury of all charges. A joint death penalty hearing commenced the next day. On July 31, 1981, the same jury found the existence of statutory aggravating factors and the nonexistence of mitigating factors, justifying a sentence of death. The presiding judge sentenced Bracy and Collins to death on September 9, 1981.[125] Hooper was tried separately, convicted of murder, and also sentenced to death.[126]

The chief prosecution witness at the trial of Bracy and Collins was one Morris Nellum, who was an admitted participant in the crimes.[127] In exchange for his cooperation, the State agreed that Nellum would plead guilty to three counts of concealing a homicidal death, with a prison sentence of three years.[128]

At trial, Nellum testified that on November 12, 1980, Lacey, Pettigrew, and Holliman were taken from an apartment on the South Side of Chicago, driven to a viaduct at Roosevelt Road and Clark Street, and shot to death.[129] Nellum testified to the involvement of both Bracy and Collins in the abduction and shooting.[130]

On cross-examination, Nellum stated that he did not know the reason for the killing, although Hooper later told him that the victims had been robbed.[131] He admitted "that he lie[d] when he ha[d] to," although he maintained that his statements to police in this case were truthful.[132] This was contradicted in part by his admission that he originally told police that he was unaware of the location of the murder weapons but later took police to the lake where they were recovered.[133] Nellum also testified that he decided to cooperate with authorities after he was told that he would not be charged with murder, and they would, instead, recommend a three-year sentence in exchange for his guilty plea to three counts of concealing a homicidal death.[134] Nellum's credibility was also impeached on the basis of inconsistencies in his testimony about other, more peripheral details.[135]

Neighbors who testified placed Bracy and Collins with Hooper, Nellum, and the victims at the time that the crimes were committed.[136] There was also evidence that Bracy had stolen one of the murder weapons from an acquaintance, and forensic evidence linked a rope found in the victims' apartment with rope found at the murder scene.[137] Both Bracy and Collins raised alibi defenses.[138]

On a joint appeal, Bracy and Collins's primary argument was that the evidence was insufficient for a jury to find them guilty of the murders beyond a reasonable doubt. As the Illinois Supreme Court stated it, Bracy and Collins "argue that Nellum's testimony was unworthy of belief, given that he admitted his participation in the crimes and therefore had a motive to lie in order to escape a murder prosecution; that he was shown to have lied about knowing the victim Lacey and about the location of the handguns; that his testimony conflicted with statements of other prosecution witnesses; and that his testimony was directly contradicted by defense witnesses."[139] The court's dispatch of this contention was succinct. "Stated simply," the majority wrote, "the resolution of the defendants' guilt or innocence depended on the credibility of the witnesses and the weight given their testimony."[140] "Here, the jury was fully cognizant of the infirmities in Nellum's testimony and was instructed that his testimony was to be viewed with suspicion. Nevertheless the jury chose to believe Nellum over the defense witnesses, and after reviewing the record, we are not prepared to say that their conclusion was unreasonable."[141]

Bracy and Collins also argued that they were denied a fair trial because the jury was allowed to hear that certain prosecution witnesses, including Nellum, were in protective custody;[142] that the trial judge erred in allowing the State to impeach defense witnesses on collateral matters;[143] and that there were several instances of prosecutorial misconduct during closing argument that denied them due process of law. The court summarily rejected these arguments as well. On the issue of prosecutorial misconduct, the majority noted that defense lawyers failed to object to most instances at the time of trial.[144] Concerning those to which objection was made, the court found no prejudice. Although one prosecutorial comment "would have been better left unsaid,"[145] that was (in the court's view) true of "many statements often made during the course of a trial."[146]

Bracy and Collins also argued that they were prejudiced by the seating of a juror who was the wife of a judge who had previously sentenced Bracy to twelve to thirty-six years in prison for another crime. This was a fact of which all members of the jury—due to a defense attorney's questioning and alleged "gross incompetence"—were made aware.[147] The court's majority noted that although defense counsel were aware of this juror's identity, "no objection was raised . . ., nor was any allegation of prejudice asserted in defendants' written motion for a new trial." Although the court acknowledged that this was a serious issue, it held that failure to challenge this juror at the time of the impaneling of the jury precluded review on appeal.[148]

Bracy and Collins also challenged their sentences of death on various grounds. They argued that the trial judge dismissed a juror for cause who expressed equivocal belief in the death penalty; refused a request for a continuance, to allow them to prepare for the death penalty phase of the trial; and permitted testimony about other crimes allegedly committed by Bracy, but of which he had not yet been convicted.[149] All were rejected by the appellate court as well.[150] The court's opinion concluded: "The clerk of this court is directed to issue mandates setting Tuesday, September 24, 1985, as the date on which the sentences of death entered in the circuit court of Cook County are to be executed. The defendants shall be executed by lethal injection in the manner provided by section 119–5 of the Code of Criminal Procedure of 1963 (Ill. Rev. Stat. 1983, ch. 38, par. 119-5). Certified copies of the mandates in this case shall be furnished by the clerk of this court to the Director of Corrections, to the warden of Stateville Correction Center, and to the warden of the institution wherein the defendants are confined."[151]

There the matter stood for eight years.

The Corruption of Thomas J. Maloney

In April 1993—some twelve years after the Bracy-Collins verdict, and while Bracy and Collins fought execution on death row—former Cook County, Illinois, Circuit Court judge Thomas J. Maloney was convicted of racketeering conspiracy, racketeering, extortion under color of official right, and obstruction of justice.[152] Maloney was one of eighteen dishonest judges exposed and convicted through "Operation Greylord," an intensive federal investigation of judicial corruption in Chicago.[153]

He was also the judge who had presided over Bracy and Collins's trial.

Maloney served as a judge on the Circuit Court of Cook County from the time of his appointment in 1977 until his retirement in 1990.[154] During a six-week trial that involved more than forty witnesses, the jury heard evidence of "[Maloney's] career as a corrupt felony trial judge."[155] His corrupt specialty was the conducting of bench trials in felony criminal cases, in which he took bribes in exchange for delivering acquittals or lenient sentences. The jury found that Maloney had agreed to fix four cases, including three murder cases, and obstructed justice in relation to the investigation of those bribes.[156] The Government's Brief, filed in the Seventh Circuit Court of Appeals, summarized the evidence as follows:

> *The Chow Murder Case:* Lenny Chow was a hit man from New York who murdered people for the On Leong—[an] . . . organization involved in illegal gambling, narcotics, and murder. Tr. 1790–93, 1803, 1988.[157] In 1981, the State of Illinois charged Chow and three others with a variety of crimes for shooting a man named William Chin in Chicago's Chinatown. Tr. 1784, 1790–92. As judge in the case, Maloney accepted a bribe and acquitted Chow and his co-defendants of murder. Tr. 1789, 1808, 1811, 1880. . . .[158]
>
> [The fix was arranged through a corrupt politician, Pat Marcy, and a corrupt attorney, Robert Cooley.] Marcy and Cooley had worked together to fix dozens of prior cases, Marcy in most instances coordinating the fixes with the judges. Tr. 1774–75, 1809–12, 1844–47.[159]
>
> . . . .

. . . Marcy [who was in contact, through others, with Maloney] . . . told Cooley to quote a $50,000 "fee" to the On Leong [for the fix] because the On Leong had a lot of money. Tr. 1788–89, 1801–02. When Cooley . . . met [a representative of the On Leong] . . . a few days later, Cooley said he could provide a guaranteed result, through a bench trial, for $100,000. Tr. 1803–06. When [the representative] asked if Cooley could "do it any cheaper," Cooley said that [the On Leong] . . . could take a jury trial for $50,000, but then there would be no guaranteed result. Tr. 1806. [The representative] . . . replied, "We don't want that," and said that he would need to consult with others before he committed. Tr. 1806–07, 1809.[160]

[Upon leaving,] . . . Cooley went directly to . . . [the others involved in the fix and reported] that he thought the On Leong would agree to a $100,000 fee. Tr. 1809–10. When Cooley asked if he could keep $50,000 of the larger "fee," Marcy balked, saying "The Judge wants a lot of money in this one." Tr. 1810–11. Several days later, [the On Leong] . . . agreed to the $100,000 charge. Tr. 1815, 1818.[161]

. . . .

The Chow bench trial [before Maloney] took place [on] August 10–13, 1981. Tr. 1860, 1863. During the first day, Cooley [did not relinquish the role of lead defense counsel], . . . as Maloney had directed. Tr. 1862–68. . . . [A]fter court that day, Cooley went to Counselor's Row. Tr. 1864. "The judge is pissed," Marcy reported. Tr. 1866. "I told you to take a back seat [in the trial]." Id. Marcy then directed Cooley henceforth to keep quiet in court. Tr. 1868. . . .

Disobediently, Cooley continued to cross-examine state witnesses the next day. Tr. 1870. . . . Marcy [reported] . . .

that Maloney was still "pissed" that Cooley continued to take an active role in the case. . . . "You go in there," Marcy scolded, "and . . . shut up." Tr. 1873–74.[162]

. . . .

On August 13, 1981, Maloney acquitted Lenny Chow and a co-defendant of murder. Tr. 1880. In rendering his verdict, Maloney attempted to cover himself by simply fabricating a significant quantum of proof that had never come in at trial. Tr. 2257–63. For example, to undermine the testimony of a nurse who Maloney conceded to have been credible, Maloney falsely claimed that the nurse had equivocated in her testimony. Tr. 2258, 2260–62. Although the nurse repeatedly testified to having heard Chin name Lenny Chow as the man who had shot him, Maloney contrived that the nurse had testified that Chin might have said his killer was "Benny" or "Kenny." . . . Tr. 2261–62. The Chow trial record revealed that [in fact] the nurse neither wavered in her testimony nor ever mentioned [those] names. . . . Id. In addition, Maloney fabricated evidence that the assailants' first shot had hit Chin (preventing him from making an identification) and that Chin could not have seen his attackers because a canopy obstructed his view. Tr. 2262–63.[163] [Maloney directed a verdict for another of the Chow murder defendants; the fourth did not appear for trial.]

The Rosario Double Murder Case: . . . In or about 1979 or 1980, William Swano represented Wilfredo Rosario [who was charged] in a double murder case before Maloney. Tr. 2446–48. [Prior to that trial,] Swano filed several motions, including a motion to quash the arrest and a motion to suppress the critical evidence in the case, Rosario's confession, on the ground it was involuntary. Tr. 2448–50. Late in the summer of 1980, Swano talked about Rosario to Lucius Robinson, the personal bailiff and bagman for former Cook County Judge Maurice Pompey. Tr. 161, 397–402, 499–53, 455–56, 467, 2450–54. . . .[164]

During his years in the Circuit Courts of Cook County, Robinson received "hundreds" of bribes, from "hundreds" of lawyers, including William Swano. Tr. 400, 454, 2452. . . . Robinson told [FBI agent Terry] Hake on tape to "[l]et me know who you got cases in front of . . . and I'll tell ya, if I can, or can't." . . . In a follow-up conversation . . ., Hake presented Robinson with a list of some twenty-five felony judges in the Cook County court system. Tr. 248, 252, 260. . . . Robinson checked off the names of only three judges whom he could bribe. Tr. 263. Thomas Maloney was one of those three judges. Id.[165]

Robinson . . . later informed Swano that Maloney would accept $2,000–$2,500 to fix the [Rosario] case. Tr. 2453–54. As Swano had requested, Maloney appeared briefly in a courthouse hallway. Tr. 2254–55. Swano relayed [Robinson's statement] that he could help Swano with his case before Maloney, prompting Maloney's reply, "He's [Robinson's] my guy, deal with him." Tr. 2455. Shortly thereafter, Swano gave Robinson $2,500 cash in two installments. Tr. 2455–58.

Maloney granted Swano's motion to suppress Rosario's confession, "[t]he sole piece of evidence against [Rosario]. . . ." Tr. 2458.[166]

. . . .

The Roby Case: In 1981 and 1982, the State charged Ronald Roby in five separate deceptive practices cases. Tr. 746–48, 2462. Roby hired William Swano as his attorney. Tr. 843, 2461.

Roby feared he would be imprisoned. . . . Tr. 842–43, 2462–63. Swano moved to consolidate all of the cases, pending before a variety of judges, to Maloney's docket. Tr. 2463. . . . During late summer or early fall of 1982, Robinson informed Swano that he had arranged the fix. Tr. 2465–66. Swano then told Roby that for a "fee" of $5,000, the case against him would be "taken care of." Tr. 846, 848. . . .

Roby paid Swano in increments, giving him the last payment on September 3, 1982, the day Roby pleaded guilty to all charges. Tr. 849–50, 2467, 2469.

During a plea conference in Maloney's chambers, the State sought penitentiary time. . . . Tr. 2467. [However, Maloney] sentence[d] Roby to three years' probation. . . . Tr. 2468. . . .

Shortly after the resolution of the case, Swano passed the bribe money to Robinson, who in turn gave it to Maloney. . . . Tr. 462–64, 2467.[167]

. . . .

The Jones Murder Case: In December 1981, the State charged Owen Jones with felony murder for beating a man to death with a pipe during a burglary. Tr. 2470–72. . . .

Anxious that her son be acquitted, Jones's mother hired Swano. Tr. 2470, 2474. . . . Swano told Robinson that he wanted an acquittal, and Robinson said he would speak to Maloney. Tr. 2474–75.

When Swano appeared in court on the Jones case a couple of weeks later, attorney Robert McGee approached him. Tr. 2475–76. . . . McGee related that because Robinson had become "too hot," Maloney wanted Swano to deal through McGee instead. Tr. 2477. . . . McGee told Swano that there was no way that Maloney could acquit Jones on the facts of the case and that the best Maloney could do was to acquit Jones on felony murder, convict him for voluntary manslaughter, and impose a nine[-]year sentence. Tr. 2478. . . .

Swano told Jones's mother he could guarantee a nine-year sentence, in return for which Jones's mother agreed to pay between $4,000 and $5,000 for the fix. Tr. 2480–81, 2483. In the late summer or early fall of 1982, Jones's mother gave the bribe money to Swano, who duly transferred it to McGee. Tr. 2481–83.

Swano tried the case before Maloney . . . during September and October of 1982. Tr. 2484–85. . . . At the end of the trial, Maloney made good on the fix. . . . Maloney acquitted Jones of murder, convicted him of voluntary manslaughter and, a month later, sentenced Jones to nine years' imprisonment. Tr. 2487–88.[168]

. . . .

The Hawkins-Fields Double Murder Case: On April 28, 1984, El Rukns [gang members] Earl Hawkins and Nathan Fields shot Jerome "Fuddy" Smith and Talman Hickman to death in a narcotics turf battle. . . . Tr. 1022, 1489–91, 1504–05, 1507–11, 1514, 2536–37. In June 1985, the State charged Hawkins and Fields with the murders and the following month Maloney received the assignment of the case. Tr. 1534–35. Ultimately, William Swano came to represent Hawkins. Tr. 1539, 1541. Swano assured his client that he could "work with Judge Maloney" because he had "worked with him before." . . . Tr. 1537–41.

In late 1985 or early 1986, Swano told Hawkins that they needed about $20,000 for the bribe. Tr. 1544. . . . [This was later reduced to $16,000.][169]

. . . .

[During the ensuing months, Maloney repeatedly continued the case while Swano attempted to secure the bribe money from the El Rukns. On June 17, 1986, the first day of trial, the El Rukns passed the $16,000 in cash to Swano.]

. . . .

During the first two days of the Hawkins/Fields bench trial, Swano and another defense attorney cross-examined the State's three eye-witnesses. Tr. 2667. . . . At 11:23 a.m., on Thursday, June 19, McGee telephoned Swano in the anteroom outside of [Maloney's] . . . chambers. Tr. 2668; 3699–3700. Speaking in code, McGee told Swano that he needed to "give the books [i.e., the money] back that [Swano] had given him the other day" because the State's witnesses were too good. Tr. 2669.[170]

. . . .

On Friday, June 20, as Swano was leaving a sidebar during trial, he and Maloney had a quick, discrete [*sic*] exchange. Tr. 2682; 3237–40. Swano said, "We've got an agreement on this, I'm going to live up to my bargain, you've got to live up to yours." Tr. 2682.[171]

. . . .

Swano presented the defense case on Monday, June 23 and Tuesday, June 24. Tr. 2685–86. The State presented its rebuttal, and on June 26, Maloney took the case under advisement. . . . Tr. 2687–88. On the evening of June 26, McGee phoned Swano and told him that Maloney was reneging on the case fix. Tr. 2688. . . .

. . . [Later in his chambers,] Maloney picked up the same file folder filled with cash that Swano had given McGee ten days earlier . . ., and handed it back to Swano. Tr. 2690.

[On June 27, Maloney] ... found Hawkins and Fields guilty of murder. Tr. 2691. On September 19, 1986, [Maloney] ... sentenced the two to death in accordance with a jury sentencing recommendation. Tr. 2704–07.[172]

During Maloney's sentencing hearing, the government offered evidence that "Thomas Maloney's life of corruption was considerably more expansive than proved at trial."[173] Prior to his elevation to the bench, Maloney—as a criminal defense attorney—bribed judges to ensure that mob figures escaped prosecution or conviction. "[B]y the time Maloney ascended the bench in 1977, he was well groomed in the art of judicial corruption, an art that he could practice at least until 1986, when he correctly perceived that he was under the watchful eye of the FBI."[174]

On July 21, 1994, Maloney was sentenced to 189 months in prison.[175]

The Critical Question

In August 1993, William Bracy—by virtue of protracted postconviction proceedings, still alive and on death row—filed a Petition for a Writ of Habeas Corpus in United States District Court. Although Maloney was not bribed in Bracy's case, it was undisputed that Maloney had accepted bribes in other cases during and around the time of Bracy's trial.[176] Bracy sought habeas corpus relief on the ground that Maloney's corruption "permeate[d] his judicial conduct" and denied Bracy a fair trial.[177]

When a nonbribing criminal defendant is convicted by an otherwise corrupt judge, there are two factual arguments that he might make in an attempt to demonstrate prejudice in his case.

First, he might argue that in an attempt to garner bribes, the corrupt judge penalized nonbribing defendants by treating them more harshly. An allegation of this—of *retaliatory bias*—was raised during Maloney's trial. For instance, Swano testified about his representation of James Davis, who was charged with armed robbery in 1985. As an appellate judge described this testimony, "By this time Swano had already bribed Maloney on a number of occasions. But after investigating the prosecution's case against Davis, Swano concluded that it would be unnecessary to bribe Maloney in order to obtain an acquittal in this case: three witnesses to the robbery knew the two perpetrators and said that Davis was not one of them; Davis had an alibi; and the victim of the crime, who had initially identified Davis as one of the perpe-trators, had confessed uncertainty about the identification. Swano was [therefore] confident '[t]he case was a not guilty in any courtroom in the building.' . . . To Swano's surprise, . . . Maloney convicted his client after a bench trial. Swano took this as a lesson that 'to practice in front of Judge Maloney . . . we had to pay.' "[178]

Alternatively, a nonbribing criminal defendant might argue that because the corrupt judge favored the defense in cases that were "fixed," he had an incentive to favor the prosecution in other cases in order to "balance" the scales and deflect attention from his courtroom. The idea here is one of *compensatory bias*. As one of the United States Supreme Court justices stated during the argument in Bracy's case, "[I]f a trial in which there was no known bribery is sandwiched between trials in which there was bribery, or was conducted at a time when bribes were being solic-ited and arranged in other cases, there is good reason to believe, certainly in [an] . . . elected system [of judges] . . ., that it would be in a judge's interest to look tough in a case in which he could be tough at no cost to himself."[179]

Both arguments were made by Bracy. Proving retaliatory or compensatory bias is, however, notoriously difficult. Since no bribe was solicited or offered in Bracy's case, there was no way for Bracy to prove—short of Maloney's confession—that Maloney's decisions in his case were, in fact, for corrupt retaliatory reasons or to further corrupt compensatory agendas. As Judge Rovner of the Seventh Circuit wrote, "[E]xcept in rare cases in which the judge's agenda is obvious, we cannot expect to autopsy a trial and find evidence that the cancer of the judge's corruption has invaded her decisionmaking."[180]

The nearly insuperable difficulties in proving retaliatory or compensatory bias on the part of an otherwise corrupt judge are aptly illustrated by the case of *United States ex rel. Guest v. Page*,[181] another case that grew out of the Operation Greylord investigation. Guest was convicted of murder and sentenced to death by electrocution by Cook County Circuit Judge Maurice Pompey.[182] Evidence uncovered during the Operation Greylord investigation, and by Guest's postconviction attorneys, established the generally widespread scope of Judge Pompey's corruption. Numerous witnesses interviewed by the FBI claimed that Pompey routinely accepted cash bribes in exchange for favorable dispositions in serious criminal cases.[183] An FBI agent testified that he gave money to influence Pompey in a case that occurred around the time of Guest's trial.[184] Lucius Robinson, who was Pompey's personal bailiff, testified that he passed bribes to Pompey on hundreds of occasions.[185] The files of the U.S. attorney indicated that corrupt defense attorneys would routinely request that their cases be assigned to Pompey.[186]

Despite this evidence and more, however, the reviewing federal judge reached the "difficult conclusion" that Guest's challenge to his conviction could not succeed.[187] "Although counsel's commendable efforts have revealed much disturbing evidence," the judge wrote, "the Court must conclude that Guest has not satisfied the heavy burden of proving . . . Pompey's actual bias."[188] Although evidence of Pompey's corruption was overwhelming, Guest had failed to prove that Pompey "engaged in compensatory bias [i.e., unduly harsh treatment of a nonbribing defendant] *in his case.*"[189]

Similarly, in *United States v. O'Sullivan*,[190] Frank Dower challenged his 1988 conviction in Cook County court on charges of murder and armed violence on the ground that the judge who tried his case (Maloney) was corrupt. The reviewing federal judge summarily dismissed his claim, stating that "Dower has offered nothing that could even arguably tie his conviction, either expressly or impliedly, to Judge Maloney's corruption."[191]

Indeed, it is precisely because of such proof problems that convictions rendered in cases *in which bribes are taken* are presumed to be corrupt.[192] A verdict rendered by a bribed judge is presumed to be invalid, no matter how powerful the case against the defendant or how fair the judge's rulings appear to have been.[193]

Thus, Bracy's appeal, as a practical matter, hinged on whether a similar presumption of corruption could be made in his case. The critical question was this: could Maloney—having acted corruptly in one (or more) instances—*be presumed* to have acted corruptly in others? In an article headlined "Justices Weigh How to Deal with Taint of Corrupt Judge,"[194] the *New York Times* reported the following colloquy during the United States Supreme Court argument on this point: " 'You're saying that once on the take, a judge can never be trusted to be unbiased,' Justice Anthony M. Kennedy said to Gilbert H. Levy [Bracy's lawyer]. . . . Mr. Levy replied, 'Someone with so little concern for his oath of office that he takes bribes to fix murder cases' should . . . be presumed to have presided over a fundamentally corrupt courtroom."[195]

There are two ways in which such a presumption of corruption might operate. First, there is the approach that because a judge acted corruptly in bribed cases, we can legitimately presume—as an evidentiary matter—that he acted corruptly in nonbribed cases as well. For instance, we might presume that it is more likely than not that Maloney exacted a penalty from nonbribing defendants, or favored the prosecution in such cases in order to "balance" the scales in his courtroom.

The key characteristic of this presumption is that it is *transaction-based*. Under this approach, evidence of corruption in one transaction can be used to establish (on a presumed basis) evidence of corruption in another, if the facts are right (e.g., the case is one where retaliation was possible or where the idea of "balancing" is plausible). This is a theory that Bracy's lawyers explicitly advanced.[196]

Corruption as capture-by-evil reflects a different approach. Under this theory, a judge such as Maloney—who has been proven to have acted corruptly in one (or more) instances—is deemed to be "captured by evil" such that his courtroom, and all of his actions, are deemed to be corrupt. It is not the particulars of the later transaction that are the focus; rather, it is the *character* and *qualifications* of the presiding judge. For instance, during oral argument in the United States Supreme Court, Bracy's lawyers raised this specter:

[Bracy's counsel]: [T]he character of the person who . . . assume[s] . . . his oath and office . . . [is relevant] in determining whether or not there was a due process violation.

. . . .

[Bracy's counsel]: . . . I think that it's more than an inference about . . . how the person will behave. It's a—if you will . . . *a structural defect.* . . .

[Question]: So any time a judge has taken one bribe, all his decisions have to be set aside?

[Bracy's counsel]: That is the inference. . . .

. . . .

[Bracy's counsel]: [I]n judicial proceedings, when Judge Maloney took an oath to be fair, he wasn't, and I think it's certainly a fair and logical inference to draw from that that he would be *dishonest or self-interested* [*across the board*].[197]

At one point, the situation was likened to one where there is "an imposter as the judge."[198]

The first approach—that certain facts suggest a particular, evidentiary presumption—is certainly the more conventional legal approach. For instance, when a trial judge has a pecuniary interest in the outcome of a case, we presume that he cannot be trusted to be fair and demand his removal.[199] Indeed, since the situations justifying such evidentiary presumptions are generally described as those where "the trial judge is discovered to have had *some basis* for rendering a biased judgment, [and] his actual motivations are hidden,"[200] the possibility that a corrupt judge's engagement in retaliatory or compensatory bias would seem to be a prime example.

There are, however, serious logical problems with the use of an evidentiary presumption of this kind in a corruption case.

Because of its evidentiary nature, the "basis" for rendering a biased judgment must be *particular*, not theoretical. In other words, there must be something particular about the later transaction that makes the operation of the presumption more than mere philosophical predilection or complete speculation. Thus, when a presumption of this kind is used, the law generally requires "*some connection* . . . between the judge and one or more of the participants in the litigation."[201] Regarding retaliatory bias, it is possible to logically infer that because Bracy did not offer Maloney a bribe, the judge was likely biased against him. However, when one considers the vast number of cases that Maloney handled,[202] the logic of this conclusion becomes seriously attenuated. Since Maloney (presumably) was bribed in only a small fraction of cases, is it reasonable to assume that he retaliated against the defendant in *every* nonbribed case? When we consider it more carefully, there is nothing about Bracy's case that makes the possibility of retaliation more than complete speculation.

The second presumption—that of compensatory bias—fares no better. A judge, as a human being, has all kinds of general biases and prejudices—including, perhaps, looking tough for colleagues or an electorate. Maloney had a reputation as a "hanging judge,"[203] but under our system of justice this philosophical predilection would not, alone, afford ground for complaint. There has to be more—there has to be something about this defendant's transaction, with this judge, that supports a particular suspicion or temptation for prosecutorial bias or punitive toughness.

In fact, there was nothing of this type about his case to which Bracy could point. If scrutiny of the Bracy/Maloney transaction is the focus, there is nothing particular about that transaction that supports a suspicion of law-and-order toughness beyond that theoretically present in every case in which Maloney presided.[204] And a presumption of the practice of compensatory bias in *all* cases goes too far. As reviewing courts observed, "We do not know whether he practiced [compensatory bias] . . . in *any* case; and he would have been unlikely to practice it in every case."[205] "[T]he evidence does not establish that an interest in covering up wrongdoing or motivating lawyer bribe payments pervaded every action taken by Maloney."[206]

Bracy tried to bolster his claim of compensatory bias by pointing out that Maloney—at his own sentencing hearing—claimed that the convictions and sentences of Bracy and Collins were "a credit to his record as a judge and evidence that he was not corrupt."[207] This statement, however, really proves little. As a reviewing judge observed, "It was natural for Maloney, at his sentencing for accepting bribes from criminal defendants, including defendants in murder cases, to point to a case before him in which the murderers had been convicted and sentenced to death."[208]

Bracy's attempt to prove that he was the victim of judicial bias or prejudice—through an evidentiary presumption or otherwise—was also made more difficult by the mechanics of the prosecution of his case. First, Bracy was tried by a jury, not the judge. Thus, Maloney's opportunity to exercise retaliatory or compensatory bias was limited to the making of rulings during trial, not the ultimate finding of guilt or innocence. As the federal appellate court observed in Bracy's case, "It is [only] in cases tried to the bench that the judge as decision-maker must shoulder full responsibility for the decision."[209]

In addition, those rulings about which Bracy did complain were committed by law to the "sound discretion" of the trial judge. Maloney's allowance of wide (and arguably irrelevant) cross-examination of defense witnesses, his excusal of a juror who expressed ambiguous views about the death penalty, his refusal to give Bracy's requested jury instructions, his denial of a continuance before the sentencing phase of the trial began, and so on, could very well have affected the outcome. However, the explicit commitment of these rulings to the trial judge's discretion made the proof of their prejudice extremely difficult. As one reviewing court succinctly put it, "[Bracy and Collins] do not point to any particular adverse ruling that would have been more favorable to them before another judge."[210] "This may be a case in which *any* judge would have ruled in favor of the government in the instances of which defendants complain."[211]

The failure of evidentiary presumptions leaves us in an untenable position. By all accounts, Maloney was "a racketeer sending men to the death chamber in the name of the State."[212] Yet a defendant who was tried by this judge is left, seemingly, with no legal complaint whatsoever.

If Bracy is to obtain relief, it must be under the second approach. What we have—and what purely evidentiary presumptions do not capture—is the presence of a judge who is *captured by evil* and who should not, as a result, be permitted to sit in judgment of any case.

Under this idea, the true intuition that we have, and the presumption that follows, in fact, is this: that a judge such as Maloney, who has been proven to have acted corruptly in one or more instances, is "captured by evil" such that his courtroom and all of his actions are presumed to be corrupt. Our outrage about Maloney's presence on the bench does not depend upon the particularities of the Maloney/Bracy transaction; we accept that the particularities of corrupt decisions, emanating from a corrupt mind, may never be known. It was not what Maloney did, *but who he was*, that causes us outrage and undermines the outcome of Bracy's case.

The appellate court opinions that were rendered in Bracy's case echo this basic intuition. Reviewing courts agreed that the assumption that "a judge's corruption is likely to permeate his judicial conduct rather than be encapsulated in the particular cases in which he takes bribes . . . is plausible."[213] They agreed that the judicial corruption of Maloney and his colleagues "tainted the judicial system of Illinois, caused unjust acquittals, jeopardized convictions, tarnished the legal profession, and raised profound doubts . . . about the entire political culture of the state."[214] They agreed that Maloney "was corrupt,"[215] that the "cancer" of his corruption "invaded [his] decisionmaking,"[216] and that his activities were a "defilement" of any semblance of judicial process.[217]

Indeed, as one reads the descriptions of Maloney in court documents, virtually every classic element of corruption as "evil" and Maloney as "captured" is vividly presented. Maloney, in these portrayals, was a dangerous hypocrite who fooled observers. He was "sinister."[218] He was a "degenerate," a "Mafia factotum," with a "depraved" character.[219] He lived a "life of corruption"; he "corrupt[ed] justice"; he was "shown to be thoroughly steeped in corruption through his public trial and conviction."[220] "His deviation from the path of righteousness was not . . . momentary and uncharacteristic; it was cold, calculated, and spanned a period of years, if not the entirety of his tenure on the bench."[221] Maloney's bribe taking was not "something external to his personality, or . . . some severable part of it"; he was "a criminal," "remove[d] . . . from the category of the 'average' man."[222] He "willingly abandon[ed] his oath and yield[ed] to the coarsest of [his] proclivities."[223] He was "no more . . . an impartial arbiter . . . than a delusional megalomaniac who locks a judge in the closet, dons a black robe, and hoodwinks everyone."[224] He was beyond the human pale, neither understandable nor reformable.[225]

The idea that there simply *was no judge* of any competence in the *Bracy* case was expressed in the following colloquy during oral argument, between justices of the United States Supreme Court and government counsel:

Question: May I ask . . . a basic question, Ms. Preiner? Suppos[e] instead of a judge who's accused of bribery and so forth, this man had been tried by an accountant or a law clerk or somebody else who was not properly elected to office and was not a lawyer, . . . but you look at the record and he got a fair trial. Would that be subject to setting aside?

Ms. Preiner: I believe it would be. . . . I believe that . . . at [a] minimum you are entitled to a trial by a judge and a jury. If we have an imposter as the judge, I believe that—

Question: And so the question is whether he had a judge here?

Ms. Preiner: Whether he had—yes, a duly elected judge, and he was tried by the judge and a jury.

Question: Do you think it's better to be tried by a corrupt judge than by an accountant, for example?

. . . .

Question: . . . [Y]ou haven't had a trial, in the ordinary sense, if it's been done before a kangaroo court. There's just been no trial in the accepted sense, and the question of whether you had a fair trial is different from the question of whether you had a trial.[226]

With such descriptions of a sitting judge, the next step would seem to be obvious: there can be no presumption of fairness or due process in that judge's court. When faced with this obvious conclusion, however, the courts that reviewed Bracy's case faltered. Rather than follow the "captured" presumption to which they—themselves—apparently subscribed, the reviewing courts, at this critical point, refused to see Maloney's corruption—as a remediable, legal matter—in other than strictly transactional terms. As framed by those courts, the question remained whether Maloney's corruption—in the sense of a perversion of judgment—could be proven in the handling of Bracy's case.[227] For those courts, the focus remained whether—in the Bracy/Maloney transaction—there was harm to Bracy's interests, something not yet proven in the case.[228] There was (as one reviewing judge put it) no substantial evidence "that . . . the jury's findings were tainted" by the "collateral corruption" in which Maloney engaged.[229]

The outcome in both reviewing courts was undoubtedly influenced by the stark judicial choice that Bracy's case presented. If Bracy was entitled to relief on a theory of presumed corruption, so were thousands of other defendants whose cases had been tried in the corrupt judge's court. As one reviewing judge noted, "A principled acceptance of . . . [Bracy's] argument would require the invalidating of tens of thousands of civil and criminal judgments, since Judge Maloney alone presided over some 6,000 cases during the course of his judicial career and he is only one of eighteen Illinois judges who have been convicted of accepting bribes."[230]

Denial of a remedy, however, is viscerally unsatisfactory on its own terms. If a judge "is corrupt," and his courtroom "is corrupt," how can we say—as a positive matter—that a fair trial was conducted, and justice done, in that judge's court? As Judge Rovner argues in dissent in Bracy's case, "What are we to say to Bracy . . ., that [he] had the right to an honest, impartial judge but that the breadth of past corruption in the Illinois judiciary makes it too costly for us to enforce that right? [Is he] . . . to become the latest victim[] of Maloney's bribetaking, and we his accomplices . . . ?"[231] It is the universal rule that a judge who is indicted for accepting bribes will be immediately removed from active service, and if he is convicted—for even one bribe—he will be removed permanently from the bench.[232] It is highly ironic to argue that Bracy's conviction should remain intact when, had Maloney's corruption been known at the time of trial, he would never have been permitted to have heard the case.

In addition, it is not the individual injustice that inheres in the acts of the corrupt judge (bad as those might be) that causes our deepest alarm in these cases; it is what that behavior says about our ability to believe in the *system* of law and the *system* of justice. The statement of a reviewing judge in Bracy's case—that absent a showing of actual prejudice, what remains is simply an "abstract interest in procedural fairness"[233]—strikes us as missing the point altogether. The issue here is not simply the unfairness to Bracy (or another individual) versus the social costs of questioning Maloney's judgments; there is the additional consideration of the systemic costs and systemic dangers that judicial corruption presents. A judge is not simply another public servant; he is a "carefully protected eminence," "the trustee of the assurance of justice."[234] "The solemnity of legal procedure and the perpetuation of traditional forms—such as the judicial robes, the bailiff's incantations . . . —all bespeak the [judge's] exalted station."[235] When this solemnity is exposed as a fabricated farce, our confidence in the system of justice is fundamentally shaken.[236] Compounding this truth is our incredulity at the system's apparent inability to rectify this situation, and, instead, its decision to simply affirm the corrupt judge's actions. Whatever the legal rationales for this outcome, the fact remains that for the judiciary (and society) to embrace such judgments is to "embrace [their] . . . stain" and "the judicial service of [the] outlaws" who produced them.[237] It is to endorse the actions of "a racketeer" who judged men in the powerful name of the state.[238]

Indeed, it is because of these damaging systemic costs that proof of prejudice to individual litigants in judicial corruption cases has no bearing on the judge's criminal prosecution. Famous defendants have asserted, and failed in, this defense. We recall that Sir Francis Bacon, English Lord Chancellor, argued that his bribe taking never influenced his decisions, and that sometimes he decided against the payers of bribes.[239] He conceded, however, that even if he were the "justest chancellor," he was deserving of "the justest censure," a judgment in which Parliament readily obliged.[240]

In the 1930s, Martin T. Manton, a United States circuit judge, was convicted of corruptly conspiring to obstruct the administration of justice and to defraud the United States. Evidence at trial established that an associate of Manton approached litigants, claiming that he was intimately acquainted with Manton and— by reason of that intimacy—able to procure favors for the parties in Manton's court.[241] In exchange for these "favors," Manton expected and received sums of money as gifts and loans. On appeal from his conviction, Manton complained that the trial judge "refused to charge the jury that they might consider . . . whether his decisions [in those cases] . . . were [nonetheless] correct."[242] The appellate court swiftly rejected this defense, stating that "we may assume for present purposes that all of the cases in which Manton's action is alleged to have been corruptly secured were in fact rightly decided. But the unlawfulness of the conspiracy here in question is in no degree dependent upon the indefensibility of the decisions which were rendered in consummating it. Judicial action, whether just or unjust, right or wrong, is not for sale; and if the rule shall ever be accepted that the correctness of judicial action taken for a price removes the stain of corruption and exonerates the judge, the event will mark the first step toward the abandonment of that imperative requisite of even-handed justice."[243]

As stated in a recent case, it is not necessary that a corrupt judge be shown to have decided wrongly; such a judge, through his actions, deprives the public of its "intangible right" to an independent and untarnished judicial system, and that is sin enough.[244]

It is these *systemic* dangers and *systemic* damage that the idea of corruption as capture-by-evil serves to so powerfully express. As a dispositionally depraved individual, a corrupt judge (in this view) presents not only the danger of individual injustice but also the problem of *the very presence of evil* on the bench. Corruption as capture-by-evil imagines an external, powerful, and corrosive force, which possesses the afflicted individuals. It is a "cancer" or "virus" or "disease" that threatens not only those afflicted, but also the institutions of government of which they are a part.

The idea of corruption as capture-by-evil thus serves, in such cases, to identify and vindicate vital interests of which other, transactional ideas of corruption have no cognizance. The competing interests in such cases are not simply those that a transactional model identifies. They are more than an assessment of the odds of wrongful treatment of the individual accused. Of the available legal ideas of corruption, only capture-by-evil vindicates our intuitions about individual risks of unfairness *and* the reality of systemic failure. The trial of an individual by a judge such as Maloney cannot be what our system guarantees; yet only through the presumptions that underlie capture-by-evil is any legal purchase given to that fact.

What about the dangers that the use of the idea of corruption as capture-by-evil entails? Several are undoubtedly present in this case. For instance, there is little doubt but that Maloney was prosecuted for both character and acts. Whatever the act-based focus required for conviction, Maloney's character—as "sinister," "depraved," and "remove[d] . . . from the category of 'average man'"—undoubtedly influenced closing arguments, judicial commentaries, sentencing, and other aspects of his prosecution. There is also little doubt, when one reads the printed words of the paper record, that Maloney's prosecution and sentencing were emotionally charged. He might have been convicted on the basis of the proof of particular acts and criminal elements; but the danger of taint from unruly emotions, character evidence, and collateral punishment was real. Although our inclination might be that Maloney would have deserved whatever he got, it must be asked whether this is an appropriate legal response to his case. Under our system of justice, even the most heinous offender is entitled to focused, dispassionate prosecution and fair sentencing.

That said, we still feel unmoved by such risks in this case. Perhaps the evidence of guilt is too strong, the emotions of condemnation too obviously justified, to give the costs of the idea of corruption as capture-by-evil anywhere near the power of the utility of that idea in Maloney's (or a similar judge's) case. If ever there was a case of judicial corruption that highlighted corruption's costs, if ever there was a case of judicial corruption in which we needed an assertion of moral principles, if ever there was a case in which there was a clear danger of both individual and systemic harm—this case was it. Whatever the usual concerns with procedural fairness to the accused, they pale when stacked against the practical and moral imperatives that corruption as capture-by-evil achieves in this case.

Of greater concern, perhaps, are the *societal* costs that the use of the idea of corruption as capture-by-evil involves. As noted above, use of this idea presents the prospect that hundreds (or, as in Maloney's case, thousands) of a corrupt judge's judgments would be deemed suspect, with the injured entitled to seek some kind of remedy.

Consider, for instance, a 2007 New York case, in which a state supreme court (trial) judge was convicted of accepting bribes to manipulate the outcome of divorce proceedings in his court.[245] Judge Gerald P. Garson presided on the bench for about five years and handled nearly eleven hundred cases involving child custody and financial disputes.[246] The prosecution alleged that he arranged with divorce lawyers "to take cash, dinners, and cigars in exchange for courtroom assignments and other favored treatment."[247] The prosecutor argued that "'Supreme Court Judge Gerald Garson became corrupt Supreme Court Judge Gerald Garson, disgraceful Supreme Court Judge Gerald Garson, disgraced Supreme Court Judge Gerald Garson.'"[248] As a result of his conviction, hundreds of divorce cases—previously closed— were reopened.[249]

Criminal cases are more difficult. Even in these cases, however, a corrupt judge has been held to taint all convictions. For instance, two state court judges in Pennsylvania were recently indicted for accepting kickbacks in exchange for sending juveniles to two privately run youth detention facilities.[250] A press account described the scheme as follows:

Things were different in the Luzerne County juvenile courtroom, and everyone knew it. Proceedings on average took less than two minutes. Detention center workers were told in advance how many juveniles to expect at the end of each day—even before hearings to determine [the defendants'] . . . innocence or guilt. Lawyers told families not to bother hiring them. They would not be allowed to speak anyway.

· · · ·

Last month, the law caught up with Judge Mark A. Ciavarella Jr., 58, who ran that juvenile court for 12 years, and Judge Michael T. Conahan, 56, a colleague on the County's Court of Common Pleas.

In what authorities are calling the biggest legal scandal in state history, the two judges [have been charged] . . . in a scheme that involved sending thousands of juveniles to two private detention centers in exchange for $2.6 million in kickbacks.[251]

· · · ·

The judges worked in tandem, beginning in 2002, with Judge Conahan controlling the budget and Judge Ciavarella overseeing the juvenile courts. They shut down a detention center run by the county and began sending the youngsters to newly built detention centers run by PA Child Care and a sister company, Western PA Child Care.

Judge Ciavarella has said he did not sentence juveniles who did not deserve the punishment, but the numbers suggested a different story: he sent one in four of the juvenile defendants to the detention centers . . ., while the rate elsewhere in the state was 1 in 10.[252]

According to Marsha Levick, deputy director of the Juvenile Law Center in Philadelphia, who alerted the FBI, children "were being locked up for minor infractions," such as shoplifting a four-dollar bottle of nutmeg or putting up a MySpace page that taunted a school administrator.[253]

On February 11, 2009, the Pennsylvania Supreme Court appointed senior judge Arthur E. Grim of Berks County Court to review the juvenile cases Ciavarella had handled.[254] Grim subsequently testified at a public hearing that the " 'almost routine disregard for the rights of juvenile offenders' was known to lawyers, court staff, and school authorities, yet went on for six years or more."[255] The scandal, in his words, "grew out of 'unfettered power, greed, opportunity, and intimidation.' "[256] Grim concluded "that *all* juvenile adjudications and consent decrees entered by Ciavarella between January 1, 2003 and May 31, 2008, are tainted."[257]

The Pennsylvania Supreme Court pondered the question of remedy:

> [The question is] how to address and remedy the travesty of juvenile justice that Ciavarella perpetuated in Luzerne County. . . .
>
> . . . .
>
> The transcripts reveal a disturbing lack of fundamental process, inimical to any system of justice, and made even more grievous since these matters involved juveniles. . . .
>
> . . . .
>
> Ciavarella's admission that he received [more than $2.6 million in] . . . payments, and that he failed to disclose his financial interests arising from the development of the

juvenile facilities, thoroughly undermines the integrity of all juvenile proceedings before Ciavarella. Whether or not a juvenile [in a particular case] was represented by counsel, and whether or not a juvenile was committed to one of the facilities which secretly funneled money to Ciavarella and Conahan, this Court cannot have any confidence that Ciavarella decided any Luzerne County juvenile case fairly and impartially. . . .

. . . [A]ll juvenile adjudications and consent decrees entered by Ciavarella between January 1, 2003 and May 31, 2008, are tainted.[258]

The court ordered that all adjudications and consent decrees entered by Ciavarella between January 1, 2003, and May 31, 2008, be vacated; that all convictions be expunged; and that possible retrial be limited to only those juveniles who were afforded counsel, were not sent to the offending facilities, and had not received final discharge either from commitment, placement, probation, or other disposition.[259] Under this order, an estimated sixty-five hundred convictions were overturned, including those involving serious crimes. Approximately ten cases could be retried, and the court specified that in those cases, the defense of double jeopardy could be asserted "in support of an argument that reprosecution should not be permitted."[260]

The court in this case squarely faced the implications of Ciavarella's corruption, and made the only intellectually honest response. Unable to determine—in fact—which outcomes were affected, the court simply held that the system had failed in all. Whatever the societal costs of this action, it was, in the court's judgment, the only acceptable choice.

If the wholesale release or retrial of juvenile offenders is costly, the wholesale release or retrial of adults convicted of crimes is more costly yet. When considering the societal cost of such remedies, it must be assumed that many defendants convicted by a corrupt judge remain incarcerated, and therefore—barring successful retrial—the voiding of convictions will mean that the guilty and dangerous might well go free.

The societal costs of the idea of corruption as capture-by-evil, and the remedies that it logically compels, are, therefore, far from trivial. The idea that convictions should be overturned is a steep cost to pay for the acts of a corrupt judicial actor. If, however, a judge is "thoroughly corrupt"—if he is an "imposter," who has donned judicial robes—there would seem, in all honesty, to be no other choice. We use the language of capture-by-evil because it fits the true character of the case. The actions of such an individual cannot be a legitimate part of the machinery of law.

THE CORRUPT CAMPAIGN

In 1983, Elizabeth Drew published what has been called "the *Silent Spring* of the political environment."[261] In *Politics and Money: The New Road to Corruption*,[262] Drew documented the "river of money" that flows through American politics to candidates for public office. Although money has always been a part of American political campaigns, she argued that the role that money played in American politics was different both in scope and in nature from what had gone before.[263]

The situation that Drew reported was not simply the presence of competing interests, or the presence of money in politics, but the obsession of politicians with the raising of money and the pleasing of those (donors) who might give more. As a "young lawyer-lobbyist" quoted by Drew put it, " 'If you went into a typical senator's or congressman's office a few years ago, almost no one knew who the contributors were or who was coming to the fund-raisers. Now almost every staff member is involved: everybody is asked to give money, to get people to give money. . . . When you talk to someone on Capitol Hill, inevitably the conversation turns to how much money the member has raised, where he's getting it, where he can get more.' "[264]

In meticulous detail, Drew described how the machinery of fund-raising distorted the legislative process. For example, she described how one representative "followed one of the fashions in fund-raising by establishing a special club—this one called the Speaker's Club—for those who [were] . . . especially generous: the admission charge [was] . . . five thousand dollars a year for an individual and fifteen thousand dollars a year for a political action committee [PAC]." A senator established a similar organization in the Senate, as did both the House and the Senate Republican campaign committees, and the Democratic and Republican National Committees. When the House member was asked what club members get, "he responded quickly and honestly. 'Access. Access. That's the name of the game. They meet with the leadership and with the chairmen of the committees. We don't sell legislation; we sell the opportunity to be heard.' "[265]

The "river of money" that Drew described has continued to flow since her book was published. In 1976, the average cost of winning a U.S. Senate seat was $610,026; by 1992, it had escalated to $3.8 million.[266] Spending in House races totaled $60.9 million in 1976, and increased to $326.9 million by 1992.[267] In 1974, congressional candidates received $12.5 million from PACs; by 1990, this figure had climbed to $150.6 million.[268] This represented more than a 500 percent increase after adjustment for inflation.[269]

During the same period, public confidence in government plummeted. A public opinion poll conducted in 1964 found that 76 percent of Americans trusted the government to do what was right most or all of the time; by 1994, only 21 percent of the public had such faith.[270] One study concluded, on the basis of citizen interviews, that "[p]eople believe two forces have corrupted democracy. The first is that lobbyists have replaced representatives as the primary political actors. The other force, seen as more pernicious, is that campaign contributions seem to determine political outcomes."[271]

The Federal Election Campaign Act (FECA), enacted in 1971 and extensively amended in 1974,[272] was the first comprehensive attempt by Congress to regulate the financing of congressional and presidential campaigns.[273] It was enacted in the wake of the Watergate scandal and revelations of big money contributors to Richard Nixon's presidential campaign—the largest being W. Clement Stone, who contributed more than two million dollars.[274] The Act's primary thrust was to implement reform through the regulation of political campaign contributions and expenditures. It also provided a system for public funding of presidential campaign activities, and established the Federal Election Commission to administer and enforce the legislation.

Less than two years after its enactment, the United States Supreme Court considered the constitutionality of the Act in the watershed case of *Buckley v. Valeo*.[275] The results were mixed. All expenditure limits, except those by political parties, were struck down on First Amendment grounds.[276] On the other hand, contribution limits, disclosure requirements, record keeping requirements, and public financing provisions were upheld.[277] In the course of upholding these provisions, the Court articulated the prevention of the "actuality and appearance of corruption"[278] as the critical government interest in this field.

What the *Buckley* majority believed the "actuality and appearance of corruption" to involve was the subject of some elaboration in the Court's opinion. First, the Court cited actual quid pro quo arrangements: "To the extent that large contributions are given to secure a political *quid pro quo* from current and potential office holders, the integrity of our system of representative democracy is undermined."[279] Although the actual incidence of such arrangements is difficult to know, the Court noted that "the deeply disturbing examples surfacing after the 1972 election demonstrate that the problem is not an illusory one."[280] In addition, and of almost equal concern, is "the impact of the appearance of corruption stemming from public awareness of the opportunities for abuse inherent in a regime of large individual financial contributions."[281] Quoting an earlier case, the Court stated that "Congress could legitimately conclude that the avoidance of the appearance of improper influence 'is also critical . . . if confidence in the system of representative Government is not to be eroded.' "[282]

Thus, that the "actuality and appearance of corruption" encompasses more than the criminal giving and taking of bribes was clear.[283] However, a vast range of conduct and potential governmental interests stretches beyond this point. Does the "appearance of corruption," for instance, target only those situations where there is a danger of quid pro quo arrangements? Or does this also include broader concerns about undue political influence and the power of money in political campaigns?

Throughout the next two decades, the Court followed a generally expansive path in the understanding of corruption and public interests in the electoral context. For instance, in *Austin v.*

Michigan Chamber of Commerce,[284] the Court upheld state limitations on "independent" corporate campaign expenditures (i.e., those not controlled by or coordinated with a candidate) on the ground that "corporate dominance" of the political process would introduce a "different type of corruption . . .: the corrosive and distorting effects of immense aggregations of wealth that are accumulated with the help of the corporate form."[285] In *Federal Election Commission v. Colorado Republican Federal Campaign Committee,*[286] the Court upheld limits on spending by political parties when that spending was coordinated with a candidate's campaign. Although the idea of quid pro quo relationships between political parties and their own candidates is illogical, the Court reasoned that political parties could be used by donors to circumvent contribution limits and as conduits for contributions that were intended to foster a sense of obligation. Abuses of both kinds, the Court reasoned, would "exacerbate the threat of corruption and apparent corruption" that contribution limits were intended to prevent.[287]

In *McConnell v. Federal Election Commission,*[288] decided in 2003, this trend toward broad understandings of corruption and legitimate government interests in the campaign finance context continued. At issue in *McConnell* was the Bipartisan Campaign Reform Act of 2002 (BCRA),[289] which targeted the "soft money loophole"—money contributed to political parties, and previously unregulated by the FECA—and issue advertising intended to influence federal election campaigns. In upholding the BCRA's central provisions, the Court emphasized the dangers presented by "great aggregations of wealth"[290] and by "big money campaign contributions."[291] Corruption caused by money in politics, the Court stated, takes several forms. First, there is the danger of cash-for-votes, or express or implied quid pro quo agreements.[292]

In addition to quid pro quo arrangements, there is the broader problem of "politicians too compliant with the wishes of large contributors"—in other words, the suspected problem of the effect of obligation or undue influence on an officeholder's judgment.[293] Finally, there is the more diffuse but important danger that whatever the realities of influence, public confidence in the electoral process will be eroded. If citizens believe (rightly or wrongly) that government policies are simply bought and sold, they will feel no responsibility for the successful functioning of government.[294]

From these cases, the following understandings of corruption in the campaign finance context can be distilled:

1. Corruption includes proof of *actual quid pro quo agreements*, and situations with a *demonstrable danger of quid pro quo arrangements*, between contributors and candidates.

2. Corruption involves situations that fall short of a quid pro quo but that nonetheless foster a *sense of obligation* on the part of officeholders to contributors, or otherwise involve *undue influence*.

3. Corruption involves the *distortion of the political process* through concentrated wealth, such as through the spending of corporate money in political campaigns.

4. Corruption includes the *impression of control* of the political process by big donors, with resultant cynicism and alienation of the populace.

With the exception of corruption of the first type, all of these understandings go far beyond the transactional or quid pro quo model of corruption in politics.[295] Under these understandings, the concern is not with the simple existence of quid pro quo arrangements, or even the danger of quid pro quo arrangements; it is with the evil that money in politics engenders.

In the 2010 case of *Citizens United v. Federal Election Commission*,[296] the majority of the Court's justices rejected the broad conception of corruption used in prior cases, and restricted corruption in the campaign finance context to simple quid pro quo transactions. In *Citizens United*, a provision of the BCRA was again challenged on First Amendment grounds. This law prohibited corporate expenditures that expressly advocate the election or defeat of candidates, or other corporate "electioneering communications."[297] Prohibitions of this kind were addressed in *Austin* and *McConnell*, and upheld in those cases. This time, a bare majority of the Court struck down the restriction, on the ground that it violated corporate rights to political speech.[298]

In reaching this result, the majority rejected the public-interest rationales for corporate-expenditure bans that were cited in *Austin* and *McConnell*. In particular, it rejected what it called the "antidistortion interest" that *Austin* had identified—that is, " 'the corrosive and distorting effects of immense aggregations of wealth that are accumulated with the help of the corporate form and that have little or no correlation to the public's support for the corporation's political ideas.' "[299] This, the majority implied, was not related to corruption.[300] Indeed, the majority opined, corruption in the campaign context is and must be limited to quid pro quo transactions.[301] Because no evidence of corruption (in this sense) was found, Congress had no justification to restrict "corporate speech." In a particularly pointed paragraph, the majority wrote: "The *McConnell* record was 'over 100,000 pages' long . . ., yet it 'does not have any direct examples of votes being exchanged for . . . expenditures.' . . . This confirms . . . that independent [corporate] expenditures do not lead to, or create the appearance of, *quid pro quo* corruption. In fact, there is only scant evidence that independent expenditures even ingratiate [donors to lawmakers]. . . . Ingratiation and access, in any event, are not corruption."[302]

The four dissenting justices presented an entirely different picture. The majority assumes, the dissent stated, "that the only 'sufficiently important governmental interest in preventing corruption or the appearance of corruption' is one that is 'limited to *quid pro quo* corruption.' . . . This is the same 'crabbed view of corruption' that was espoused [by the dissent] . . . in *McConnell* and squarely rejected by the Court in that case."[303] The dissent pointed out that "[o]n numerous occasions we have recognized Congress' legitimate interest in preventing the money that is spent on elections from exerting an 'undue influence on an officeholder's judgment' and from creating 'the appearance of such influence,' beyond the sphere of *quid pro quo* relationships. . . . Corruption may take many forms. Bribery may be the paradigm case. But the difference between selling a vote and selling access is a matter of degree, not kind. . . . Corruption operates along a spectrum, and the majority's apparent belief that *quid pro quo* arrangements can be neatly demarcated from other improper influences does not accord with the theory or reality of politics."[304]

In addition, the dissent argued, at stake is "not only the legitimacy and quality of Government but also the public's faith therein." If the public believes in the evils of big money in politics, it will erode " 'the confidence of its citizens in their capacity to govern themselves.' "[305]

The understanding of corruption that *Austin*, *McConnell*, and the dissent in *Citizens United* reflect is a form of the idea of capture-by-evil. To the justices writing the opinions in these cases, the problem in the campaign-finance context is far more than preventing or detecting illegal quid pro quo transactions by candidates and elected officials. Rather, it is the problem of an external, explicit, "moral" bad (the influence of money), which works to distort the political process, and to whose temptations— in multifarious detected and undetected ways—candidates and officeholders may succumb. In the images found in these opinions, corruption—in the form of large campaign contributions— is a "pernicious influence" that "insinuate[s] itself" into the political process.[306] It is "corrosive and distorting."[307] It presents "a mortal danger against which effective preventative and curative steps must be taken."[308] It is a "constantly growing evil" that has shaken the confidence of the people in government.[309] It is something that must be "purge[d]" from national politics.[310]

This idea of corruption, and the reforms that it has generated, have been criticized on many grounds. These include the charges that limits on campaign contributions reinforce the status quo by hindering the ability of challengers to raise money;[311] that limits on contributions to candidates forces candidates to spend more time raising money from many small donors;[312] and others.[313] Perhaps the most trenchant critique is that which attacks the *substance* of the broad idea of corruption in this context. These writers argue that there is no hard evidence—beyond anecdotal stories—that campaign contributions actually influence legislators' conduct.[314] In this view, concern about money without proof of its dangers is "conjectural" at best, and "irrational" or "vacuous" at worst.[315] These writers speculate that concern about corrupt appearances has less to do with genuine dangers than with an inability to show actual influence on a legislator's conduct.[316]

Studies that have attempted to gather data on whether campaign contributions influence legislators' conduct as an empirical matter have proven inconclusive.[317] This is not surprising, since admission of specific instances of influence by legislators would implicate their involvement in dereliction of duty, improper influence, and bribery. In addition, the influence of favors and benefits may be subtle, shifting, and not even acknowledged by elected officials to themselves. As described by one commentator, "What happens is a gradual shifting of a man's loyalties from the community to those who have been doing him favors. His final decisions are, therefore, made in response to his private friendships and loyalties. . . . Throughout this whole process, the official will claim—and may indeed believe—that there is no causal connection between the favors he receives and the decisions which he makes. . . . [T]he whole process may be so subtle as not to be detected by the official himself."[318] Tony Coelho, former member of Congress, explained it this way: "Take anything. Take housing. . . . If you are spending all your time calling up different people that you're involved with, . . . to raise $50,000, . . . all of a sudden, in your mind, you're in effect saying, 'I'm not going to go out and develop this new housing bill that may get the Realtors or . . . the builders or . . . the unions [or other contributors] upset. You know, I've got to raise the $50,000; I've got to do that.' "[319]

The scarcity of admissions of improper influence does not mean, of course, that we should choose to believe that it does not exist. At the very least, as Fred Wertheimer and Susan Manes have observed, "[t]here is an inherent problem with a system in which individuals and groups with an interest in government decisions can give substantial sums of money to elected officials who have the power to make those decisions."[320] The bottom line, as expressed by Dale Bumpers, former senator from Arkansas, is: "Every Senator knows I speak the truth when I say

[that] bill after bill has been defeated in this body because of campaign money."[321]

In addition—and perhaps more important—the empirical claim must be seen for what it is. The key to the empirical critics' position is this: corruption is composed of acts that have actually influenced a legislator's conduct.[322] *If* (as such critics assume) we posit that "actual" corruption is the existence of successful quid pro quo transactions, then the conclusion that anything "less" than this is simply a poor substitute inexorably follows. This does not, however, answer the primary question, which is this: Are there broader government interests—*perhaps even more critical government interests*—that corruption as capture-by-evil identifies?

We are concerned—in this area—not only with the damage caused by *particular acts* or *particular votes* but also with the damage to broad, institutional processes that money in politics presents. We must be concerned not only with the possible quid pro quo transaction but also with the *public suspicion* that government policies and public offices are "bought and sold"[323]—a suspicion that free-wheeling spending by powerful interests in the campaign arena inevitably creates.

Indeed, of all government interests in this context, the maintenance of popular belief in the legitimacy of the political system is by far the most critical. Studies have repeatedly found that instances of quid pro quo corruption and (more important for our purposes) *the perception of a culture* of quid pro quo corruption destroy government legitimacy. For many years, political scientists have reported the effects of clientelism and cronyism on popular belief in government.[324] As one study succinctly put it, "[C]lientelism and related corruption (in the form of vote-buying and bribery) . . . decreas[e] trust for the political system, which is viewed as being at the service of the highest bidder."[325] Studies of the political systems in France, Chile, Germany, Italy, Mexico, Nicaragua, El Salvador, Costa Rica, Bolivia, Paraguay, Japan, and the United States confirm what—perhaps—is obvious: that actual quid pro quo corruption and public belief *in the opportunity for* quid pro quo corruption erode the legitimacy of government.[326]

In a recent United States Supreme Court case, Justice Souter summarized the effects of big campaign contributions in the American context this way: "What high-dollar [donors] . . . get is special access to the officials they help elect, and with it disproportionate influence on those in power. . . . As the erstwhile officer of a large American corporation put it, 'Business leaders believe—based on experience and with good reason—that . . . access gives them an opportunity to shape and affect governmental decisions. . . .' . . . Voters know this. Hence, the . . . consequence of the demand for big money to finance publicity: pervasive public cynicism. A 2002 poll found that 71 percent of Americans think Members of Congress cast votes based on the views of their big contributors, even when those views differ from the Member's own beliefs about what is best for the country."[327]

What critics of capture-by-evil conceptions of corruption in this context miss is that the individual corrupt transaction is only a small part of the larger problem of real or perceived corrupt institutional capture.[328] Transactional crimes may be the most familiar and obvious example of perversion of the political process; however, their true importance lies not in the particular government interests that are sacrificed in each case, but in the larger message that they send. The larger concern is the maintenance of public faith in government. Toward that end, all aspects of campaign corruption must be recognized, and addressed by prophylactic measures.[329]

This admixture of concerns about individual and institutional corruption is vividly illustrated in another, peculiarly American campaign context: that of the *elected* state court judge. Although federal judges are appointed (for life), trial and appellate judges are elected by the populace in thirty-nine states. These judges are elected by the public after campaigns that are often virtually indistinguishable from legislative and executive races.[330] Judges in election campaigns often amass "million-dollar war chests, [and engage in] attack advertising and even outright distortion of an opponent's record" in efforts to win reelection.[331] For instance, a publication by a citizens' group reported that a total of $9,166,450 was raised by seven justices of the Texas Supreme Court in their election campaigns.[332] It was predicted that in Ohio, "more than $5 million and possibly as much as $12 million" would be spent in the year 2000 during a battle for a single state Supreme Court seat.[333] The awakening of interest groups to the power of money in judicial races was described by a lobbyist for Pennsylvanians for Effective Government (PEG): "The business community woke up in the late 1980s and realized that there are three legs to the government stool—the executive branch, the judicial branch, and the legislative branch. We were playing quite well for over a decade in two of those three and [came to realize that judges] . . . are the arbiters of the final interpretation of all rules and regulations that are passed by the legislature. Consequently, in '89 to the present, PEG periodically got involved in statewide appellate court races, most of those being Supreme Court races."[334]

The result—as observed by David Barnhizer, a prominent commentator—is that "many judicial candidates are consciously and unconsciously selling their votes on issues. Judges need to attract contributions both for their own campaigns and to keep the funds and other forms of political support away from potential competitors. Judges do this by crafting messages that signal to the contributors that [they] . . . are willing to provide what the donors want in exchange for their money."[335] For instance, "[i]n recent years, races for the Alabama Supreme Court have turned into multimillion-dollar spending sprees fueled by business groups and plaintiff[s'] lawyers."[336] Jere Beasley, Montgomery attorney and former Alabama lieutenant governor, accurately predicted that the elections of 2000 would be a spending blowout, when five of the nine seats on the Supreme Court were at stake.[337] "'[B]usiness interests will try to elect justices who will support their agenda[s],'" he predicted. "'They [will try] . . . to elect a Supreme Court that will put the stamp on binding arbitration.'"[338]

The problem, Barnhizer observed, "is far more pervasive, destructive, and subtle than ordinary criminal bribery intended to obtain a particular outcome in a specific case."[339] "The corruption of the judiciary includes deliberate wrongdoing in exchange for financial contributions. But it also involves more subtle judicial behavior shaped to fit the contributors' agendas. . . . Even if judicial corruption through decisions that favor special interests is not empirically demonstrable, the public's perception will be that judicial decision-making favors special interests to which the judge is obligated through financial or other campaign support."[340]

In 2006 the *New York Times* examined campaign contributions received by justices of the Ohio Supreme Court, and the justices' subsequent behavior when hearing cases involving contributors.[341] The study concluded that justices of the Ohio Supreme Court "routinely sat on cases after receiving campaign contributions from the parties involved or from groups that filed supporting briefs. On average, they voted in favor of contributors 70 percent of the time."[342] One justice, Terrence O'Donnell, voted for his contributors 91 percent of the time during the period 1994–2006.[343] "[J]ustices almost never disqualified themselves from hearing their contributors' cases. In the 215 cases with the most direct potential conflicts of interest, justices recused themselves just 9 times."[344] Did most of these justices favor contributors in their decision making? It is impossible to know. However, in a survey of 2,428 state court judges conducted by the reform organization Justice at Stake, almost half said that they believed that campaign contributions influenced the decisions of their colleagues.[345] This suspicion is not lost on the public. Surveys indicate " 'that generally 75 percent of the people believe that [judicial campaign] contributions influence decisions.' "[346]

As a result—as in other campaign contexts—concerns about the influence of money in judicial campaigns goes far beyond the transactional or quid pro quo idea of corruption. The concern is not simply about the existence of actual quid pro quo arrangements, or even the danger of quid pro quo arrangements; it is about damage to the broad, institutional interest that citizens believe in the integrity of the courts of their states.

Very recently, all of these issues—and the United States Supreme Court's response—were vividly illustrated by the case of *Caperton v. A. T. Massey Coal Co.*[347] In August of 2002, a state court jury in West Virginia found A. T. Massey Coal Company liable in a civil lawsuit brought by Hugh Caperton, who had alleged fraudulent misrepresentation, concealment, and tortious interference with contract. A judgment of $50 million was entered against Massey.[348]

The state trial court subsequently denied Massey's posttrial motions challenging the verdict and the damages award. After the verdict, but before an appeal, West Virginia held its 2004 judicial elections.[349] Don Blankenship, Massey's chairman, chief executive officer, and president—"knowing [that] the Supreme Court of Appeals of West Virginia would consider the appeal in the case"—backed an attorney, Brent Benjamin, who sought to replace Justice McGraw on the court.[350] The United States Supreme Court described Blankenship's efforts as follows:

> In addition to contributing the $1,000 statutory maximum to Benjamin's campaign committee, Blankenship donated almost $2.5 million to "And For the Sake of the Kids," a political organization formed under 26 U.S.C. §527. [This] . . . organization opposed McGraw and supported Benjamin. . . . This was not all. Blankenship spent, in addition, just over $500,000 on independent expenditures . . . for direct mailings and letters soliciting donations as well as television and newspaper advertisements [supporting Benjamin]. . . .
>
> To provide some perspective, Blankenship's $3 million in contributions were more than the total amount spent by all other Benjamin supporters and three times the amount spent by Benjamin's own [campaign] committee.[351]

Benjamin won the election, 53.3 percent to 46.7 percent.[352]

Before the West Virginia high court heard the case, "Caperton moved to disqualify now-Justice Benjamin under the [federal] Due Process Clause and the West Virginia Code of Judicial Conduct, based on the conflict [of interest] caused by Blankenship's campaign involvement."[353] Benjamin, who (under court rules) personally decided this motion pertaining to himself, denied it on the ground that there was " 'no objective information . . . to show that this Justice has a bias for or against any litigant, that this Justice has prejudged the matters which comprise this litigation, or that this Justice will be anything but fair and impartial.' "[354]

The hearing of the case by the West Virginia high court proceeded. The $50 million verdict against Massey was reversed in a 3–2 vote. Justices Benjamin, Davis, and Maynard composed the majority; two other justices (Starcher and Albright) dissented. The majority of the court found that " 'Massey's conduct warranted the type of judgment rendered [below] in this case' " but reversed on two independent (and, by all accounts, flimsy) state law grounds.[355]

Caperton sought rehearing, and moved to disqualify Justice Benjamin on the basis of Blankenship's support for Benjamin's campaign. He also moved to disqualify Justice Maynard, who was discovered to have vacationed with Blankenship in the French Riviera while the case was pending in the court. Massey, in turn, brought a motion to disqualify Justice Starcher (one of the dissenters) on the ground that his public criticism of Blankenship's role in the 2004 judicial election revealed that he was biased.

In response to these motions, Justice Benjamin refused to recuse himself; Justice Maynard and Justice Starcher complied. In announcing his recusal, Starcher stated bitterly that "Blankenship's bestowal of his personal wealth, political tactics, and 'friendship' have created a cancer in the affairs of this Court."[356]

The West Virginia high court then granted a rehearing of the case, with Benjamin now the acting chief justice. He selected two state court judges, Cookman and Fox, to replace the two recused justices. The court reheard the case, and again reversed the jury's verdict in a 3–2 vote.[357] While the rehearing was pending, an independent public opinion poll found that more than 67 percent of responding West Virginians doubted that Benjamin would be fair or impartial in the case.[358]

The question before the United States Supreme Court was whether these events denied Caperton due process of law under the federal Constitution. The Court held that it did. The Due Process Clause, the majority wrote, "has been implemented by objective standards that do not require proof of actual [judicial] bias."[359] Rather, the question is "whether, 'under a realistic appraisal of psychological tendencies and human weakness,' the [facts] . . . pose[] such a risk of actual bias or prejudgment" that the situation cannot be tolerated.[360] Although judicial campaign contributions do not always create a sufficient presumption of bias, "Blankenship's campaign efforts had a significant and disproportionate influence in placing . . . Benjamin on the case."[361] That—"coupled with the temporal relationship between the election and the pending case—offer a possible temptation to the average . . . judge" to depart from an impartial standard.[362]

The majority's approach to this case—from the focus on broad institutional interests, to the adoption of a posture of prophylaxis—echoes the idea of campaign corruption as a dangerous, systemic evil, which may tempt judges beyond their endurance and corrode the system of justice of which they are a part. This is more than the ferreting out of instances of quid pro quo corruption; it is an endorsement of the idea that we cannot trust—indeed, *cannot afford to trust*—individuals such as Benjamin to act noncorruptly, whatever assurances they give and what- ever the lack of evidence of instances of quid pro quo corruption there might be. This vindicates our deepest, visceral convictions about what this case involves. Would anyone truly believe that Benjamin—or any elected judge in his position—would not "feel a debt of gratitude to Blankenship for his extraordinary efforts" in his election campaign?[363] And that in the light of that gratitude, we can simply trust the judge's sense of right to ensure impartial justice? Indeed, our belief in the individual and institutional dangers here is so strong that we (and the Court) are willing to engage in a prophylactic act that does not exist in other campaign finance contexts: we *disqualify* the decision maker (judge) from acting in the donor's case.

There are, therefore, strong reasons for employing the broad, enveloping idea of corruption as capture-by-evil in the legislative, executive, or judicial campaign context. The question that remains is whether there are any countervailing drawbacks to the use of this idea in our thinking about corrupt election campaigns.

Institutional objections to the identification of campaign finance evils in broad, prophylactic terms fall into several categories. First, there is the objection that this idea admits of no limiting principle. If the prevention of the evil of distorting influence in elections is the touchstone, there is no reason to limit the targets of prophylaxis to large monetary contributions. *Any* significant monetary or nonmonetary campaign contribution should be suspect, including (for instance) offers of media exposure, access to union or other interest-group membership lists, endorsement by prominent people, and so on.[364] All contributions (and acts) by supporters have the potential to influence legislative, executive, and judicial candidates; if influence without more is the test, there is no obvious line where "benign" support ends and "corrupt" influence begins.

In addition, it has been argued that the broad prophylactic measures that this conception of corruption demands may have unforeseen and ultimately undesirable consequences. For instance, any chosen array of prohibited or "corrupt" contributions would have different effects on particular candidates, political parties, and contributors. Different candidates and political parties are dependent on contributors with different identities and contribution patterns, making the effects of any scheme of prophylaxis of unpredictable and unequal consequence to candidates and causes.[365] For example, incumbents enjoy a notorious general advantage over challengers,[366] with the result that restricting contributions may hurt challengers far more than the incumbents whom they are trying to unseat.[367] Incumbents enjoy widespread name recognition and the advantage of ready media access for "official" duties and pronouncements—advantages that a challenger must generally spend to achieve. In addition, restrictions on the size of campaign contributions favor the candidate with the larger pool of identified donors. As one critic put it, contribution limits benefit "those candidates who have in place a database of past contributors, an intact campaign organization, and the ability to raise funds on an ongoing basis from PACs [who want to back winners[368]]. This . . . group consists almost entirely of current officeholders."[369]

Such objections undoubtedly have some merit. The extension of electoral corruption from the narrow idea of real (or suspected) quid pro quo arrangements to the broader idea of *institutional* capture by undue influence vastly extends government power in an area fraught with uncertainties and the dangers of favoritism and the protection of vested interests. No matter how much we weigh these concerns, however, the bitter truth remains: the corrupting influence of campaign money is a critical concern in this arena, and it is not—to the public—merely a stand-in for unprovable transactional crimes. A system that winks toward the dangers of undue influence breeds its own cynicism in politics. As Justices Stevens and O'Connor, writing for the majority in *McConnell*, expressed it, "Just as troubling to a functioning democracy as classic *quid pro quo* corruption is the danger that office holders will decide issues not on the merits or the desires of their constituencies, but according to the wishes of those who have made large financial contributions. . . . Even if it occurs only occasionally, the potential for such undue influence is manifest. And unlike straight cash-for-votes transactions, such corruption is neither easily detected nor practical to criminalize. The best means of prevention is to identify and to remove the temptation."[370] Rather than being seen as something that "[c]ater[s] to irrational fears,"[371] campaign finance reform that uses the idea of capture-by-evil is better seen as the only practical way to address this critical interest of government.

Corruption as capture-by-evil has distinct benefits and costs in each of the contexts we have examined. In the case of the corrupt politician, the use of this idea serves to reinforce justified moral condemnation, but there are serious problems with the demonization of offenders or (paradoxically) the reluctance to brand as "corrupt" offenders who do not fit the demonized idea. In the case of the corrupt judge, those dangers also exist, but the need for absolute public confidence in the integrity of American justice *and* its verdicts makes the case for the use of capture-by-evil and its consequences stronger. In the case of the campaign finance reform, the positive case for the use of capture-by-evil is the least complicated. Since campaign-contribution corruption and its prevention by nature involve prophylactic measures, rather than after-the-fact criminal prosecutions, concern about individual injustice toward particular accused officials is minimal. Both costs and benefits, in this context, are primarily institutional—making the preponderance of benefits an easy call.

What capture-by-evil accomplishes in all of these contexts is to remind us that corruption has powerful effects that extend beyond damage created to particular persons as the result of particular acts. There may be serious costs that should restrict its use; but the function of this idea is both clear and powerful. It reminds us that corruption challenges norms. It reminds us that corruption destroys our ability to believe in the impartiality of law. It reminds us that corruption threatens—through its capture of politicians and judges—public trust in the entire system of government.

7 CORRUPTION AND MORAL VALUES

Some Implications for Government

The idea of corruption as capture-by-evil stresses corruption's roots in moral ideas. Corruption, as commonly understood, is not simply a violation of law or the breach of a public duty; it is the engagement in evil, the transgression of deeply held moral norms.

This chapter explores the implications of this idea of corruption in various practical contexts of government. The strength of this idea of corruption is its recognition that corruption operates—inherently—as an alternative moral system, which thrives when the previously existing normative system is weakened or discarded. This explains why an increase in corruption has so often been associated with regime change, democratization efforts, and the institution of market-based reforms. It also explains why "moral" campaigns are a critical part of the politics of corruption control.

CORRUPTION AS AN ALTERNATIVE MORAL SYSTEM

The interplay of corruption as capture-by-evil and moral ideas is complex. Most obviously, corruption as capture-by-evil involves the violation of otherwise firmly established moral norms. However, as previously discussed,[1] it involves more than this. It also involves the conviction that corruption, by its very nature, challenges the continued existence of previously accepted norms. To employ the language that is so often used to describe corruption, corruption is a *virus* or a *cancer* because it has the power to destroy the organism of which it is a part. It can destroy the individual who is affected; it can, by contagion, spread to others and destroy them; and it can, by extension, destroy the system of social norms and underlying moral ideas that are there to constrain it. In short, corruption both violates and *subverts* the existing social and moral order, by suggesting a plausible, apparently self-serving order to replace it.

Consider, for instance, the condition of a "culture of corruption," which is widely described in academic and popular corruption accounts. In a particularly cogent statement, a senior researcher for the Chinese Communist Party described a culture of corruption in the following terms: "Not only is corruption widespread in the economic spheres of finance, securities, real estate, land leasing, and construction, but it also has emerged and is growing in politics, culture, and all aspects of social life— in the party, government, and [nonpolitical] organizations. . . . Cases tend to involve more people, some cases as many as tens or even hundreds of individuals. . . . Improper conduct is repeatedly prohibited, only to reappear in new forms. The spread of corruption to executive departments of the party and government and departments responsible for law enforcement and discipline becomes more serious by the day."[2]

The current situation in Russia provides another contemporary example. In a recent Reuters report, it is stated that more than half of Russian citizens believe that bribing officials is the necessary and best way to "solve problems."[3] "Fifty-five percent of respondents . . . said they believed that 'bribes are given by everyone who comes across officials' in Russia. . . . Russians . . . pay bribes to obtain better medical services, prefer to 'buy' their driving licenses, bribe police when caught violating traffic rules, or pay to ensure that their child can dodge the draft or get a place at the right school. Ten percent confessed they had even paid to arrange funerals for relatives or loved ones. Only 10 percent . . . believe[d] that only 'cheats and criminals' bribed officials."[4] On a higher level, "powerful individuals or groups [in Russia] . . . use material rewards or physical threats to reshape the state."[5] "[I]n contrast to mere bribe-making, to secure access to a good or an exception to existing rules, interested parties exploit the malfeasance of officials to change the rules (laws, judicial rulings, or bureaucratic regulations)" in their favor.[6]

Beliefs about the corruption of others undermine contrary norms and encourage corrupt activities, lest the actors miss the benefits of corruption and be taken as fools. As political scientist Melanie Manion has written, "[W]hat most fundamentally distinguishes countries with rampant corruption from those where corrupt activities are unusual is not the content of rules but their relevance. . . . Moral squeamishness about acting corruptly (and illegally) is likely to be little or great, depending on whether such violations are common or exceptional. If public officials and ordinary citizens obtain their information about social values by observing the pattern of transactions around them, then what is normal (in a descriptive sense) may become acceptable (in a moral sense)."[7] If corruption is the usual medium of exchange in the world that citizens know, they will also know that they are at a serious comparative disadvantage if they fail to engage in it.[8]

Corruption is an alternative normative and moral system that thrives as previously existing social and moral constraints decay. Because of this character, corruption may be particularly problematic in situations involving regime change, democratization efforts, and the establishment of market-based reforms.

CORRUPTION, REGIME CHANGE, AND NEOLIBERAL POLITICAL REFORM

Moving from corruption as a theoretical idea, to corruption as an actual factual matter, is hazardous. As one moves from the idea of corruption that motivates legal, political, and popular analysis, to the *fact* of corruption as experienced (for instance) in particular national contexts, generalization invariably breaks down. The causes of corruption, its particular forms, and its potential control must be appreciated in context. Forms of corruption vary from country to country, and from national subgroup to national subgroup. The same is true of the reasons for its growth, and the reasons for its demise. As World Bank economist Daniel Kaufmann has stated, "[C]ountry-specific understanding [at the least] is imperative."[9] The diversity that characterizes corruption's forms and reasons does not, however, preclude the identification of particular settings or factors that frequently recur. It is with that general goal in mind that we shall proceed.

Links between corruption and political instability and regime change have been drawn by many observers.[10] For instance, particular case studies that support this linkage have involved the countries of Latin America, Eastern Europe, the former Soviet Union, Sierra Leone, Mozambique, Burundi, Uganda, and the former Zaire.[11] The relationship between corruption and regime change is often described in symbiotic terms: corruption provokes regime change, and then the institutions that might otherwise control corruption are rendered ineffective due to the political upheaval.[12] Even though the ultimate governmental outcome—for instance, the adoption of a democratic system—might "engender powerful antibodies against corruption,"[13] through the institution of a free press, an independent judiciary, greater transparency in government, and other reforms, corruption will often intensify in the short or medium term.[14] Typical explanations for corruption's increase during such times include the weakening of political and legal institutions, the removal of authoritarian controls, the suspension of resources for corruption-fighting efforts, and greater opportunities for corruption as the result of bureaucratic structural confusion and lines of authority being up for grabs.[15]

There is, however, another common characteristic of conditions during times of political turbulence that is directly related to the growth of corruptive forces. Corruption—as the idea of capture-by-evil vividly projects—is directly related to the degree of *anti*corruption norm internalization and adherence among citizens. Although it is conceivable that the occurrence of governmental upheaval will—out of the starting gate—strengthen moral standards, it is more likely that it will be accompanied by social upheaval and the destabilization of existing norms. For antisocial self-seeking to be constrained, there must be a contrary normative structure in place, and belief in that normative structure by the populace. In an atmosphere of uncertainty and the rejection of the prior social order, the acceptability of unrestrained, illegal self-seeking that is the core of corrupt conduct may be enhanced for public figures and ordinary citizens alike. In an atmosphere of profound governmental upheaval, with social restructuring and reordering, new norms will be tentative. Individuals will be adrift as new normative pronouncements replace the old, and new ideas replace what were contrary (if often flawed) social and cultural commitments. Without deep cultural and social constraints, there is often little to inhibit the grasping impulse to participate in spoils that "everyone else" seems to be extorting.

The suspected association of a moral vacuum of this type with the growth of corruption has been associated with the modernization of traditional societies,[16] the experience of post-colonial societies,[17] and postsocialist transitions.[18] One of the most striking examples of the intertwined effects of political upheaval, the destabilization of prior norms, and corrupt activities is that of post-Maoist China. Although corruption was certainly prevalent in China prior to that time, the end of the Maoist era was accompanied by " 'a fantastic increase' " in corrupt irregularities, "as well as the emergence and growth of new forms of corruption."[19] One Chinese commentator wrote that attempts to curb corruption by exhorting moral standards during this era were "made difficult by the confusion over changing values."[20] As a result, there were "lower psychic costs for officials choosing to engage in corruption."[21] In contemporary China, this transitional problem persists. It is estimated that in recent years some four thousand officials have fled overseas with some $50 billion in embezzled money.[22]

In contemporary Nigeria, a similar situation is described by commentators. Corruption in Nigeria is often stated to be a "paradox," in that Nigerians simultaneously engage in the corruption that is rife in their country and bitterly complain about it.[23] In part, this ostensibly paradoxical behavior is practical: Nigerians "must navigate—indeed, participate in—corruption if they are to achieve even their most mundane and reasonable aspirations."[24] It is also the product of transition between a traditional moral economy, in which reciprocity, kinship, and personal allegiance dictate forms of sociability and social obligation, and one governed by the ethos of a neoliberal, postcolonial governmental system.[25] In the resulting conflict between traditional and neoliberal moral codes, "Nigerians sense that their state and society have become increasingly amoral—with elites pursuing wealth and power without regard for the consequences, and ordinary people seeking money by all means available."[26]

In sum, the strength and coherence of moral norms is a vital part of corruption's common causes. It is also a vital part of strategies for corruption's control. In addition to structural strategies such as an elimination of bureaucratic discretion and increased transparency in governmental decision making, most successful anticorruption campaigns have included acknowledgment of this moral element. Whether called "public education," the repair of a "breakdown in ethical values," or "positive public integrity initiatives," the objective is the same: the fostering of coherent and internalized normative constraints in both public and private actors.[27]

Consider, for instance, the anticorruption strategies employed in Hong Kong. In the 1960s, corruption in Hong Kong was as common as it is in mainland China today.[28] Today, "Hong Kong offers an example of a successful government-coordinated 'equilibrium switch' from widespread corruption to clean government."[29] The anticorruption effort pursued in Hong Kong utilized three strategies: legal prosecution of the corrupt, institutional changes to reduce opportunities for corruption, and educational campaigns to change underlying norms.[30] Manion describes the third effort as follows:

> From the outset, the governor [of Hong Kong] recognized that the success of the anticorruption effort could not

rely on enforcement and prevention alone. The Independent Commission Against Corruption [ICAC] Ordinance . . . charge[d] the commissioner to 'educate the public against the evils of corruption' and 'enlist and foster public support' in fighting corruption. . . . The commissioner summarized the role of the [corruption-fighting Community Relations Department] . . . as "a vast exercise in public education, or re-education" and acknowledged that the exercise would be a "long-term business." . . . [P]ublic education involve[d] four major, closely related responsibilities: (1) to propagate widely the role of the ICAC and its reliability as an anticorruption agency; (2) to educate the Hong Kong community about the legal concept of corruption; (3) to mobilize ordinary citizens and officials to cooperate in enforcement . . .; and (4) to increase the psychic costs and social disapproval of corrupt activities.[31]

The last was the most ambitious, and involved "moral education, [as] an effort to change private values and their social expression."[32] Moral education included heightened awareness of the evils of corruption, the importance of honesty and self-discipline, and individuals' rights and societal responsibilities.[33] In particular, moral education attempted to inculcate values that raised the psychic costs of participating in corruption, or not reporting it. "[T]he ICAC aim[ed] to have these values expressed socially, as norms whose violation incurs disapproval in the community."[34] At one point, the ICAC head wrote: " 'An important manifestation that the new environment has been accepted will be when we, as a community, and especially community leaders and those in authority, begin to indicate to those who are known to be corrupt, to those who indulge in unethical business behaviour, that they and their kind are unacceptable in decent society, that they are without honour and are not wanted in Hong Kong.' "[35]

CORRUPTION AND THE MOVE TO A MARKET ECONOMY

Political transitions that involve increased corruption are often economic transitions as well. In particular, transitions to a liberal democratic order have often been accompanied by transitions to a market-based economy. The question that arises is whether the move to a market economic system has any independent corrupting effect.

From an observational standpoint, an increase in corruption has been associated with a transition to market capitalism in important instances.[36] This result is counterintuitive, from some perspectives, since market reforms that lower trade barriers, eliminate unnecessary regulations, and reduce the power and discretion of officials should reduce the opportunities for official extortion and corruption.[37]

The reasons that have been advanced for the link between market economics and corruption have focused on the underdevelopment of complementary institutions.[38] In particular, countries that have experienced this phenomenon have offered weak policing and law enforcement controls. As Robert Leiken has observed, where corruption is systemic, market reforms may be counterproductive.[39] "Loosening government controls can facilitate illicit . . . economic activity."[40] Market-driven economic reforms "may expose old ways of doing business . . ., but they may also introduce new opportunities for corruption and bring new players into the game."[41]

Such conventional explanations undoubtedly have varying degrees of empirical truth in different situations. What I would like to explore is less experience-based and, in a sense, more theoretical. It is this: Is there anything *intrinsic* to the market model that encourages a corrupt ethos?

This is a difficult and complex question. There are, however, persuasive arguments that market values—whatever their virtues, in an economic sense—can cut against values that are important in the containment of corruption.

Corruption—as understood in this book—is, at core, the idea of self-involvement, self-indulgence, and the loosening and discarding of the restraints of social bonds.[42] Corruption, in this sense, is notoriously driven by decay in trust in social institutions.[43] Formal rules that are presupposed to generate social welfare goods—including justice and some measure of equal opportunity—lose their legitimacy, as having little or no relevance to the successful pursuit of individual advantage.[44] As Manion has written, "[F]ormal rules reflect the government's proclaimed commitment to a predictable, normatively rationalized, social order. The government supplies these rules as a public good and manages their enforcement. . . . When officials openly and routinely ignore rules about allocation of goods and services requiring their actions, then the system of order that in theory is backed up by government's coercive power loses its meaning. Some alternative system of order [—i.e., corruption—] then exists."[45]

Reflection upon this description of the corruption process reveals two primary assumptions. First, there is the assumption that in a noncorrupt governmental order there are certain societal norms and public goods that must be placed beyond the ethos of individual determination, competition, and grabbing. For instance, "[l]egislative decisions are not supposed to be for sale to the highest bidder . . ., even though democracy coexists with markets for many goods."[46] The second assumption is that it is the blurring of the line between those transcendent societal norms and the sphere of individual self-interest that urges descent into corruption's spiral. For instance, we (as a society) place the equal application of the law, the unimpaired judgment of legislators, the impartiality of judges, and other transcendent societal norms above the exigencies and struggles generated by interpersonal competition and individual grabbing. It is when those transcendent norms are *subverted* to contrary self-interest that the phenomenon of corruption occurs.

Enter, at this point, the ethos of markets. In a liberal democratic system, markets must function in a manner that is restrained by the society's articulated public norms. Public norms and institutions both support the operation of markets and restrain their excesses.[47] On the supportive side, public laws enforce market contracts and provide venues for dispute resolution. On the restraining side, public laws establish standards for fair play and distributional issues of societal wealth and power.[48] A market system must be accompanied by "[c]lear and accepted boundaries and distinctions . . . between state and society; public and private roles and resources; personal and collective interests; and market, bureaucratic, and patrimonial modes of allocation. . . . Without such boundaries major economic interests may dominate politics or powerful politicians [or business interests] can plunder the economy."[49]

The problem posed by a market ethos is that it tends to deny, of its own nature, the existence of countervailing, nonmarket public norms and goods. As Michael Johnston has observed, "[L]iberal political and economic processes are *asymmetrical* in significant ways. Democratic politics rests not only on open competition, but also on normative assumptions about equality and fair play encapsulated by the notion of 'one person, one vote.' Self-interest generally drives the process, but contention among such interests must stay within certain boundaries. . . . Markets, by contrast, incorporate few presumptions of equality, either in process or outcome. . . . Gains are presumed to be private and separable, rather than public and aggregated."[50] If the line between public norms and private norms is blurred, or if market ideas fill a vacuum left by deteriorated or discredited societal institutions, the result can be an unrestrained grabbing and competition for spoils. "If politics has become a mere extension of markets—or if a substantial proportion of people *believe* that it has—the system risks losing the trust of citizens and its ability to . . . make legitimate, genuinely *public* policies. The core problem is not lawbreaking as such, but rather the widespread perception that the whole system, and with it the opportunities and guarantees supposedly provided to citizens," has become a question of supply and demand, dictated only by wealth and power.[51]

In contemporary China, for instance, the rise of market capitalism has created a "crisis of values."[52] Rejection of Maoist economic policy has transformed the normative environment.[53] Manion writes that "[r]eform replaced the Maoist rhetoric of economic equality with a 'trickle-down' economic strategy that unabashedly encouraged some to get rich first (and others later). In the post–Cultural Revolution context, the 'transformation of economic ethics [was] nothing short of astonishing. . . .' [There was] a 'general blurring of boundaries between legitimate and illegitimate economic and social behavior and to an increasing sense of normlessness.'" "In the new normative climate, officials who chose to engage in corruption had less cause for moral qualms about it."[54]

Today, in China, "[o]fficial corruption . . . has contributed to the deepening moral vacuum and cynicism felt by many ordinary Chinese when making money is paramount. Petty corruption is commonplace. Peddlers sell false expense-account receipts outside train stations. Doctors demand 'red envelope' payments from patients. Graduate students bribe scholarly journals to publish their work."[55] In the absence of widespread moral or ethical buy-in, the enactment of laws to establish anticorruption norms will be of limited influence.

Similar phenomena have been observed during market transitions in other countries, including those in Africa, the former Soviet Union, and Eastern Europe.[56] In Mozambique, for instance, corruption spread rapidly with the abrupt shift from socialism to a capitalist system in 1987. David Stasavage has observed that "corruption today [in Mozambique] has become morally acceptable in a way that it was not ten years ago."[57] Possible reasons include the installation of "a particularly unbridled form of capitalism" that has legitimated an ethos of unrestrained self-seeking to get ahead.[58] In former Soviet bloc countries, the public sphere was something that was neither cultivated nor respected by the citizenry during socialist years.[59] With a transition to a market economy, identification of the citizenry with public values is, if anything, even more uncertain.[60] To compound the problem, the impersonal norms of a market system do not present a compelling, competing ideology to self-seeking; if anything, they appear (from the popular point of view) to ideologically reify it.[61]

Roger Williams, in a seminal article, observed that "corruption essentially privatizes moral life." In a corrupt society, "[s]ocial relations are dominated by self-interest. . . . [C]ivic virtue and social responsibility are displaced and discarded in favour of an intense competition for spoils."[62] The introduction of a market system is not necessarily destructive of the idea of a public weal or public interest; indeed, in most countries, the two operate in an integrated manner, governing intertwined areas of human life. The problem occurs in those settings where the identification of citizens with the public weal is weak. In such cases, corruption—or unbridled self-seeking, in defiance of common interests—can be fueled by the self-interested core of the market norm.

CORRUPTION, MORALITY, AND POLITICS: A REPLY TO SKEPTICS

The idea that corruption's moral aspect should be an important part of corruption analyses and national control strategies has been heavily criticized in some quarters.[63] Most cogently, it has been argued that moralizing about corruption—even if it reflects some truth—is a practical, indeed counterproductive, waste of time.[64]

Consider, for instance, the critique of U.S. anticorruption efforts by Frank Anechiarico and James Jacobs.[65] Anechiarico and Jacobs begin by acknowledging that corruption is a serious problem and that its control is a challenge for all governments.[66] Where they part company with mainstream positions is in the "unreflective acceptance [by mainstream theorists] of the reigning anticorruption project and its prescription for more of the same."[67]

The general thesis of the authors is that "the anticorruption machinery" implemented in the United States during the 1980s and 1990s "has had profound, complicating, and often negative implications for the organization and operation of public administration."[68] For instance, complicated reporting and "transparency" requirements have bogged down administrative actions; conflict-of-interest rules have been woodenly implemented, regardless of whether prohibited parties are in fact the most qualified for public office or contracts; whistle-blowers have been protected in their employment status, regardless of their competence as employees; and other efficiency concerns.[69]

Anechiarico and Jacobs are particularly sharp in their criticism of what they call "moral entrepreneurs."[70] Moral entrepreneurs are obsessed with scandal and push unrealistic moral standards that serve only to increase mistrust in government and fuel a relentless anticorruption project.[71] "Demands for higher levels of job-related and personal morality in public officials inevitably lead to disappointment, public accusation, scandal, hand-wringing, righteous indignation, and reform."[72] This effect is intensified by the fact that "[c]orruption sells. Exposing hypocrisy and wrongdoing among those sworn to create, administer, or enforce the law makes for compelling reading or viewing. The higher the rank of the corrupt official, the greater the human drama and spectacle."[73] The costs are direct: "Moral entrepreneurs are likely to be so concerned with stopping corruption, or at least with appearing that way to the media and the public, that they give slight, if any, thought to the costs of implementing their vision. In the aftermath of serious scandal, concerns about guaranteeing integrity and about the appearance of integrity trump efficiency. Rarely is the integrity/efficiency trade-off even considered."[74]

There is no doubt that there is a public fascination with corruption and the fall of the powerful—indeed, with all evil, of whatever kind. The idea of corruption as evil always carries dangers of hysteria and prosecutorial excess, as was discussed above.[75] It is also a theoretical certainty that *too much* rigidity or *too much* bureaucratic accountability might deleteriously affect the efficiency of government. Moral invocations against corruption—like those against any undesirable behavior—can result in rules and prosecutions that are excessively rigid, or abusive.

The critique by Anechiarico and Jacobs, however, seems to go beyond the idea that morally based strategies should be implemented with more temperance. The authors appear to argue, in addition, that there is something about morality qua morality that makes morally based understandings of corruption and corruption-control strategies inherently suspect. For instance, in support of their critique, they cite the fact that more than one thousand public officials in the United States were indicted or convicted for corruption offenses between 1970 and 1977, and during the eight-year Reagan administration, more than one hundred federal officials met the same fate.[76] The meaning of these statistics, however, is not self-evident. Anechiarico and Jacobs seem to assume that these numbers—on their face—must be excessive. But there is little evidence given of this, other than the fact that in these prosecutions, a moral impetus (presumably) was involved.[77]

Assuming that "moralism" has run amok in the United States is particularly tenuous in view of the admitted difficulties in measuring the level of corrupt activity, in the United States or elsewhere, or the effects—if any—of particular anticorruption strategies. There is a general consensus that some societies are more plagued by corruption than others, and that currently, at least, the United States is perceived as less corrupt than many other countries.[78] This observation, however, hardly proves the excessive nature of the moral imperative in this country. First, as Anechiarico and Jacobs acknowledge, there is no widely accepted way to measure levels of corrupt activities in the past or in the present.[79] The problem of public corruption in the United States might be more, or less, than public perceptions indicate. In addition, there is—as Anechiarico and Jacobs agree—no way "[t]o determine whether the anticorruption project as a whole, much less any particular anticorruption initiative, has reduced corruption."[80] They use this point to argue that it cannot (therefore) be assumed that expanding the anticorruption project will be successful in corruption suppression.[81] However, the converse is also true. If we do not know the impact of past efforts, we cannot assume that cutting back on those strategies will have no deleterious effects.

In short, lack of knowledge about corruption's existence or deterrence hardly leads inexorably to the conclusion that there is currently an excess of moral zeal in combating corruption in the United States, or elsewhere. The fact that "[c]orruption seems to persist and even flourish [in the United States] despite threats, scores of arrests, administrative sanctions, prosecutions, organizational reshuffling, stings, undercover operations, intensive monitoring, and operational initiatives to strengthen central [governmental] authority"[82] does not necessarily mean that current anticorruption strategies should be curbed; it can just as easily signal that those strategies should be intensified.

On an international level, studies of societies that have deteriorated into a culture of corruption, and those that have recovered from rampant corruption, acknowledge the importance of the moral imperative in civic attitudes and public affairs.[83] Robert Rotberg, who has long studied corrupt societies, has recently written of the importance of moral values and the political leadership to enforce them:

[O]fficials and politicians steal from the state and cheat their fellow citizens because of a prevailing permissive ethos. . . . Once it becomes known that certain kinds or all kinds of corrupt behavior are acceptable, then all self-interested maximizers (nearly all of us) will hardly want to miss good opportunities to secure and then to employ official positions for private gain. Whatever one's views of human nature and human fallibility, if the prevailing political culture tolerates corruption, nearly everyone will seek opportunities to be corrupt.

. . . .

Corruption begets more corruption. . . . Breaches of norms, sliding norms, or the development of new norms are easily communicated throughout a political system. . . . Civil societies may rail at corrupt practices, journalists may investigate and uncover scandals, and prosecutors may bring egregious offenders before courts, but the acceptability and the prevalence of corrupt practices depends more on leadership actions than on formal mechanisms of accountability. . . . [S]uch mechanisms are insufficient, absent strong leadership, to stanch the natural human tendency to put self interest over national interest and emulation over conscience.

. . . .

[I]t is only from the establishment of political cultures that enshrine values antithetical to corruption that effective institutions of accountability and oversight emerge.[84]

In corrupt societies, C. Raj Kumar has written, corruption becomes "a way of life" in the public and private lives of citizens. Public corruption not only affects the quality of government; it has the power to "shape the character, values, and actions of individuals in their private [lives]."[85]

Ultimately, the question is individual. As Hartmut Schweitzer has observed, even under conditions most favorable to corruption, not all people act corruptly.[86] It is individual to leaders, and individual to lesser officials and common citizens. Shall the prevailing ethos be one of corruption, or not?

In one of the best recent examinations of individual moral decision making in collective contexts, Herbert Kelman and Lee Hamilton discussed the phenomenon of human obedience to orders by superiors that were known at the time to be illegal or immoral.[87] Among the subjects discussed was the way to enhance the independent judgment of individuals in the face of such orders. The key, Kelman and Hamilton wrote, is to sensitize people to the "opposing forces" of contrary personal values and moral standards.[88] Such personal values, supported collectively, give an individual the sense of obligation, the standing, and the courage to deviate from ordered acts.[89] Thus, they wrote, in the prescriptions that follow, "we focus on the development and buttressing of social norms, societal practices, and situational cues that would increase sensitivity to opposing forces linked to moral values. Changes in social structures, educational experiences, and group supports need to be designed to counteract" the tendency of individuals to suspend independent judgment and unthinkingly follow the orders of authorities.[90]

An individual decision to engage in corrupt conduct is different in many ways from an individual decision to follow the command of illegal or immoral authority. Corrupt activity is rarely commanded by organizational leaders, although it is possible to imagine such a case. There is, however, a fundamental commonality in both cases. An individual must choose, in both cases, to engage in conduct known by that individual—on some level—to be forbidden by some external moral standard. And in both cases, the psychological environment in which that step is taken is societally as well as individually constructed.

Prosecutions, bureaucratic controls, transparency requirements, and other anticorruption efforts are merely the reflection of an underlying social ethos. Whether called "morality" or another name, that underlying ethos—encouraged by collectivities and reflected in the attitudes and decisions of each individual—will be determinative of the societal outcome. Its importance cannot be overestimated. It not only matters; it is the name of the game.

CORRUPTION AND MORAL CHOICE

As Michael Johnston has written, "[C]orruption is not something that 'happens to' a society."[91] There are reasons for a society's descent into corruption, and those reasons generate strategies for reform. The erosion of a moral ethos—of individual restraint and societal identification—is not the only factor involved, but it is a fundamental one.

Institutional reforms are important. It is important that opportunities and incentives for corrupt behavior be reduced, and that individual incapacitation and general deterrence be pursued through criminal prosecution of wrongdoers. The fact remains, however, that institutional reforms cannot prevent the corrupt behavior of thousands of individuals—public officials and private citizens—if they are dedicated to grabbing whatever they can in every public and private transaction. There is no way to reduce all opportunities or to prosecute all lawbreakers—particularly when those who enforce the rules are also, presumably, corrupt. The corrupt ethos that pervades such a society must, itself, be attacked. There must be an alternative moral and ethical system which is aggressively advocated, and which is eventually regarded by officials and citizens as in their best individual and collective self-interest. A different normative system must be internalized by individuals and institutionalized as policy. This is true whether we are speaking of individual, national, or international action.[92]

8 CODA

Corruption and the Rule of Law

The idea of the rule of law is of unquestioned importance in the liberal democratic political tradition. Indeed, it is—in some form—essential to human interaction. The idea of the rule of law is the centuries-old solution for mediating interhuman conflict over applicable moral principles and for controlling the despotism of rulers.[1] The law, as conceptualized by this idea, is an articulated set of rules, objectively enforced. The importance of the rule of law in Western jurisprudence has been expressed in ringing terms: "[L]aw becomes necessary to make life in society tolerable. . . . Given the [contentious] nature of man, law is the highest form of social organization . . . which we can in fact achieve."[2]

Corruption as capture-by-evil poses a difficult problem for rule-of-law ideals. The idea of corruption as capture-by-evil is a largely "degenerate" or "incommensurable" concept when used as a part of law. By inflaming decision makers with religiously infused ideas of evil, perversion, defilement, and sin, the idea of corruption as capture-by-evil implicitly challenges the very notion that objective, neutral, rule-based concepts can capture the essence of corruption. For instance, the assertion that a judge is "captured by evil," and has "defiled" justice and her court, is not compatible with the idea that legal decisions are forged from publicly accessible norms and articulated through dispassionate and objective standards.[3] Corruption as capture-by-evil appears to stake the following claim: neutral, rational, general, and impartial rules might be adequate in most contexts but are not adequate in this. Corruption is an evil with many tentacles, and it cannot be captured or controlled by conventional ideas of law.

One might argue that the ostensible conflict between corruption as capture-by-evil and the idea of the rule of law is overstated; that law is often not the objective, articulated, rule-based creature that this comparison suggests. For instance, there are situations in which the law has previously not spoken, or in which no current societal consensus exists. For example, conventional legal principles often fail when confronted by technological advances, and some notoriously contentious legal issues—such as abortion, capital punishment, and physician-assisted suicide—are ones on which no broadly based societal consensus exists.

Even in these cases, however, there is an awareness of the purposes of the rule of law, and an explicit attempt to hew as close as possible to the rule-of-law ideal. When dealing with questions about patenting life-forms, or new surveillance techniques, or the content of notions of cruel and unusual punishment or medical privacy, legislatures and courts do not issue instructions or decisions that invoke raw notions of good and evil, salvation and damnation. Even when the idea of the rule of law necessarily fails, the contemporary Western ideology of law nonetheless strives to operate within a universe of knowable and articulable standards, logical and demystified, with neutral content and operation. The idea of the rule of law may necessarily fail in marginal situations, but the commitment to replicate its processes remains. The idea of corruption as capture-by-evil is different. Its processes and assumptions invoke very different sources and emotions.

When evaluated against the rule of law, then, corruption as capture-by-evil seems to enjoy a profoundly negative assessment. In addition to dangers of emotionally laden decision making, explored in a prior chapter,[4] this idea of corruption invites standardless decision making and unarticulated—indeed, unknowable—reasons for decisions.

There is, however, an interesting twist that often accompanies degenerate or incommensurable concepts. Such concepts may simply (and unacceptably) contradict a dominant and justified theory, and that is the end of it. *Or* they may successfully challenge that theory, in a way that illuminates its flaws.

Does corruption as capture-by-evil have the latter function, in any way, when considering its challenge to the rule of law?

In fact it does, in two ways. First, the idea of corruption as capture-by-evil reminds us, forcefully, of the shallow nature of written laws and written codes. The rule of law, which written laws exemplify, is obviously of critical importance; however, it cannot *of itself* justify the laws of which it is composed. Oppressive majorities and mobs can create laws; tyrants and despots can enforce laws; corrupt governments can transform laws, until they accomplish the ends that corruption requires. By explicitly and jarringly retaining its core moral reference, corruption as capture-by-evil reminds us of these realities. It reminds us that as much as the rule of law is justifiably venerated, it is only as good as the moral code on which it is based. There must be an assumed moral reference, a moral grounding, for the *authority* of law to be complete.

Corruption as capture-by-evil also points out the limits of the idea of the rule of law in another way. It points out that the power of law, however crafted and justified, is limited, and that more is needed to enforce critically important norms.

In the United States, we tend to have an exaggerated sense of the power of law. There is, as one commentator put it, a "peculiarly American view that the world can be reimagined and reinvented through the rule of law."[5] We tend to believe that if the right rules are crafted, and strenuously enforced, deviance from ideal norms will cease. It is the belief that the problem of lawbreaking is one of societal design, not individual volition.

The idea of corruption as capture-by-evil, with its squarely moral focus, contradicts this model. It invokes the intuition that law alone is inadequate to control corruption, whether in this country or others. Law enforcement, administrative reform, and other external, structural changes may be crucial, but they are not enough. Corruption—and, by implication, all societal deviance— is an individual moral question. It involves individual convictions and individual decisions regarding good and evil, right and wrong, societal cohesion and the chaos of unmitigated individual self-seeking.

The idea of corruption as capture-by-evil reminds us that decisions by individual citizens to adhere to societal norms is not only a question of the existence of the rule of law; it is also a question of individual choice. It is a question of whether an individual will respect the restraints of social bonds or breach them. It is—to use the language of corruption, and to paraphrase a popular song—whether the individual will serve "the Devil or . . . the Lord."[6]

CONCLUSION

It is fair to say, after our examination, that corruption is a troubled concept in law. The traditional understandings of corruption, used in law—corruption as the breach of duty, corruption as the quid pro quo transaction, corruption as illegality or inequality, and so on—capture parts of this idea, but not all. Animating these technical and rational understandings in spirit and practice is another, quite incommensurable concept. Corruption, under this deeper (and popular) understanding, is a raw moral idea. It invokes ideas of "depravity" and "evil," human frailty and temptation. It is the capture of individuals and political systems by corrosive, distorting, and decomposing forces. It is the loosening and discarding of the restraint of social bonds. It is the capture by evil of one's soul.

This idea of corruption—although ubiquitous in popular *and* legal accounts—has remained unexamined because, perhaps, we would not like what we would find. This idea, with its medieval and religious undertones, does not fit with our system of legal thought. Law is supposed to be knowable and rationally articulable, with disciplined, neutral content and careful operation. Corruption as capture-by-evil is none of these things. It is intuitive, emotionally driven, and prone to distortion and excess. It is inarticulable in traditional legal terms. It contradicts the idea of careful, uniform standards and judgment.

The costs of corruption as capture-by-evil for the operation and administration of law are severe. It sees "the corrupt" in terms of persons, not acts. As a result, it fears and punishes character. This affects both the substance of accusations and their proof. It invites—indeed, expects—broad association with crimes of general "immorality" and vice. It defies exculpatory accounts or usual claims to rehabilitation. It anticipates emotion-laden prosecutions and rests uncomfortably with the foundational idea of variable criminal culpability. It invites standardlessness and collateral punishment for character and acts that are not a part of the crime charged. It is so extreme in its characterization of the accused that it in fact *undermines* the conviction of lawbreakers who do not fit the "evil" image that this idea demands.

Faced with such realities, the conclusion might well be drawn that corruption as capture-by-evil is an illegitimate concept and should be banished from law. Apart from the serious question of whether this could be done (even if we wished to do so), there are strong arguments for this idea's critical functions. Corruption as capture-by-evil asserts, in a powerful and undeniable way, the costs of corruption for societies and governments. It affirms the need for a moral response to what is, at core, a moral problem. It recognizes, and captures as a part of law, the systemic harm that corrupt acts accomplish. It forces us to face the fact that there is more to corruption than traditional breach-of-duty or quid pro quo formulations acknowledge.

Where do we come out, then, in the end? One conclusion might be that capture-by-evil is an essential idea in politics and culture—where its strengths are manifest, and its dangers less damaging—but that it should not be used in law. To some extent, this might be accomplished. Corruption as capture-by-evil could be forbidden in the context of individual prosecutions. Prosecutors could be unable to invoke it, and judges could certainly be prohibited from citing it in their statutory interpretations, sentencing decisions, and other contexts. One could argue, quite persuasively, that in the context of individual criminal adjudications, the dangers of individual unfairness outweigh the idea's prophylactic and norm-enforcing functions. We do not need to invoke the idea of evil when considering an individual defendant's fate in the judicial dock.

The success of such efforts would, of course, be mixed. Attitudes by jurors, prosecutors, and judges are brought into the courtroom. The emotions generated in popular culture and politics obviously affect law. The idea of the corrupt as evil, and corruption as capture-by-evil, will bleed into the courtroom if it is a powerful force outside. However, the fact that this idea—like all extralegal ideas—will retain influence in legal prosecutions does not mean that we should therefore throw up our hands and invite it in with vigor. To the extent that the idea of capture-by-evil can be excluded from the context of individual criminal prosecutions, the better argument is that it should be.

This does not address, however, the other contexts—both legal and nonlegal—in which the idea of corruption as capture-by-evil is essential, and unparalleled, in its expression of the real harm that corrupt individual acts and actors pose. When there is a corrupt judge, the damage of his acts goes beyond the demonstrable effects on individual defendants to the foundation of the legal system and its courts. Remedies for the presence of corrupt judicial actors must acknowledge that reality. Transactional approaches are not adequate in this context. Similarly, when the question is the adoption of prophylactic measures regarding corrupt transactions in politics, the idea of systemic harm that corruption as capture-by-evil exemplifies must be given the recognition that it, in fact, presents. In such cases, the idea of corruption as some kind of "contained transaction" is inadequate. What is at stake is the perversion, and the perceived perversion, of the apparatus of government. As corruption as capture-by-evil so well states, the stakes in such cases are not simply the punishment of bad actors; they are the rectifying, through *systemic* actions, of the implicit challenge that has been posed to the system of government and its foundational norms.

Finally, corruption as capture-by-evil has a more subtle, but important, role. This idea, by stressing individual capture by evil forces, reminds us of the reality of human frailty, and the role of moral accountability in social relations and law. Law is, in the end, nothing more than the implementation by force of the societal consensus that underlies it. If individual decision makers—tomorrow—reject that consensus, the mystique and power of the law collapses. For this, temptations abound. The voice to act corruptly, in just this instance, persistently whispers. In the end, whether governments fail or courts act justly is left to the individual decisions of each of us.

NOTES

INTRODUCTION

1. *See* J. Peter Euben, *Corruption*, in *Political Innovation and Conceptual Change* 220, 243 (Terence Ball, James Farr, & Russell L. Hanson eds., 1989).

2. *See* Laura S. Underkuffler, *Agentic and Conscientic Decisions in Law: Death and Other Cases*, 74 Notre Dame L. Rev. 1713, 1734 (1999).

CHAPTER 1. EXPLORING CORRUPTION

1. James C. Scott, *Comparative Political Corruption* 3 (1972).

2. Judicial opinions often state this view. *See, e.g., United States v. Poindexter*, 951 F.2d 369, 391 (D.C. Cir. 1991), *cert. denied*, 506 U.S. 1021 (1992) (Mikva, C.J., dissenting in part) ("corruptly" defined as acting in a manner "inconsistent with a legal duty") (internal quotation marks deleted).

3. *See* Robert Klitgaard, *Controlling Corruption* 3–4 (1988) (discussing illegal acts commonly believed to constitute corrupt behavior).

4. *See* John Gardiner, *Defining Corruption*, in *Coping with Corruption in a Borderless World: Proceedings of the Fifth International Anti-Corruption Conference* 21, 26 (Maurice Punch, Emile Kolthoff, Kees van der Vijver, & Bram van Vliet eds., 1993). *See also* Michael Johnston, *Political Corruption and Public Policy in America* 8 (1982) ("Corruption is abuse of a public role for private benefit in such a way as to break the law (or other formal administrative regulations . . .). ") (emphasis deleted).

5. *See, e.g.,* Scott, *supra* note 1, at 4 ("relying heavily on legal norms in defining corruption, while it too has shortcomings, seems the most satisfactory alternative").

6. *See* Susan Rose-Ackerman, *Corruption and Government: Causes, Consequences, and Reform* 9 (1999) ("Payments are corrupt if they are illegally made to public agents with the goal of obtaining a benefit or avoiding a cost.").

7. Gardiner, *supra* note 4, at 26.

8. Scott, *supra* note 1, at 5.

9. Associated Press, *China Plans Crackdown on Media: The Government Says It Wants to Stop Fake Reporters Soliciting Bribes*, Portland Press Herald, Aug. 16, 2007, at A8.

10. *See* Scott, *supra* note 1, at 4.

11. *See id.* at 96 (footnote omitted). *See also* Jennifer L. McCoy & Heather Heckel, *The Emergence of a Global Anti-Corruption Norm*, in *Global Society in Transition: An International Politics Reader* 217, 220 (Daniel N. Nelson & Laura Neack eds., 2002) (corruption is a broad term for a variety of issues, including bribery, ethics violations, illegal asset accumulation, violations of procurement regulations, political nepotism, cronyism, campaign finance violations, money laundering, and others).

12. *See* Scott, *supra* note 1, at 112 (as the political machine matures, the inducements it offers are "more typically embodied in general legislation, whereas previously they had been particularistic and often outside the law").

13. Scott recognizes the potential divergence between what "legality" provides and what "corruption" means; his solution is an injunction that we must, among other strategies, "avoid the *a priori* moral judgments that the term 'corruption' popularly connotes." *Id.* at 6. This is, however, more easily said than done—as his subsequent divergence from this principle, in his discussion of machine politics, illustrates.

14. *See* Mark Philp, *Conceptualizing Political Corruption*, in *Political Corruption: Concepts & Contexts* 41, 46 (Arnold J. Heidenheimer & Michael Johnston eds., 2002). The possible disjunction between the law and deeper moral notions in this context is discussed by John Gardiner. He writes: "In Nazi Germany during World War II, Jews were forbidden by law to emigrate. If a passport inspector took 1,000 DM from a Jewish family and approved its departure, could his act be called 'corruption'?" Gardiner, *supra* note 4, at 27.

15. Indeed, this is tacitly recognized by writers who attempt to enhance the notion of simple illegality with other glosses. For instance, when describing why money laundering is an act of corruption, one commentator reminds us that "the *sine qua non* to [*sic*] money laundering is to 'clean' the 'dirty' money by making it appear to have the smell of lawful proceeds of commerce rather than the stench of criminality." Wilmer Parker III, *Every Person Has a Price?*, in *Corruption: The Enemy Within* 87, 89 (Barry Rider ed., 1997).

16. John G. Peters & Susan Welch, *Political Corruption in America: A Search for Definitions and a Theory*, 72 Am. Pol. Sci. Rev. 974, 974–975 (1978) (footnote omitted).

17. *See* David H. Bayley, *The Effects of Corruption in a Developing Nation*, in *Political Corruption: Readings in Comparative Analysis* 521, 522 (Arnold J. Heidenheimer ed., 1978).

18. *See* Arnold J. Heidenheimer, *The Context of Analysis*, in *Political Corruption: Readings in Comparative Analysis, supra* note 17, at 3, 4.

19. *See* Samuel P. Huntington, *Political Order in Changing Societies* 59 (1968). *See also* Carl J. Friedrich, *The Pathology of Politics: Violence, Betrayal, Corruption, Secrecy, and Propaganda* 127 (1972) ("Corruption is a kind of behavior which deviates from the norm actually prevalent or believed to be prevalent in a given context, such as the political.").

20. *See* J. S. Nye, *Corruption and Political Development: A Cost-Benefit Analysis*, in 61 Am. Pol. Sci. Rev. 417, 419 (1967); Morris Szeftel, *Corruption and the Spoils System in Zambia*, in *Corruption: Causes, Consequences and Control* 163, 165 (Michael Clarke ed., 1983) ("corruption is behaviour which deviates from the norms, rules, and duties governing the exercise of a public role or office for purposes of private gain").

21. *See* Ibrahim F. I. Shihata, *Corruption—A General Review with an Emphasis on the Role of the World Bank*, in *Corruption: The Enemy Within, supra* note 15, at 255, 258.

22. *See* Arnold A. Rogow & H. D. Lasswell, *The Definition of Corruption*, in *Political Corruption: Readings in Comparative Analysis, supra* note 17, at 54, 54.

23. M. McMullen, *A Theory of Corruption*, 9 Soc. Rev. 181, 183–184 (1961). *See also* Simon Rottenberg, *Corruption as a Feature of Governmental Organization: Comment*, 18 J. L. & Econ. 611, 611–612 (1975) (corruption is "the collection of a private charge for doing something that a nominal, relevant rule requires to be done without the payment of that charge").

24. Robert C. Brooks, *The Nature of Political Corruption*, in *Political Corruption: Readings in Comparative Analysis, supra* note 17, at 56, 59.

25. *See, e.g.,* Rose-Ackerman, *supra* note 6, at 14, 9 (corruption involves self-seeking, "personal enrichment and the provision of benefits to the corrupt"); Gunnar Myrdal, *Corruption as a Hindrance to Modernization in South Asia*, in *Political Corruption: Readings in Comparative Analysis, supra* note 17, at 229, 232 (corruption involves "private gain by dishonest dealings"); George C. S. Benson, Steven A. Maaranen, & Alan Heslop, *Political Corruption in America* xiii (1978) ("*Political corruption* is a general term covering all illegal or unethical use of governmental authority as a result of considerations of personal or political gain."); Bayley, *supra* note 17, at 522 ("corruption includes improper and selfish exercise of power and influence attached to a public office or to the special position one occupies in public life") (internal quotation marks omitted).

26. Bayley, *supra* note 17, at 522.

27. Nye, *supra* note 20, at 419 (footnote omitted).

28. As Matthew Bunn suggests, this approach can be extended to include activities by private citizens that constitute a breach of the public trust. *See* Matthew Bunn, *Corruption and Nuclear Proliferation*, in *Corruption, Global Security, and World Order* 124 (Robert I. Rotberg ed., 2009).

29. *See* Michael Johnston, *Right and Wrong in American Politics: Popular Conceptions of Corruption*, in *Political Corruption: Concepts & Contexts, supra* note 14, at 173, 178–190 (discussing survey results for many of these and other potentially "corrupt" acts).

30. Consider, for example, the difficulties we encounter in the articulation of workable and consistent understandings of duties in the campaign finance area. Requiring an explicit quid pro quo transaction—of money for influence—will fail to capture the most sophisticated (and perhaps most corrupt) transactions, since in such cases, no mention of the "payoff" for the "influence" received will be made at all. Mention of a "problem" simply will be made, and influence—in response to the benefit received—will be exercised. Indeed, in highly sophisticated transactions, "[corrupt] exchange resembles social exchange." Heidenheimer, *supra* note 18, at 18.

In addition, when the contributing parties are constituents, there are difficult questions surrounding when exchange of attention and favors is a corrupt exchange, and when it is simply the ordinary grist of politics. *See* Walter Lippmann, *A Theory about Corruption*, in *Political Corruption: Readings in Comparative Analysis, supra* note 17, at 294, 295 ("[T]he exchange of favors is the elemental and essential motive power which operates the semi-private machinery inside the political parties which in their turn operate the official machinery of government."). Often, whether we view attempts to influence legislators as corrupt or noncorrupt will depend upon deeper notions of governance, such as whether we see legislators as simple implementers of constituents' desires or as trustees bound to exercise independent judgment for the benefit of a broader public good. *See, e.g.*, Theodor Eschenburg, *German Attempts at the Legal Definition of Parliamentary Corruption*, in *Political Corruption: Readings in Comparative Analysis, supra*, at 404, 407, and Daniel H. Lowenstein, *Political Bribery and the Intermediate Theory of Politics*, 32 U.C.L.A. L. Rev. 784, 831–843 (1985) (discussing political theories— such as "mandate," "trusteeship," and "pluralist"—in the context of bribery and candidates for legislative office).

31. *See, e.g.*, Nye, *supra* note 20, at 417–419; Colin Leys, *What Is the Problem about Corruption?*, 3 J. Mod. Afr. Stud. 215, 215–217 (1965).

32. Friedrich, *supra* note 19, at 130.

33. Nathaniel H. Leff, *Economic Development through Bureaucratic Corruption*, in *Political Corruption: Readings in Comparative Analysis, supra* note 17, at 510, 510.

34. As one commentator has framed it, under the breach-of-duty model the corrupted man and the man opposing him may be simply "'men of two worlds,' partly adhering to two standards which are incompatible." Leys, *supra* note 31, at 221.

35. *See, e.g.*, José Veloso Abueva, *The Contribution of Nepotism, Spoils, and Graft to Political Development*, in *Political Corruption: Readings in Comparative Analysis, supra* note 17, at 534, 534 (official nepotism, spoils, and graft contribute to political unification and stability, popular participation in public affairs, and higher levels of political and administrative achievement); Huntington, *supra* note 19, at 64 (corruption provides "immediate, specific, and concrete benefits to out-of-power groups").

It should be noted that claims of the beneficial effects of (breach-of-duty) corruption have been hotly contested, as an empirical matter, and largely discredited. *See, e.g.*, Rose-Ackerman, *supra* note 6, at 9–26 (claimed economic benefits of corruption fail to adequately consider the inefficiency of illegal markets and the costs involved in their undermining of the general legitimacy of government); Pranab Bardhan, *Corruption and Development: A Review of Issues*, 35 J. Econ. Lit. 1320, 1327–1330 (1997) (alleged benefits of corruption are overwhelmed by its adverse effects on investment and growth); Paolo Mauro, *The Effects of Corruption on Growth and Public Expenditure*, in *Political Corruption: Concepts & Contexts, supra* note 14, at 339 (recent empirical evidence indicates that corruption has other, harmful economic consequences); Shihata, *supra* note 21, at 256–260 (same).

36. *See, e.g.*, Klitgaard, *supra* note 3, at 24 ("corruption occurs when an agent *betrays* the principal's interests in pursuit of her own") (emphasis added); Leslie Palmier, *Bureaucratic Corruption and Its Remedies*, in *Corruption: Causes, Consequences and Control, supra* note 20, at 207, 208 ("In brief, . . . corruption may be defined as the acquisition of forbidden benefits by officials or employees, so bringing into question their loyalty to their employers." "It is the weakening of loyalty that is at the heart of the offence.").

37. *See* H. A. Brasz, *The Sociology of Corruption*, in *Political Corruption: Readings in Comparative Analysis, supra* note 17, at 41, 41; Vladimer Orlando Key Jr., *The Techniques of Political Graft in the United States* 389 (1936).

38. *See* Jacob van Klaveren, *The Concept of Corruption*, in *Political Corruption: Readings in Comparative Analysis, supra* note 17, at 38, 38 ("corruption means that a civil servant abuses his authority" for private gain); Peter Csonka, *Corruption: The Council of Europe's Approach*, in *Corruption: The Enemy Within, supra* note 15, at 343, 350 (corruption is "about the abuse of power, or more accurately, improbity in the decision-making process").

39. *See* James Lindgren, *The Theory, History, and Practice of the Bribery-Extortion Distinction*, 141 U. Pa. L. Rev. 1695, 1704–1708 (1993); Jacob van Klaveren, *Corruption as a Historical Phenomenon*, in *Political Corruption: Readings in Comparative Analysis, supra* note 17, at 67, 69; Philp, *supra* note 14, at 41, 42.

40. *See, e.g.*, Klitgaard, *supra* note 3, at 19 (corruption involves an agent who "betray[s] her role as a public servant for her own private interests"); Philp, *supra* note 14, at 42 (in public corruption, the official "violat[es] . . . the trust placed in him by the public"); Shihata, *supra* note 21, at 260 ("In all cases [of corruption], a position of trust is . . . exploited to realize private gains. . . .").

41. *See, e.g.*, Syed Hussein Alatas, *Corruption: Its Nature, Causes and Functions* 2 (1990) ("[T]he essence of corruption . . . can be described as stealing through deception in a situation which betrays a trust."). *See also* Niklas Luhmann, *Trust and Power* 4–17 (1979), and Carol M. Rose, *Trust in the Mirror of Betrayal*, 75 B.U. L. Rev. 531, 557–558 (1995) (discussing the general importance of trust in personal and institutional relations).

42. *See* Friedrich, *supra* note 19, at 86, 109–112 (no positive changes could occur in a political system "if some men were not willing to betray the old order to the emergent one").

43. Brasz, *supra* note 37, at 42 (emphasis added). *See also* David Brooks, *The Culture of Exposure*, N.Y. Times, June 24, 2010 (Journalists believed that "there [was] . . . a secret corruption deep down" in government. "It became the task of journalism to expose the underbelly of public life, to hunt for impurity, assuming that the dark hidden lives of public officials were more important than the official performances [themselves].").

44. Brasz, *supra* note 37, at 42, 43 (footnote omitted) (emphasis added). *See also* Alatas, *supra* note 41, at 2 (the essence of corruption is "stealing through deception in a situation which betrays a trust"); John Warburton, *Corruption as a Social Process: From Dyads to Networks*, in *Corruption and Anti-Corruption* 221, 224–225 (Peter Larmour & Nick Wolanin eds., 2001) (describing the secrecy of corrupt transactions).

45. Key, *supra* note 37, at 387 n.1.

46. *See* Lowenstein, *supra* note 30, at 829–830.

47. *Id.* at 830. *Cf.* Alatas, *supra* note 41, at 2 (corruption involves "secrecy of execution except in situations which allow powerful individuals or those under their protection to dispense with it"). Our reluctance to characterize open, conditional campaign contributions as bribes probably has more to do with our uncertainty as to whether this transaction—at its core—is criminal or corrupt conduct than it does with the distinction between openness and secrecy.

48. Robert Williams, *Corruption: New Concepts for Old?*, in 20 Third World Q. 503, 510 (1999).

49. Susan J. Pharr, *Public Trust and Corruption in Japan*, in *Political Corruption: Concepts and Contexts, supra* note 14, at 835, 853.

50. *See, e.g.,* Carl J. Friedrich, *Corruption Concepts in Historical Perspective*, in *Political Corruption: Concepts & Contexts, supra* note 14, at 15, 29–31 (the idea of equality before the law provides the setting for the modern and specific sense of corruption); Denis Osborne, *Corruption as Counter-culture: Attitudes to Bribery in Local and Global Society*, in *Corruption: The Enemy Within, supra* note 15, at 9, 28 ("Bribes create inequalities. A corrupt system is unfair."); Shihata, *supra* note 21, at 260 (corruption involves the "grant[ing] [of] special favours [which] undermines the general obligation to apply public rules without discrimination"). *See also* Alatas, *supra* note 41, at 8–10 (corruption violates notions of fair play). Some anchor the idea of equality in explicitly broader-than-legal obligations. *See, e.g.,* Shihata, *supra,* at 260–261 (corruption involves "[a]ttempts to influence the position holder, through the payment of bribes or an exchange of benefits or favours, in order to receive in return a special gain or treatment not available to others . . ., even if the gain involved is not illicit under the applicable law").

51. *See, e.g., United States v. North,* 910 F.2d 843, 881–882 (D.C. Cir. 1990), *cert. denied,* 500 U.S. 941 (1991) ("corruptly" involves an act done with an intent to obtain an improper advantage "inconsistent with official duty and rights of others"). *Accord, United States v. Ogle,* 613 F.2d 233, 238 (10th Cir. 1979), *cert. denied,* 449 U.S. 825 (1980); *United States v. Reeves,* 752 F.2d 995, 999 (5th Cir.), *cert. denied,* 474 U.S. 834 (1985).

52. The theory of equality has been particularly prominent in the identification of the corrupt nature of large campaign contributions. *See, e.g.,* David A. Strauss, *Corruption, Equality, and Campaign Finance Reform,* 94 Colum. L. Rev. 1369, 1370 (1994) (arguing that corruption in the campaign finance context is actually "derivative" of concerns about inequality in citizen access and influence).

53. For instance, bribery is "paying to receive better than fair treatment"; extortion is "paying to avoid worse than fair treatment." Ian Ayres, *The Twin Faces of Judicial Corruption: Extortion and Bribery,* 74 Denv. U. L. Rev. 231, 1235 (1997).

54. Tina Rosenberg, *Latin America's Magical Liberalism,* Wilson Q., Autumn 1992, at 58, 62.

55. *See, e.g.,* Robert S. Getz, *Congressional Ethics: The Conflict of Interest Issue* 67 (1966).

56. *See, e.g.,* Edgar Lane, *Group Politics and the Disclosure Idea,* 17 W. Pol. Q. 200, 205 (1964); Cass R. Sunstein, *Political Equality and Unintended Consequences,* 94 Colum. L. Rev. 1390, 1392 (1994).

57. *See, e.g.,* U.S. Const. amend. I.

58. *See, e.g.,* Gardiner, *supra* note 4, at 28 (most would "probably feel uncomfortable using the term corruption in all situations where the political process produces policies which do not benefit everyone equally").

59. Williams, *supra* note 48, at 509.

60. *See, e.g.,* Thomas Burke, *Corruption Concepts and Federal Campaign Finance Law,* in *Political Corruption: Concepts & Contexts, supra* note 14, at 645, 659 ("All standards of [political] corruption rest on some notion of what

constitutes an ideal political community."). *See also* Lowenstein, *supra* note 30, at 831–843, and Getz, *supra* note 55, at 53–68 (discussing "mandate," "trusteeship," and "pluralist" theories in the context of bribery and the actions of candidates for public office).

61. *See* Williams, *supra* note 48, at 508 (in the bureaucratic context, "rule following is anticipated"; bureaucratic organizations "characteristically operate on the basis of clear lines of authority and accountability," making it possible, in principle, to distinguish proper and improper actions).

62. *See, e.g.,* Arnold J. Heidenheimer, *Introduction: The Analysis of Electoral and Legislative Corruption,* in *Political Corruption: Readings in Comparative Analysis, supra* note 17, at 361, 368.

63. James Blitz, *Blow to Blair as Blunkett Goes,* Fin. Times (London), Dec. 16, 2004, at 1.

64. Mary Dejevsky, *Don't Be Fooled: Blunkett Is Guilty of a Serious Offence,* The Independent (London), Dec. 22, 2004, at 25. Another letter writer recalled how Prime Minister Tony Blair, Blunkett's boss, campaigned on a slogan of "No sleeze, bribery, or corruption." The Express (Scottish edition), Dec. 15, 2004, at 42.

65. National Public Radio broadcast, Dec. 7, 2004. Transcript available at http://nl.newsbank.com/nl-search/we/Archives (last visited Dec. 9, 2004).

66. Michael Johnston, *Measuring the New Corruption Rankings: Implications for Analysis and Reform,* in *Political Corruption: Concepts & Contexts, supra* note 14, at 865, 875.

67. Williams, *supra* note 48, at 505. *See also* Robert C. Brooks, *Apologies for Political Corruption,* in *Political Corruption: Readings in Comparative Analysis, supra* note 17, at 501, 507 ("The very essence of corruption is self-interest regardless of public interest."); Carl J. Friedrich, *Political Pathology,* 37 Pol. Q. 70, 74 (1966) (corruption exists when a power holder is induced "by monetary or other rewards . . . to take actions which favour whoever provides the reward and thereby does damage to the public and its interests").

68. Arnold A. Rogow & Harold Lasswell, *Power, Corruption, and Rectitude* 132 (1963).

69. *See, e.g.,* Barry Hindess, *Good Government and Corruption,* in *Corruption and Anti-Corruption, supra* note 44, at 1, 5 (a government that "pursues factional interests rather than the common interests of the community . . . [is] corrupt").

70. Heidenheimer, *supra* note 62, at 369.

71. Frank J. Sorauf, *The Conceptual Muddle*, in *Nomos V: The Public Interest* 183, 184 (Carl J. Friedrich ed., 1962).

72. As Arnold Heidenheimer puts it, the question is exactly *"whose evaluation* of the public's interest is to be operationalized?" Heidenheimer, *supra* note 18, at 6 (emphasis added).

73. Scott, *supra* note 1, at 3–4.

74. *See* Huntington, *supra* note 19, at 61.

75. *See, e.g.,* Bayley, *supra* note 17, at 528, 529; Leff, *supra* note 33, at 516 ("entrepreneurs and corrupted officials . . . [may] produc[e] a more effective [economic] policy than the government").

76. Franklin E. Zimring & David T. Johnson, *On the Comparative Study of Corruption*, 45 Brit. J. Criminology 793, 807 (2005).

77. *See id.* at 795, 797–798, 800.

78. *See id.* at 796.

79. *See id.* at 795.

80. *Id.* at 801.

81. *Id.*

82. *Id.*

83. *See id.*

84. *Id.* at 797.

85. *Id.*

86. *Id.* at 795.

87. *See id.*

88. *Id.* at 798.

89. *Id.* at 807.

90. *See id.* at 800.

91. *See id.* at 798 ("exclud[ing] from corruption acts where the actor's deviation from legal standards was objectively trivial").

92. *See, e.g.,* Bruce L. Benson, *A Note on Corruption by Public Officials: The Black Market for Property Rights*, J. Libertarian Stud. 305 (Summer 1981); Bruce L. Benson & John Baden, *The Political Economy of Governmental Corruption: The Logic of Underground Government*, 14 J. Legal Stud. 391 (1985).

93. *See* Benson & Baden, *supra* note 92, at 392; Benson, *supra* note 92, at 306.

94. Benson & Baden, *supra* note 92, at 392 (quoting *The Economics of Property Rights* 3 (Eirik G. Furubotn & Svetozar Pejovich eds., 1974)).

95. *Id.* at 392–393.

96. *Id.* at 393.

97. *Id.*

98. *Id.*

99. *Id.* at 393.

100. *See* Robert O. Tilman, *Black-Market Bureaucracy*, in *Political Corruption: Readings in Comparative Analysis, supra* note 17, at 62, 62.

101. *See id.*

102. *See* Benson & Baden, *supra* note 92, at 393–395.

103. *See id.* at 392–393.

104. Leff, *supra* note 33, at 510.

105. *See* Benson & Baden, *supra* note 92, at 392–393. The observations of David Bayley are typical of this view. Although corruption has costs, "it is not necessarily antipathetic to the development of modern economic and social systems." "Governments have no monopoly upon correct solutions. . . ." "Corruption may serve as a means for impelling better choices, even in terms of government's expressed goals." Bayley, *supra* note 17, at 521, 528.

106. Most contemporary scholars agree that these theories seriously underestimate corruption's other costs—particularly, the costs involved in damage to the accountability and transparency of government. *See, e.g.,* Bardhan, *supra* note 35, at 1327–1330; Mauro, *supra* note 35, 339; Paul D. Hutchcroft, *The Politics of Privilege: Rents and Corruption in Asia*, in *Political Corruption: Concepts & Contexts, supra* note 14, at 489, 493–495; Jean-François Médard, *Corruption in the Neo-Patrimonial States of Sub-Saharan Africa*, in *Political Corruption: Concepts & Contexts, supra*, at 379. *See also* Michael Johnston, *Syndromes of Corruption: Wealth, Power, and Democracy* 18 (2005) ("[S]trong theory and evidence suggest that corruption delays and distorts economic growth, rewards inefficiency, and short-circuits open competition. . . ."), and *id.* at 26–28 (citing studies). Such routine problems are in addition to those that corrupt states pose to international security and other issues of global welfare. *See* Robert Legvold, *Corruption, the Criminalized State, and Post-Soviet Transitions*, in *Corruption, Global Security, and World Order, supra* note 28, at 194.

107. Van Klaveren, *supra* note 38, at 38, 39.

108. *See, e.g.,* Rose-Ackerman, *supra* note 6, at 2–5, 14; Klitgaard, *supra* note 3, at 19–23; Michael Beenstock, *Economics of Corruption* (1977).

109. *See, e.g.,* Rose-Ackerman, *supra* note 6, at 2, 9 (distinguishing between productive and nonproductive rent-seeking (or corrupt) activity. For instance, "[b]ribes [may] clear the market." "Bribes [may] act as incentive bonuses." "Bribes [may] lower costs.").

110. *Id.* at 3. For instance, "[t]he official seeks to maximize his or her gains, not the optimal level of services. . . . If several officials have authority over the allocation of scarce benefits, the problems can multiply as each tries to extract a share of the gain." *Id.* at 14.

111. *See id.* at 4, 17, 22–23.

112. *See id.* at 2–3.

113. *Id.* at 5.

114. *Id.*

115. *Id.*

116. *See, e.g.,* Hindess, *supra* note 69, at 4 ("non-economic corruption" includes situations in which "[a] government puts pressure on police and [the] judiciary to protect its friends and to penalise its opponents"; "[a] ruling party appoints judges . . . and uses the courts to destroy the political opposition"; "[a] government uses its powers to discriminate systematically in favour of some sections of the population and against others"; and so on).

117. *See, e.g.,* Rose-Ackerman, *supra* note 6, at 25 (acknowledging that individual bribes "sometimes not only benefit the payer and the recipient but also enhance overall efficiency or fairness").

118. *See id.* at 9 (defining corruption as payments *"illegally* made to public agents with the goal of obtaining a benefit or avoiding a cost") (emphasis added).

119. *See* Klitgaard, *supra* note 3, at 21–24; Flavio M. Menezes, *The Microeconomics of Corruption,* in *Corruption and Anti-Corruption, supra* note 44, at 119, 119.

120. Philp *supra* note 14, at 50.

121. *Id.* at 42 (footnotes omitted) (emphases added). Philp specifies that "the core of [the] . . . fourth condition is the *intention* to act for private gain (one is not less corrupt for being unsuccessful)." *Id.* at 42 n.1.

122. Alatas, *supra* note 41, at 2 (footnote omitted) (emphases added). Alatas states that "[t]he last mentioned is important to distinguish corruption from other types of criminal behaviour." For example, when an official is bribed to issue a business license, he acts as the issuer (one capacity) and acquires the bribe (second and contradictory capacity). "This characteristic distinguishes corruption from theft, burglary, and embezzlement." *Id.*

CHAPTER 2. THE IDEA OF CORRUPTION

1. John T. Noonan Jr., *Bribes* 702 (1984).

2. *Id.* at 702–703.

3. *See id. See also* Robert Klitgaard, *Controlling Corruption* 11 (1988).

4. Noonan, *supra* note 1, at 582.

5. *See, e.g.,* 15 U.S.C. § 78dd-2(a) (2006) (Foreign Corrupt Practices Act) ("It shall be unlawful for any domestic concern . . . to make use of the mails or any means or instrumentality of interstate commerce *corruptly* in furtherance of an offer, payment, [or] promise to pay . . . anything of value to . . . any foreign official for the purpose of . . . influencing any act or decision of such foreign official. . . .") (emphasis added); 18 U.S.C. § 201(b)(1) (2006) (general federal bribery statute) ("Whoever . . . directly or indirectly, *corruptly* gives, offers or promises anything of value to any public official . . . with intent . . . to influence any official act" shall be guilty of bribery.) (emphasis added); 18 U.S.C. § 666(a)(1)(B) (2006) (bribery in federal programs) ("Whoever, . . . being an agent of an organization, or of a State, local, or Indian tribal government . . . *corruptly* . . . accepts or agrees to accept, anything of value from any person, intending to be influenced or rewarded in connection with any business . . . of such organization, government, or agency," in connection with a federal program, is guilty of bribery.) (emphasis added).

6. *See* statutes in note 5, *supra. Cf. United States v. Sun-Diamond Growers*, 526 U.S. 398, 404–405 (1999) ("[F]or bribery there must be a *quid pro quo*—a specific intent to give or receive something of value *in exchange* for an official act.") (emphasis in original).

7. Daniel H. Lowenstein, *Political Bribery and the Intermediate Theory of Politics*, 32 U.C.L.A. L. Rev. 784, 798 (1985). *See also* Noonan, *supra* note 1, at 644 (" '[C]orruptly' . . . apparently add[s] something to the description of the crime, but what? . . . [T]he word could be considered mere rhetoric, specifying nothing as to the elements of criminality to be proved."). The superfluity of this term in the bribery context is generated by the fact that there can be no innocent or lawful giving of money or other value to an official *in exchange* for his official act. *See, e.g., United States v. McCormack*, 31 F. Supp.2d 176, 177–178 (D. Mass. 1998) (interpreting 18 U.S.C. § 666(a)(2)) (equating "intent to influence or reward" a government official with " 'corrupt' intent"). This should be distinguished from those cases where the conduct (the attempt to influence) could have been done for innocent or lawful reasons. Compare, for instance, *United States v. Farrell*, 126 F.3d 484, 489 (3d Cir. 1997) ("corrupt persuasion" of someone to refuse to cooperate with a federal inquiry, in violation of 18 U.S.C. § 1512(b) (federal witness tampering statute) requires more than knowing and intentional persuasion that someone not testify, since failure to testify could be on wholly legitimate grounds, such as an exercise of the right against self-incrimination).

8. *See, e.g., United States v. Alfisi*, 308 F.3d 144, 149 (2d Cir. 2002) (the "corrupt" intent element establishes that "bribery involves the giving of value to procure a specific official action from a public official"); *United States v. Strand*, 574 F.2d 993, 996 (9th Cir. 1978) ("corrupt" intent requires a "*knowing* acceptance of money for *financial gain, in return for* violation of . . . official duty, with the *specific intent* to violate the law") (emphasis in original).

9. *See, e.g., United States v. Fenster*, 449 F. Supp. 435, 438 (E.D. Mich. 1978) (difference between the federal bribery statute and the statute that simply outlaws illegal gratuities "consist[s] in the higher degree of criminal knowledge and purpose betokened by the adverb 'corruptly'" (found in the first text, and not in the second)). *See also* Lowenstein, *supra* note 7, at 803 ("The word's very function is to group together actions and situations that generally have a certain descriptive character *and* that are regarded as seriously wrong.") (emphasis in original) (footnote omitted).

10. *United States v. North*, 910 F.2d 843, 881 (D.C. Cir. 1990), *cert. denied*, 500 U.S. 941 (1991) (interpreting 18 U.S.C. § 1505, dealing with obstruction of Congress). *See also Arthur Andersen LLP v. United States*, 544 U.S. 696, 705 (2005) (" 'corrupt' and 'corruptly' are normally associated with wrongful, immoral, depraved, or evil [acts]") (interpreting 18 U.S.C. §§ 1512(b)(2)(A) and (B), making it a crime to "knowingly us[e] intimidation or physical force, threate[n], or corruptly persuad[e] another person . . . with intent to . . . cause" that person to "withhold" documents from an official proceeding); *United States v. Ryan*, 455 F.2d 728, 734 (9th Cir. 1972) (corruption involves "an evil or wicked purpose") (interpreting 18 U.S.C. § 1503, making it a crime to "corruptly . . . endeavor[] to influence, obstruct, or impede . . . the due administration of justice"); *United States v. Jacobs*, 431 F.2d 754, 759 (2d Cir. 1970), *cert. denied*, 402 U.S. 950 (1971) (antibribery laws are attempts to prevent the "evil" of corruption in public life) (interpreting 18 U.S.C. § 201(b), general federal bribery statute); *Farrell*, 126 F.3d at 488 n.2 (characterizing "corrupt" as "morally degenerate and perverted") (internal quotation marks omitted).

11. Wilmer Parker III, *Every Person Has a Price?*, in *Corruption: The Enemy Within* 87, 87 (Barry Rider ed., 1997) (quoting John T. Noonan).

12. *See, e.g.*, Carl J. Friedrich, *The Pathology of Politics: Violence, Betrayal, Corruption, Secrecy, and Propaganda* 130–131 (1972); J. Peter Euben, *Corruption*, in *Political Innovation and Conceptual Change* 220, 223–242 (Terence Ball, James Farr, & Russell L. Hanson eds., 1989).

13. *See, e.g.*, Friedrich, *supra* note 12, at 127–141; Maryvonne Génaux, *Early Modern Corruption in English and French Fields of Vision*, in *Political Corruption: Concepts & Contexts* 107, 107–117 (Arnold J. Heidenheimer & Michael Johnston eds., 2002).

14. *Le Dictionnaire de l'Académie Françoise, dedié au Roi* (Geneva, 1981) (reproduction of the 1st ed., Paris, 1694), vol. 1 (corruption s.s.v.: "fig., de toute dépravation dans les moeurs, et principalement de celle qui regarde la justice . . .").

15. Samuel Johnson, *A Dictionary of the English Language* 154 (2006) (reproduction of the edition published by C. & J. Rivington, London, 1826).

16. Robert Williams, *Corruption: New Concepts for Old?*, in 20 Third World Q. 503, 504 (1999).

17. Arnold J. Heidenheimer, *The Context of Analysis*, in *Political Corruption: Readings in Comparative Analysis* 3, 4 (Arnold J. Heidenheimer ed., 1978).

18. Parker, *supra* note 11, at 87 (footnote omitted).

19. Robert C. Brooks, *Apologies for Political Corruption*, in *Political Corruption: Readings in Comparative Analysis, supra* note 17, at 501, 505, 506. *See also* Robert C. Brooks, *The Nature of Political Corruption*, in *id.* at 56, 58.

20. Ronald Wraith & Edgar Simpkins, *Corruption in Developing Countries* 17 (1963). *See also* Edward C. Banfield, *The Moral Basis of a Backward Society* 83–101 (1958) (describing members of a corrupt society as "amoral familists").

21. Klitgaard, *supra* note 3, at 23.

22. *See* Colin Leys, *What Is the Problem about Corruption?*, 3 J. Mod. Afr. Stud. 215, 216 (1965).

23. *See* Colin Leys, *New States and the Concept of Corruption*, in *Political Corruption: Readings in Comparative Analysis, supra* note 17, at 341, 341.

24. Bayless Manning, *The Purity Potlatch: Conflict of Interests and Moral Escalation*, in *Political Corruption: Readings in Comparative Analysis, supra* note 17, at 307, 307, 308.

25. *Id.* at 308.

26. *See id.* at 308–312.

27. *See, e.g.*, Thomas Burke, *Corruption Concepts and Federal Campaign Finance Law*, in *Political Corruption: Concepts & Contexts, supra* note 13, at 645, 646; Euben, *supra* note 12, at 222.

28. Syed Hussein Alatas, *Corruption: Its Nature, Causes, and Functions* 17 (1990).

29. *Id.* at 29.

30. *Id.* at 71.

31. *See* Burke, *supra* note 27, at 646.

32. St. Augustine, *The City of God* 444 (Marcus Dods trans., 1950).

33. Anselm of Canterbury, *On the Fall of the Devil*, in *Anselm of Canterbury, The Major Works* 191, 206–207 (Brian Davies & G. R. Evans eds., 1998).

34. St. Thomas Aquinas, *Summa Theologica: Complete English Edition in Five Volumes* (Fathers of the English Dominican Province trans., 1948), vol. I, 249–250.

35. John Calvin, *Calvin: Institutes of the Christian Religion* (Ford Lewis Battles trans., 1960), vol. II, 1311.

36. Jonathan Edwards, *Original Sin* 107, 128, 130, 132 (Clyde A. Holbrook ed., 1970).

37. *See, e.g.*, Immanuel Kant, *Religion within the Limits of Reason Alone* 25, 28, 30, and *passim* (Theodore M. Greene & Hoyt H. Hudson trans., 1960); Jean-Jacques Rousseau, *Preface to "Narcissus,"* in Jean-Jacques Rousseau, *The Discourses and Other Early Political Writings* 92–106 (Victor Gourevitch trans., 1997); Jean-Jacques Rousseau, *Observations*, in Rousseau, *supra*, at 46; Jean-Jacques Rousseau, *Last Reply*, in Rousseau, *supra*, at 65–72; Marquis de Sade, *Justine, Philosophy in the Bedroom, and Other Writings* (Richard Seaver & Austryn Wainhouse trans., 1965).

38. Kant, *supra* note 37, at 25.

39. *Id.*

40. Rousseau, *Preface to "Narcissus,"* in Rousseau, *supra* note 37, at 100.

41. *See* J. G. A. Pocock, *The Machiavellian Moment* 506–552 (1975).

42. *Id.* at 548.

43. *See* Stephen Hutcheon, *Eighteen to Face Court Charges over $3 Billion Beijing Fraud*, Sydney Morning Herald, April 4, 1996, at 10.

44. *Id.*

45. N. R. Kleinfield, *Chinatown Officers Said to Forge a Partnership of Vice and Greed*, N.Y. Times, June 19, 1995, at A1.

46. Nathaniel C. Nash, *Brazilian Leader Quits as His Trial Starts in Senate*, N.Y. Times, Dec. 30, 1992, at A1.

47. Edward A. Gargan, *Corruption's Many Tentacles Are Choking India's Growth*, N.Y. Times, Nov. 10, 1992, at A1.

48. John Hall, *GOP Sleaze Explosion*, Raleigh News & Observer, Jan. 9, 2006.

49. Ruth Marcus, *Corruption Runs Bone Deep*, Raleigh News & Observer, March 2, 2006.

50. Kim Long, *The Almanac of Political Corruption, Scandals, and Dirty Politics* 260 (2007).

51. *United States v. Shields*, No. 90 CR 1044, 1992 WL 43239, at 32 (N.D. Ill. Feb. 20, 1992).

52. Associated Press, *Corruption "A Cancer Destroying the Core Values" of New Jersey*, Lewiston Daily Sun, July 24, 2009, at A6.

53. Adam Nossiter, *Civil Rights Hero, Now a Judge, Is Indicted in a Bribery Case*, N.Y. Times, Feb. 14, 2009, at A9. Such associations are not a recent phenomenon in U.S. history. For instance, Daniel Webster, nineteenth-century American statesman, was investigated by Congress for financial corruption while secretary of state. "According to a political critic writing at the time, 'He is a prostitute in morals and something worse in politics. . . . Loose in many matters, tainted with fraud, fixed in profligacy, he is a living ulcer and infection.'" Long, *supra* note 50, at 44.

54. Burke, *supra* note 27, at 646.

55. H. A. Brasz, *Administrative Corruption in Theory and Dutch Practice*, in *Political Corruption: Readings in Comparative Analysis, supra* note 17, at 243, 248. *See also* Euben, *supra* note 12, at 222 ("[C]orruption involves enervation, a loss of health and power. Such loss leads to decadence. . . . Decadence implies self-indulgence, luxury, and excess. . . .").

56. Brooks, *The Nature of Political Corruption, supra* note 19, at 58.

57. *See* Walter Lippmann, *A Theory about Corruption*, in *Political Corruption: Readings in Comparative Analysis, supra* note 17, at 294, 295.

58. *See* Wraith & Simpkins, *supra* note 20, at 11, 13.

59. Friedrich, *supra* note 12, at 128.

60. Barry A. K. Rider, *Introduction*, in *Corruption: The Enemy Within*, *supra* note 11, at 1, 1. *See also* Robert Klitgaard, *International Cooperation against Corruption*, in *World Development Report*, Nov. 1977, at 2 (people "tend to think of corruption *as a sin* of government") (emphasis added).

61. Parker, *supra* note 11, at 102–103.

62. *See, e.g.*, Euben, *supra* note 12, at 222–223.

63. In an interesting example of this idea, Susan Sontag, writing of atrocities committed by American soldiers regarding Iraqi prisoners at Abu Ghraib, described their actions as "representative of the fundamental *corruptions* of any foreign occupation." Susan Sontag, *Regarding the Torture of Others: Notes on What Has Been Done—and Why—to Prisoners, by Americans*, N.Y. Times, May 23, 2004 (Magazine), at 24, 26 (emphasis added).

64. *See, e.g.*, Friedrich, *supra* note 12, at 138–139 ("The common understanding is that an official is corrupt when he accepts monetary or other reward . . . for something he should or should not do anyway, or exercises the discretion entrusted to him so as to favor his *corruptor*.") (emphasis added); Susan Taylor, *Taking the Profit out of Corruption: A UK Perspective*, in *Corruption: The Enemy Within*, *supra* note 11, at 169, 169 ("[T]he *corrupted* obtains the benefit of the bribe, [and] the *corruptor* obtains a preference or advantage over others. This advantage often leads to significant profit being made by the *corruptor*.") (emphasis added).

65. *See, e.g.*, Brasz, *supra* note 55, at 244; Rider, *supra* note 60, at 1.

66. Joseph Borkin, *The Corrupt Judge: An Inquiry into Bribery and Other High Crimes and Misdemeanors in the Federal Courts* (1962).

67. *Id.* at 15 (emphasis added). Borkin notes, furthermore, that "[a]s a rule, the corruptors fared better than the corrupted judge in material reward." *Id.*

68. Kleinfield, *supra* note 45, at A1.

69. *See* Sheryl Gay Stolberg, *Lobbyist Accepts Plea Deal and Becomes Star Witness in a Wider Corruption Case*, N.Y. Times, Jan. 4, 2006, at A1.

70. *See* Ana Marie Cox, *Political Theater of the Absurd*, N.Y. Times, Jan. 5, 2006, at A23.

71. Philip Shenon, *Ohio Congressman Is Said to Agree to Plead Guilty: Past Ties to Corrupt Lobbyist Are Cited*, N.Y. Times, Sept. 15, 2006, at A12. Abramoff was later described in an editorial as "the imprisoned superlobbyist who corrupted House members." *Editorial*, N.Y. Times, Feb. 28, 2008, at A26.

72. Pete Yost, *Ex-aide Admits Trying to Corrupt Rep. Ney, His Staff; His Boss, Abramoff, Is Facing Influence Peddling Charges,* Durham Herald-Sun, May 9, 2006, at A8. The aide "enumerated sixteen actions he said his old boss took on behalf of Abramoff clients." *Id.*

73. Shenon, *supra* note 71.

74. *See id.*

75. Philip Shenon, *Lawmaker Took Cash for Favors, F.B.I. Contends,* N.Y. Times, May 22, 2006, at A1.

76. *See id.* (emphasis added). Jefferson was convicted of corruption charges and sentenced to thirteen years in prison on November 13, 2009.

77. Euben, *supra* note 12, at 222. *See also* Alatas, *supra* note 28, at 5 (describing the "metastatic effects" of corruption).

78. *See* Gargan, *supra* note 47.

79. *See, e.g.,* Yufan Hao and Michael Johnston, *Corruption and the Future of Economic Reform in China,* in *Political Corruption: Concepts & Contexts, supra* note 13, at 583, 584 (corruption " 'is like a virus invading the body of the party and the state' ") (quoting former Chinese Communist Party chief Jiang Zemin).

80. *See, e.g.,* Lippmann, *supra* note 57, at 296 (corruption is a "disease . . . [of] the body politic"); Friedrich, *supra* note 12, at 131–132 (same). Alatas describes public corruption as an "infection," an "infestation." *See* Alatas, *supra* note 28, at 5, 72.

81. *See, e.g.,* Friedrich, *supra* note 12, at 135 (corruption is a "particular form of political pathology"); Martin Shapiro, *Corruption, Freedom and Equality in Campaign Financing,* 18 Hofstra L. Rev. 385, 393 (1989) (excessive political influence by the rich has been characterized as a "pathology" to be "excised").

82. *See* Brooks, *The Nature of Political Corruption, supra* note 19, at 59.

83. Ibrahim F. I. Shihata, *Corruption—A General Review with an Emphasis on the Role of the World Bank,* in *Corruption: The Enemy Within, supra* note 11, at 255, 262. As a former secretary-general of the Council of Europe stated: " 'None of our countries is immune from the disease of corruption. This disease is spreading in countries which regard or regarded themselves as old and firmly established democracies. . . . The disease is spreading in the new democracies and those countries of Central and Eastern Europe where democracy is still being built.' " Peter Csonka, *Corruption: The Council of Europe's Approach,* in *Corruption: The Enemy Within, supra,* at 343, 345 (quoting statements at the Nineteenth Conference of European Ministers of Justice, Valletta, June 1994).

84. Jonathan Salzman, *Officer Gets 26 Years in Trafficking Scheme*, Boston Globe, May 17, 2008, at A1.

85. Pub. L. No. 95–213, 91 Stat. 1496 (1977) (codified as 15 U.S.C. §§ 78dd-1, 78dd-2, 78ff (2006)).

86. Henry H. Rossbacher & Tracy W. Young, *The Foreign Corrupt Practices Act: An American Response to Corruption*, in *Corruption: The Enemy Within, supra* note 11, at 209, 224–225.

87. Lippmann, *supra* note 57, at 296. Exposure of corrupt acts means that "'the antibodies [of the democratic system] are fighting the disease.'" Larry Rohter, *Brazilians May Be Used to Corrupt Officials, but Draw the Line at Soccer Referees*, N.Y. Times, Oct. 11, 2005, at A10 (quoting anthropologist Roberto da Matta).

88. Quoted in Fin. Times, Sept. 16, 1977, at 15.

89. *See* Arnold J. Heidenheimer & Michael Johnston, *Introduction to Part I*, in *Political Corruption: Concepts & Contexts, supra* note 13, at 1, 7.

90. Friedrich, *supra* note 12, at 128. *Cf.* Maeve Cooke, *An Evil Heart: Moral Evil and Moral Identity*, in *Rethinking Evil: Contemporary Perspectives* 113, 122 (María Pía Lara ed., 2001) (moral evil is "a perversion or *corruption* of the human heart") (emphasis added).

91. Brooks, *The Nature of Political Corruption, supra* note 19, at 57.

92. Kenneth T. Young Jr., *New Politics in New States*, 39 Foreign Affairs 495, 498 (1961).

93. Alatas, *supra* note 28, at 122. Witnesses at the trial of Richard W. Reading (1882–1952), mayor of Detroit, were described in the following terms: "'Every time [the judge] . . . got a new witness to talk, it was like turning up a rotten log; the bugs swarmed out and he had to work fast before they got away.'" Long, *supra* note 50, at 177–178 (quoting Time Mag.). Spiders are also favorite images of corruption. *See, e.g.,* Cox, *supra* note 70 (describing Abramoff's "elaborate web of corruption").

94. *In the Matter of Coruzzi*, 484 A.2d 667, 668 (N.J. 1984). *See also Brief of Amicus Curiae of Concerned Illinois Lawyers and Law Professors in Support of Petitioner*, filed in *Bracy v. Gramley*, 520 U.S. 899 (1997), at 14 (question before the Court was whether the judge's "pervasive and calculated corruption infected [the defendant's trial]").

95. Johann Graf Lambsdorff, Markus Taube, & Matthias Schramm, *Corrupt Contracting: Exploring the Analytical Capacity of New Institutional Economics and New Economic Sociology*, in *The New Institutional Economics of*

Corruption 1, 1 (Johann Graf Lambsdorff, Markus Taube, & Matthias Schramm eds., 2005).

96. Conversation with Hon. Antonio Herrera, Caracas, Venezuela (June 1992). *See also* Georg Simmel, *The Philosophy of Money* 385 (Tom Bottomore & David Frisby trans., 1978) (describing how a person paying a bribe would pursue secrecy in order to protect himself against "self-negation and self-devaluation which would result from his sacrificing his personality for . . . money").

97. Rider, *supra* note 60, at 1.

98. *See, e.g.*, Csonka, *supra* note 83, at 343; Gert Vermeulen, *The Fight against International Corruption in the European Union*, in *Corruption: The Enemy Within, supra* note 11, at 333. Generally, bribery statutes in the United States do not make this distinction. *See, e.g.*, 18 U.S.C. § 201(b)(1) and § 201(b)(2) (2006) (punishing bribery of public officials, with equal reference to the giver and the recipient).

99. W. Paatii Ofosu-Amaah, Raj Soopramanien, & Kishor Uprety, *Combating Corruption: A Comparative Review of Selected Legal Aspects of State Practice and Major International Initiatives* 48 (1999); Vermeulen, *supra* note 98, at 336.

100. For instance, in Chile the payment of a bribe is a criminal offense, while the receipt of a bribe is not unless it is accompanied by other wrongdoing. *See* Sietze Hepkema & Willem Booysen, *Bribery of Public Officials: An IBA Survey*, 25 Int'l Bus. Law 415, 415 (1997).

101. Examples of reference to corrupt status are ubiquitous. *See, e.g.*, Susan Rose-Ackerman, *Corruption and Government: Causes, Consequences, and Reform* 36, 99, 101, 199 (1999); Shenon, *supra* note 71.

102. *See* Brooks, *The Nature of Political Corruption*, *supra* note 19, at 59.

103. *See* Alatas, *supra* note 28, at 6.

104. *See* Salzman, *supra* note 84, at A1, A8.

105. Denis Osborne, *Corruption as Counter-Culture: Attitudes to Bribery in Local and Global Society*, in *Corruption: The Enemy Within, supra* note 11, at 11, 28 (emphasis added). *See also* Simmel, *supra* note 96, at 384 (referring to bribery as "the 'purchase' of a person").

106. *Bracy v. Gramley*, 81 F.3d 684, 699–700, 702–703 (7th Cir. 1996), *rev'd*, 520 U.S. 899 (1997) (Rovner, J., dissenting).

107. *Bracy*, 520 U.S. at 906–909.

108. *United States ex rel. Collins v. Welborn*, 79 F. Supp.2d 898, 906 (N.D. Ill. 1999), *aff'd and rev'd in part sub nom. Bracy v. Schomig*, 248 F.3d 604 (7th Cir. 2001), *aff'd*, 286 F.3d 406 (7th Cir.), *cert. denied*, 537 U.S. 944 (2002).

109. *See* Otto Hintze, *Der Beamtenstand*, in *Soziologie und Geschichte* 72 (1964). *See also* Heidenheimer, *supra* note 17, at 16.

110. Burke, *supra* note 27, at 53 (emphasis added).

111. *In the Matter of Coruzzi*, 472 A.2d 546, 549–550 (N.J. 1984).

112. Michael Brick, *Former Judge Is Convicted of Bribery in Divorce Court*, N.Y. Times, Apr. 20, 2007, at A22.

113. Sam Dolnick, *Kerik Gets 4 Years in Prison for Tax Fraud and Lies*, N.Y. Times, Feb. 19, 2010, at A18.

114. Parker, *supra* note 11, at 102.

115. *See* Brooks, *The Nature of Political Corruption, supra* note 19, at 58.

CHAPTER 3. CORRUPTION-AS-DISPOSITION

1. For instance, whether dispositions are humanly cognizable separately from their manifestations and whether they can be reduced to the facts stated by their conditionals are questions of lively philosophical debate. *See, e.g.*, the Martin-Armstrong-Place Debate in *Dispositions: A Debate* 69–192 (Tim Crane ed., 1996).

2. *See, e.g.*, Tim Crane, *Introduction*, in *Dispositions: A Debate, supra* note 1, at 1, 1–2; U. T. Place, *Structural Properties: Categorical, Dispositional, or Both?*, in *Dispositions: A Debate, supra*, at 105, 112–122; C. B. Martin, *Final Replies to Place and Armstrong*, in *Dispositions: A Debate, supra*, at 163, 166. *Cf.* Gilbert Ryle, *The Concept of Mind* 123 (dispositional statements are those "to the effect that a mentioned thing, beast, or person, has a certain capacity, tendency or propensity, or is subject to a certain liability").

3. Martin, *supra* note 2, at 166.

4. Place, *supra* note 2, at 113 (emphasis added).

5. *See* Richard J. Bernstein, *Radical Evil: Kant at War with Himself*, in *Rethinking Evil: Contemporary Perspectives* 55, 67 (María Pía Lara ed., 2001).

6. *See id.* at 67–68.

7. Sergio Pérez, *Major Offenders, Minor Offenders*, in *Rethinking Evil: Contemporary Perspectives, supra* note 5, at 189, 191.

8. Maeve Cooke, *An Evil Heart: Moral Evil and Moral Identity*, in *Rethinking Evil: Contemporary Perspectives, supra* note 5, at 113, 118.

9. *See, e.g.,* Susan Rose-Ackerman, *Corruption and Government: Causes, Consequences, and Reform* 36, 101, 199 (1999); *Bracy v. Gramley,* 81 F.3d 684, 689 (7th Cir. 1996), *rev'd,* 520 U.S. 899 (1997).

10. *United States v. Jacobs,* 431 F.2d 754, 759 (2d Cir. 1970), *cert. denied,* 402 U.S. 950 (1971).

11. *See, e.g.,* Syed Hussein Alatas, *Corruption: Its Nature, Causes, and Functions* 6 (1990); Arnold J. Heidenheimer, *The Context of Analysis,* in *Political Corruption: Readings in Comparative Analysis* 3, 16 (Arnold J. Heidenheimer ed., 1978).

12. *See, e.g.,* Stephen Hutcheon, *Eighteen to Face Court Charges over $3 Billion Beijing Fraud,* Sydney Morning Herald, Apr. 4, 1996, at 10.

13. *United States v. North,* 910 F.2d 843, 881 (D.C. Cir. 1990), *cert. denied,* 500 U.S. 941 (1991).

14. Wilmer Parker III, *Every Person Has a Price?,* in *Corruption: The Enemy Within* 87, 102 (Barry Rider ed., 1997).

15. *Okabe v. I.N.S.,* 671 F.2d 863, 865 (5th Cir. 1982) (interpreting federal antibribery statute, 18 U.S.C. § 201(b)(3)). *See also Michel v. I.N.S.,* 206 F.3d 253, 265 (2d Cir. 2000) (moral turpitude "is . . . a question of the offender's evil intent or corruption of the mind"); *Rodriquez-Castro v. Gonzales,* 427 F.3d 316, 320 (5th Cir. 2005) ("[A] crime involves moral turpitude . . . [if it] is accompanied by a vicious motive or a corrupt mind. . . .").

16. *See* Daniel R. Coquillette, *Francis Bacon* viii (1992).

17. *Articles of Impeachment of Sir Francis Bacon, Lord Chancellor,* reprinted in Joseph Borkin, *The Corrupt Judge: An Inquiry into Bribery and Other High Crimes and Misdemeanors in the Federal Courts,* Appendix, 213–218 (1962).

18. *See* Coquillette, *supra* note 16, at 222.

19. *See id.*

20. *See* Borkin, *supra* note 17, at 5.

21. *See* Coquillette, *supra* note 16, at 222.

22. *See id.*

23. *See id.* at 223.

24. *See id.* at 222.

25. Jay Weaver, *Abramoff Sentenced to Six Years,* Miami Herald, Mar. 30, 2006.

26. One can sense the permanent nature of expulsion for corruption in the following order regarding a corrupt judge: "Judge Coruzzi engaged in misconduct in office. We therefore remove him . . . effective immediately. He shall not hereafter hold judicial office." *In the Matter of Coruzzi*, 472 A.2d 546, 558 (N.J. 1984).

27. Officeholders who survived allegations of corruption include Jonathan Belcher (1682–1757), royal governor of Massachusetts and New Jersey, and a founder of Princeton University; Eugene Schmitz (1864–1928), mayor of San Francisco; Frederick Nicholas Zihlman (1879–1935), U.S. representative from Maryland; and Albert Williams Johnson (1872–1957), U.S. district judge in Pennsylvania. *See* Kim Long, *The Almanac of Political Corruption, Scandals, and Dirty Politics* 7, 121, 152, 193 (2007); Mark Grossman, *Political Corruption in America: An Encyclopedia of Scandals, Power, and Greed* 290–291 (2003).

28. *See* Long, *supra* note 27, *passim*.

29. These were Alexander Caldwell (1830–1917), senator from Kansas, who began a new career as a bank president; William Sulzer (1863–1941), governor of New York, who won election to the state house; and Alcee Lamar Hastings (1936–), U.S. district judge in Florida, who was elected to the U.S. House of Representatives. *See id.* at 81, 137, 267–268. *See also* Grossman, *supra* note 27, at 43–45, 313–315, 154–156.

30. *See* Immanuel Kant, *Religion within the Limits of Reason Alone* 39 (Theodore M. Greene & Hoyt H. Hudson trans., 1960).

31. John T. Noonan Jr., *Bribes* 582 (1984). *Cf.* Susan Neiman, *What's the Problem of Evil?*, in *Rethinking Evil: Contemporary Perspectives, supra* note 5, at 27, 29 (what "we mean when we use the word 'evil' today: absolute wrong-doing, which leaves room for no account and no expiation").

32. Cooke, *supra* note 8, at 126.

33. *See* María Pía Lara, *Introduction*, in *Rethinking Evil: Contemporary Perspectives, supra* note 5, at 1, 4 (internal quotation marks omitted).

34. During the Spanish Inquisition in the sixteenth century, "Protestant sympathizers . . . and other persons accused of heresies [were] believed to pose a major risk to the [prevailing religious orthodoxy] and general well-being" of Spanish life. Richard L. Kagan & Abigail Dyer, *Inquisitional Inquiries: Brief Lives of Secret Jews and Other Heretics* 9 (2004). Like corruption, heresy was believed to be a visceral part of the affected person, was "contagious" to others, and had the power to change established norms. *See id.* at 8–18.

35. Ryle, *supra* note 2, at 125.

36. *See* Chapter 2.

37. *See* Gwen Ifill, *Clinton Admits Experiment with Marijuana in the 1960s*, N.Y. Times, Mar. 30, 1992.

38. Francis Markus, *China City Eyes Official Affairs*, BBC News, May 20, 2005.

39. *See, e.g.*, Crane, *supra* note 2, at 7.

40. Robbie Brown, *Ex-Mayor Gets 15 Years in Bribery, and City Pays Price*, N.Y. Times, Mar. 6, 2010, at A10.

41. *Id.*

CHAPTER 4. AN *EVIL* DISPOSITION

1. Amélie Oksenberg Rorty, *Preface: Varieties of Evil*, in *The Many Faces of Evil: Historical Perspectives* xi, xii (Amélie Oksenberg Rorty ed., 2001).

2. *See, e.g.*, *The Judgment of the Dead*, in *The Ancient Egyptian Book of the Dead* 27–28 (Raymond O. Faulkner trans., 1972); *The Book of Genesis* 2: 7–17; 3: 1–24.

3. *See* Susan Neiman, *Evil in Modern Thought: An Alternative History of Philosophy* 3 (2002).

4. Tertullian, *Adversus Marcionem* 97–99 (II.5) (Ernest Evans ed. & trans., 1972). *See also* Mark Larrimore, *Introduction: Responding to Evil*, in *The Problem of Evil: A Reader* xiv, xxi (Mark Larrimore ed., 2001).

5. *See* Amélie Oksenberg Rorty, *From Sin to Vice*, in *The Many Faces of Evil, supra* note 1, at 39, 39.

6. *See, e.g.*, St. Augustine, *The Problem of Free Choice* 212–217 (Dom Mark Pontifex trans., 1955); Peter Abelard, *Ethics*, in *Peter Abelard, Ethical Writings: His Ethics or "Know Yourself" and His Dialogue between a Philosopher, a Jew, and a Christian* 2–16 (Paul Vincent Spade trans., 1995). *See also* Rorty, *supra* note 1, at xiii.

7. *See* Rorty, *supra* note 1, at xii–xv; María Pía Lara, *Introduction*, in *Rethinking Evil: Contemporary Perspectives* 1, 3 (María Pía Lara ed., 2001).

8. *See, e.g.*, Immanuel Kant, *Religion within the Limits of Reason Alone* 17 (Theodore M. Greene & Hoyt H. Hudson trans., 1960).

9. *See* Richard J. Bernstein, *Radical Evil: Kant at War with Himself*, in *Rethinking Evil: Contemporary Perspectives, supra* note 7, at 55, 67–68.

10. *See, e.g.*, Kant, *supra* note 8, at 31–32.

11. *See, e.g., id.* at 25.

12. *See id.*

13. Lara, *supra* note 7, at 3 (quoting Joan Copjec, *Introduction: Evil in the Time of the Finite World*, in *Radical Evil* vii, xi (Joan Copjec ed., 1996)).

14. Maeve Cooke, *An Evil Heart: Moral Evil and Moral Identity*, in Lara, *supra* note 7, at 113, 121.

15. *Id.* at 126.

16. Bernstein, *supra* note 9, at 57.

17. Benedict Carey, *For the Worst of Us, the Diagnosis May Be "Evil,"* N.Y. Times, Feb. 8, 2005, at D1.

18. *See* Rorty, *supra* note 1, at xv.

19. *See id.* at xiii.

20. *See* Lara, *supra* note 7, at 2.

21. *Id.* at 3 (quoting Bernstein, *supra* note 9, at 57) (emphasis omitted).

22. *See, e.g.,* Neiman, *supra* note 3, at 9.

23. Jennifer L. Geddes, *Introduction*, in *Evil after Postmodernism: Histories, Narratives, and Ethics* 1, 1–2 (Jennifer L. Geddes ed., 2001).

24. *See, e.g.,* Andrew Delbanco, *The Death of Satan: How Americans Have Lost the Sense of Evil* 9 (1996) ("[W]e feel something that our culture no longer gives us the vocabulary to express.").

25. Neiman, *supra* note 3, at 3.

26. Susan Neiman, *What's the Problem of Evil?*, in *Rethinking Evil: Contemporary Perspectives, supra* note 7, at 27, 29.

27. Peter Dews, *"Radical Finitude" and the Problem of Evil*, in Lara, *supra* note 7, at 46, 51 (quoting Paul Ricoeur, *La critique et la conviction: Entretien avec François Azouvi et Marc de Launay* 168 (1995)) (footnote omitted).

28. Berel Lang, *Evil Inside and Outside History: The Post-Holocaust vs. the Postmodern*, in Geddes, *supra* note 23, at 11, 11. *See also* Nevitt Sanford & Craig Comstock, *Sanctions for Evil*, in *Sanctions for Evil: Sources of Social Destructiveness* 5 (Nevitt Sanford, Craig Comstock, & Associates eds., 1971) (evil is an "ancient and heavily freighted term"); Thomas Cushman, *The Reflexivity of Evil: Modernity and Moral Transgression in the War in Bosnia*, in *Evil after Postmodernism: Histories, Narratives, and Ethics, supra* note 23, at 79, 80 (evil carries "the baggage of morality, metaphysics, emotions, essentialism, [and] psychology").

29. Carey, *supra* note 17.

30. *Id.*

31. *Id.*

32. *See, e.g.*, Aristotle, *The Works of Aristotle*, vol. X, bk. III (1286a–1286b) (W. D. Ross ed., 1921); J. G. A. Pocock, *The Machiavellian Moment: Florentine Political Thought and the Atlantic Republican Tradition* 76–80 (1975) (discussing early Greek and Christian humanist works).

33. St. Augustine, *The City of God* 441–446 (Marcus Dods trans., 1950).

34. *See, e.g.*, Pocock, *supra* note 32, at 135, 258, 297, 333, and *passim*.

35. *See, e.g., id.* at 506–507, and *passim*.

36. *See* Chapter 2.

37. Jeffrey C. Alexander, *Toward a Sociology of Evil: Getting beyond Modernist Common Sense about the Alternative to "the Good,"* in Lara, *supra* note 7, at 153, 153, 167 (footnote omitted).

38. *See* Chapter 2.

39. Neiman, *supra* note 26, at 29.

40. *See* Chapter 3.

41. *Cf.* Maryvonne Génaux, *Early Modern Corruption in English and French Fields of Vision*, in *Political Corruption: Concepts & Contexts* 107, 109 (Arnold J. Heidenheimer & Michael Johnston eds., 2002) (discussing the eighteenth-century idea of corruption as the antithesis of civic virtue and salvation).

42. Robert C. Brooks, *Apologies for Political Corruption*, in *Political Corruption: Readings in Comparative Analysis* 501, 505 (Arnold J. Heidenheimer ed., 1978).

43. *See id.* at 505–506.

44. *See* Chapter 2.

45. *See* J. S. Nye, *Corruption and Political Development: A Cost-Benefit Analysis*, in *Political Corruption: Readings in Comparative Analysis, supra* note 42, at 564, 565.

46. Robert I. Simon, *Bad Men Do What Good Men Dream: A Forensic Psychiatrist Illuminates the Darker Side of Human Behavior* (1996).

47. *See, e.g.*, Carl Goldberg, *Speaking with the Devil: Exploring Senseless Acts of Evil* (1996).

48. *See id.* at xii–xiii.

49. *See id.* at 8.

50. *Id.* at 9.

51. *Id.*

52. *Id.* at 255.

53. *See id.* at 253–260.

54. *See, e.g.,* St. Augustine, *supra* note 33, at 365, 387 ("evil . . . is a name for nothing but the want of good"; the evil will "is not efficient, but deficient"); Pseudo-Dionysius Areopagite, *The Divine Names,* IV.32, 160, in *The Divine Names and Mystical Theology* (John D. Jones trans., 1980) ("evil is a privation, lack, weakness, . . . failure, non-intention, . . . non-being, and itself being in no manner whatever at all"); St. Thomas Aquinas, *Summa Theologica: Complete English Edition in Five Volumes* I.248–249 (Fathers of the English Dominican Province trans., 1948) ("by the name of evil is signified the absence of good").

55. *See, e.g.,* Larry J. Siever, *Neurobiology in Psychopathy,* in *Psychopathy: Antisocial, Criminal, and Violent Behavior* 231 (Theodore Millon, Erik Simonsen, Morten Birket-Smith, & Roger D. Davis eds., 1998) (discussing studies).

56. *See* Robert Klitgaard, *Controlling Corruption* 74–95 (1988).

57. *See id.* at 90–97.

58. *See* Syed Hussein Alatas, *Corruption: Its Nature, Causes and Functions* 122 (1990).

59. *Id.*

60. *See id.*

61. *Id.* at 184.

CHAPTER 5. CORRUPTION AS CAPTURE-BY-EVIL

1. Robert C. Brooks, *The Nature of Political Corruption,* in *Political Corruption: Readings in Comparative Analysis* 56, 56 (Arnold J. Heidenheimer ed., 1978).

2. *See* Thomas Cushman, *The Reflexivity of Evil: Modernity and Moral Transgression in the War in Bosnia,* in *Evil after Postmodernism: Histories, Narratives, and Ethics* 79, 80 (Jennifer L. Geddes ed., 2001).

3. *See, e.g.,* Michael Welner, *Defining Evil,* 6 The Forensic Echo 4–12 (1998), and Michael Welner, *Defining Evil: A Depravity Scale for Today's Courts,* http://echo.forensicpanel.com/2001/5/10/definingevil.html (last visited June 21, 2006) and https://depravityscale.org/depscale/ (last visited June 21, 2006) (describing the development of a "Depravity Scale" for use by courts, which correlates descriptions of crimes with legal definitions of acts exhibiting particular depravity, and reactions of study participants to those crimes).

4. *See, e.g., United States v. North,* 910 F.2d 843, 881 (D.C. Cir. 1990), *cert. denied,* 500 U.S. 941 (1991) (" 'corrupt' . . . means 'depraved, evil: perverted into a state of moral weakness or wickedness' ").

5. *See, e.g., United States ex rel. Collins v. Welborn,* 79 F. Supp.2d 298, 906 (N.D. Ill. 1999), *aff'd and rev'd in part sub nom. Bracy v. Schomig,* 248 F.3d 604 (7th Cir. 2001), *aff'd,* 286 F.3d 406 (7th Cir.), *cert. denied,* 537 U.S. 944 (2002).

6. See, e.g., Amélie Oksenberg Rorty, *The Banality of Evil: The Cruelty of Everyday Life,* in *The Many Faces of Evil: Historical Perspectives* 239, 240 (Amélie Oksenberg Rorty ed., 2001).

7. *See, e.g.,* Robert C. Brooks, *Apologies for Political Corruption,* in *Political Corruption: Readings in Comparative Analysis, supra* note 1, at 501, 505.

8. *See, e.g.,* Syed Hussein Alatas, *Corruption: Its Nature, Causes, and Functions* 17, 29, 71 (1990); Thomas Burke, *Corruption Concepts and Federal Campaign Law,* in *Political Corruption: Concepts & Contexts* 645, 646 (Arnold J. Heidenheimer & Michael Johnston eds., 2002).

9. *See, e.g.,* Maeve Cooke, *An Evil Heart: Moral Evil and Moral Identity,* in *Rethinking Evil: Contemporary Perspectives* 113, 122, 124–125, 128 (María Pía Lara ed., 2001); Amélie Oksenberg Rorty, *How to Harden Your Heart: Six Easy Ways to Become Corrupt,* in *The Many Faces of Evil: Historical Perspectives, supra* note 6, at 282.

10. *See, e.g.,* Peter Csonka, *Corruption: The Council of Europe's Approach,* in *Corruption: The Enemy Within* 343, 345 (Barry Rider ed., 1997).

11. *See, e.g., Bracy v. Gramley,* 81 F.3d 684, 702 (7th Cir. 1996), *rev'd,* 520 U.S. 899 (1997) (Rovner, J., dissenting); Edward A. Gargan, *Corruption's Many Tentacles Are Choking India's Growth,* N.Y. Times, Nov. 10, 1992, at A1 (quoting former attorney general of India); Fin. Times, Sept. 16, 1977, at 15 (quoting president of the World Bank).

12. *See, e.g.,* Yufan Hao & Michael Johnston, *Corruption and the Future of Economic Reform in China,* in *Political Corruption: Concepts & Contexts, supra* note 8, at 583, 584 (quoting former Chinese Communist Party chief Jiang Zemin).

13. William Ian Miller, *The Anatomy of Disgust* (1997).

14. *Id.* at 50.

15. *See id.* at 180.

16. *Id.*

17. *Id.* at 2.

18. *Id.* Compare Sharon Lamb, *The Psychology of Condemnation: Underlying Emotions and Their Symbolic Expression in Condemning and Shaming,* 68 Brook. L. Rev. 929, 931 (2003) ("Condemnation serves a social function, communicating to members of society that we don't do that (whatever the transgression might be)—that we abhor that act, that way of thinking and that lack of feeling that may have led to the transgression.").

19. *See, e.g.*, Brooks, *supra* note 1, at 57.

20. Compare Lamb, *supra* note 18, at 941 (Sex offenders are people who "evoke a fear of our own sexuality, a fear that it will spiral out of control or that it can be disgusting and ill-placed. In over-punishing sex offenders, in creating monsters, we differentiate us from them and ease our self-conscious fears about our own sexuality.").

21. *See* Chapter 2.

22. *See* Miller, *supra* note 13, at 115 ("[V]iolators of deeply held norms populate our myths, books, and movies, either as gods or as criminals.").

23. *See* Rorty, *supra* note 9, at 282–283 ("There are many ways to go wrong. Corruption covers a large scope: it can be expressed in nuance of speech and gesture as well as in overt behavior. It can be a trivial departure from what an otherwise relatively decent and civilized person normally does. . . . It can happen suddenly or gradually, imperceptively. . . . It can begin with the perception of an injury or threat; or with a vision of what seems a tantalizing good.").

24. Miller, *supra* note 13, at 202.

25. *Id.*

26. *Id.*

27. Martha C. Nussbaum, *"Secret Sewers of Vice": Disgust, Bodies, and the Law*, in *The Passions of Law* 19, 22 (Susan A. Bandes ed., 1999).

28. *See id.* at 27.

29. *Id.* at 51. *See also* Toni M. Massaro, *Show (Some) Emotions*, in *The Passions of Law*, *supra* note 27, at 80, 96 (Emotions of disgust—of a reflexive nature, to contaminants and pollutants—are linked by humans "to other, metaphorical forms of 'contamination' and 'poisoning.' These links may include associating other humans, sometimes entire groups of them, with the feeling of disgust and treating these others as objects—specifically, as objects comparable to disgusting contaminants. . . . It can lead to the actual expelling and casting aside of what is labeled disgusting, without much reflection on the fact that the offensive object actually is *not* bad . . . and thus poses no *literal* peril. . . .") (emphasis in original).

30. *See* Massaro, *supra* note 29, at 97 ("Reference to our feelings of disgust over an act . . . is simply another way of referring to whatever experiences and norms have given this emotion its cognitive content. . . .").

31. Nussbaum, *supra* note 27, at 32. *See also id.* at 50, 51 (Disgust and like emotions "place[] the murderer in a class of heinous monsters more or less outside the boundaries of our moral universe. . . . We . . . tell ourselves that the doers of heinous wrongs are monsters, in no way like ourselves.").

32. *See, e.g.,* Lucy Koechlin & Magdelena Sepúlveda Carmona, *Corruption and Human Rights: Exploring the Connection,* in *Corruption, Global Security, and World Order* 310 (Robert I. Rotberg ed., 2009).

33. Massaro, *supra* note 29, at 103.

34. Jeffrie G. Murphy, *Moral Epistemology, the Retributive Emotions, and the "Clumsy Moral Philosophy" of Jesus Christ,* in *The Passions of Law, supra* note 27, at 149, 158–159.

35. *See, e.g.,* Robert H. Frank, *The Strategic Role of the Emotions: Reconciling Over- and Undersocialized Accounts of Behavior,* 5 Rationality & Soc'y 160 (1993); Kent Oatley, *Best Laid Schemes: The Psychology of Emotions* 130–177 (1992); Ronald de Sousa, *The Rationality of Emotion* (1987).

36. *See* Susan A. Bandes, *Introduction,* in *The Passions of Law, supra* note 27, at 1, 6–7. *See also* Robert Solomon, *Passions* (1976) (arguing that emotion is a necessary part of how human beings live their lives).

37. Massaro, *supra* note 29, at 104.

38. Examples that immediately come to mind include religious persecution in all eras; the persecution of "witches" in seventeenth-century England and the American colonies; the later-discredited child molestation prosecutions in the United States in the 1980s; and others.

39. Massaro, *supra* note 29, at 98 (footnote omitted).

40. See Kim Long, *The Almanac of Political Corruption, Scandals, and Dirty Politics* 83 (2007).

41. Georgia Weekly Telegraph, Aug. 15, 1876, at 4 (quoted in Long, *supra* note 40, at 83–84).

42. Long, *supra* note 40, at 90.

43. *See id.*

44. *Id.* at 91.

45. One of the most famous was Albert Alonzo Ames (1842–1911), mayor of Minneapolis, who fled the city—with his brother, who was the chief of police—when corruption charges loomed. They were tracked to New Hampshire and arrested. "His defense to a charge of bribery rested primarily on his claim that health problems affected his sanity. . . . Found guilty at trial, he was sentenced to six years of hard labor, but before he began serving time, the state supreme court reversed the original indictment. He was tried a few more times on the original charge, but each trial resulted in a hung jury." Long, *supra* note 40, at 123–124. Other prosecutions with strong evidence but hung juries included those in the trials of Sidney Johnston Catts (1863–1936), Baptist minister and governor of Florida, prosecuted for peonage and counterfeiting; John Warren Davis (1867–1945), New York state judge, prosecuted for taking payoffs to fix cases; and Daniel John Flood (1903–1994), U.S. representative from Pennsylvania, prosecuted for conspiracy, bribery, and perjury. *See id.* at 143–144, 183, 246–247.

46. *See, e.g.,* American Law Institute, *Model Penal Code* § 2.01(1) (1962).

47. *See, e.g., State v. Thompson,* 558 P.2d 202 (Wash. 1977); *Dishman v. State,* 721 A.2d 699 (Md. 1998).

48. *See* Wayne R. LaFave, *Criminal Law* 211 (3rd ed. 2000).

49. *See* Chapter 2.

50. *See* Chapter 3.

51. *See* David M. Halperin, *One Hundred Years of Homosexuality* 15 (1990).

52. *Id.* at 15.

53. *Id.* at 16.

54. *See id.* at 8–16.

55. *Id.* at 17.

56. *Id.* at 8.

57. *See id.* at 16–17.

58. *See id.* at 24.

59. *Id.* at 24–25.

60. *Id.* at 26.

61. *Id.*

62. *Id.* at 26 (footnote omitted).

63. *Id.* (footnote omitted).

64. *See id.*

65. *Id.* at 43 (emphasis deleted).

66. *Id.* at 26.

67. *Id.* at 9.

68. Wilmer Parker III, *Every Person Has a Price?,* in *Corruption: The Enemy Within, supra* note 10, at 87, 102.

69. Halperin, *supra* note 51, at 43.

70. *See, e.g.*, Arnold J. Heidenheimer, *The Context of Analysis*, in *Political Corruption: Readings in Comparative Analysis, supra* note 1, at 3, 4; Alatas, *supra* note 8, at 13–36.

71. Halperin, *supra* note 51, at 26.

72. *Id.*

73. Laura S. Underkuffler, *Agentic and Conscientic Decisions in Law: Death and Other Cases*, 74 Notre Dame L. Rev. 1713, 1734 (1999). *See also* Lamb, *supra* note 18, at 933 ("Moral outrage and punitiveness are the response[s] to . . . incursions [onto a community's sacred values], followed by attempts to cleanse the community by distancing oneself from the offender and the offense.").

74. Criminal punishment for homosexuality is a contemporary reality in many parts of the world. *See, e.g.*, Jeffrey Gettleman, *Americans' Role Seen in Uganda Anti-Gay Push*, N.Y. Times, Jan. 4, 2010 (discussing proposed death penalty in Uganda and existing death penalties in parts of Nigeria, Iran, and Yemen).

75. *See* Nussbaum, *supra* note 27, at 22 (the loss of humanity that this view involves has been "at the root of gross evils throughout history").

76. *See, e.g.*, Massaro, *supra* note 29, at 96.

77. *Id.* at 103.

78. *Id.* (emphasis deleted).

79. "Corruption of Blood is when any one is attainted of Felony or Treason, then his Blood is said to be corrupt; by means whereof neither his Children, nor any of his Blood, can be Heirs to him, or to any other Ancestor, for that they ought to claim by him. And if he were Noble or Gentleman before, he and all his children are thereby made ignoble and ungentle." John Rastell, *Termes de la Ley: or, Certain difficult and obscure Words and Terms of the Common and Statute Laws of this Realm . . .*, 189 (1721).

80. Most famously, see Hannah Arendt, *Thinking and Moral Considerations: A Lecture*, 38 Soc. Res. 417 (1971); Hannah Arendt, *Eichmann in Jerusalem* (1963).

81. *Cf.* Nussbaum, *supra* note 27, at 52 ("If jurors are led to think that evil is done by monsters who were just born different, . . . freaky and inhuman, they will be prevented from having thoughts about themselves and their own society that are highly pertinent, not only to the equal and principled application of the law but also to the construction of a society in which less evil will exist.").

82. U.S.C. § 201(b)(1)(A) (2006) (emphasis added). Such persons "shall be fined under this title . . . not more than three times the monetary equivalent of the things of value, . . . or imprisoned for not more than fifteen years, or both." 18 U.S.C. § 201(b)(4) (2006).

83. *See, e.g.*, 18 U.S.C. § 201(c) (2006) ("Whoever . . . gives, offers, or promises *anything of value* to any public official . . . for or because of any official act performed or to be performed by such public official" shall be fined or imprisoned for not more than two years, or both.) (emphasis added). There is no mention of intent to influence in this statute, and no reference to corruption.

84. Compare, for instance, the Foreign Corrupt Practices Act, 15 U.S.C. § 78dd-2(a) (2006) (Any officer, director, employee, or agent of a domestic concern who *"corruptly* . . . offer[s], pay[s], promise[s] to pay, or authori[zes] . . . the payment of *any* money, or offer, gift, promise to give, or authorization of the giving of *anything* of value" to influence a foreign official in his official capacity shall be fined no more than $100,000 or imprisoned not more than five years, or both.) (emphasis added). For a comparison of U.S. law and that of other countries, *see* W. Paatii Ofosu-Amaah, Raj Soopramanien, & Kishor Uprety, *Combating Corruption: A Comparative Review of Selected Legal Aspects of State Practice and Major International Initiatives* 47–48 (1999).

Interestingly, only one federal statute of this type expressly calibrates lesser punishment to smaller bribes. This is the statute prohibiting the "corrupt" giving of commissions or gifts to officers of financial institutions in loan transactions. *See* 18 U.S.C. § 215(a)(1), (2) (2006). The offender "shall be fined not more than $1,000,000 or three times the value of the thing given, offered, . . . solicited, . . . [or] accepted . . ., whichever is greater, or imprisoned not more than 30 years, or both"; "but if the value of the thing given, offered, . . . solicited, [or] accepted . . . does not exceed $1,000, [he] shall be fined . . . or imprisoned not more than one year, or both." *See id.*

85. *See* 18 U.S.C. § 201(b)(1) (2006) (emphasis added) (general federal bribery statute).

86. *See* John G. Peters & Susan Welch, *Gradients of Corruption in Perceptions of American Public Life*, in *Political Corruption: Concepts & Contexts, supra* note 8, at 155.

87. *See id.* at 160–161, 165.

88. *See id.* at 168.

89. *See* Heidenheimer, *supra* note 70, at 26–27.

90. *See* text at notes 82–84, *supra.*

91. *See, e.g., United States v. North*, 910 F.2d at 881 (interpreting 18 U.S.C. § 1505) ("'corruptly' [as used in criminal law] is the adverbial form of the adjective 'corrupt,' which means 'depraved, evil: perverted into a state of moral weakness or wickedness'"); *United States v. Jacobs*, 431 F.2d 754, 759 (2d Cir. 1970), *cert. denied*, 402 U.S. 950 (1971) (interpreting 18 U.S.C. § 201(b)) (corruption involves "perfidious" conduct); *Arthur Anderson LLP v. United States*, 544 U.S. 696, 705 (2005) (interpreting 18 U.S.C. § 1512(b)) (corruption involves "depravity," "evil").

92. *United States v. Poindexter*, 951 F.2d 369, 378 (D.C. Cir. 1991), *cert. denied*, 506 U.S. 1021 (1992) (quoting *Ricks v. District of Columbia*, 414 F.2d 1097, 1106–1107 (D.C. Cir. 1968)).

93. *See* Underkuffler, *supra* note 73.

94. *Id.* at 1714.

95. *Id.*

96. *Id.* at 1714–1715.

97. *Id.* at 1715. For a discussion of this issue in the general context of criminal law, *see* Kenneth W. Simons, *Does Punishment for "Culpable Indifference" Simply Punish for "Bad Character"? Examining the Requisite Connection between Mens Rea and Actus Reus*, 6 Buff. Crim. L. Rev. 219, 302–306 (2002).

98. Underkuffler, *supra* note 73, at 1715.

99. *See id.* at 1719 (footnote omitted).

100. *See id.* (emphasis in original).

101. *Id.*

102. *See* Chapter 3.

103. *See* Stephen Hutcheon, *Eighteen to Face Court Charges over $3 Billion Beijing Fraud*, Sydney Morning Herald, Apr. 4, 1996, at 10.

104. *See* N. R. Kleinfield, *Chinatown Officers Said to Forge a Partnership of Vice and Greed*, N.Y. Times, June 19, 1995, at A1.

105. *See* Ruth Marcus, *Cunningham's Enablers*, Wash. Post, Feb. 28, 2006.

106. *See* Parker, *supra* note 68, at 102.

107. *See United States ex. rel. Collins v. Welborn*, 79 F. Supp.2d at 906.

108. *See, e.g.*, David H. Bayley, *The Effects of Corruption in a Developing Nation*, in *Political Corruption: Readings in Comparative Analysis, supra* note 1, at 521, 526; M. McMullan, *Corruption in the Public Services of British Colonies and Ex-Colonies in West Africa*, in *Political Corruption: Readings in Comparative*

Analysis, supra, at 317, 318 ("Corruption in the government involves the ultimate transfer of public funds to the pockets of politicians or officials. The businessman who has to bribe to get a government contract ultimately charges the bribe to public funds."). It has been estimated that in countries where corrupt procurement practices prevail, governments pay from 20 to 100 percent more for goods and services than they would pay under noncorrupt conditions. *See* Robert Klitgaard, *Controlling Corruption* 39 (1988).

109. Klitgaard, *supra* note 108, at 44. *See also* Gunnar Myrdal, *Corruption: Its Causes and Effects,* in *Political Corruption: Readings in Comparative Analysis, supra* note 1, at 540, 541 (quoting Government of India, Ministry of Home Affairs, *Report of the Committee on Prevention of Corruption* 44 (1964) ("Santhanam Committee Report")) (" '[A]dministrative delays are one of the major causes of corruption. . . . [Q]uite often delay is deliberately contrived so as to obtain some kind of illicit gratification.' ").

110. Ledivina V. Cariño & Josie H. deLeon, *Final Report for the Study of Graft and Corruption, Red Tape, and Inefficiency in Government* (Report for the President's Center for Special Studies, Manila, 1983), at 2 (quoted in Klitgaard, *supra* note 108, at 38).

111. *See* Klitgaard, *supra* note 108, at 40–41; McMullan, *supra* note 108, at 317–318.

112. Klitgaard, *supra* note 108, at 41.

113. *See* McMullan, *supra* note 108, at 328 (corruption acts as "an emollient, softening conflict and reducing friction"); Samuel P. Huntington, *Modernization and Corruption,* in *Political Corruption: Readings in Comparative Analysis, supra* note 1, at 492, 499 (corruption is "a welcome lubricant"); J. S. Nye, *Corruption and Political Development: A Cost-Benefit Analysis,* in *Political Corruption: Readings in Comparative Analysis, supra,* at 564, 569 (corruption is a "glue").

114. *See, e.g.,* Huntington, *supra* note 113, at 498 ("Corruption may be one way of surmounting traditional laws or bureaucratic regulations which hamper economic expansion."); Nathaniel H. Leff, *Economic Development through Bureaucratic Corruption,* in *Political Corruption: Readings in Comparative Analysis, supra* note 1, at 510, 514 (graft "can induce the government to take a more favorable view of activities that would further economic growth"; it can "provide the direct incentive necessary to mobilize the bureaucracy for more energetic action on behalf of the entrepreneurs").

115. *See, e.g.,* Peter Eigen, *A Coalition to Combat Corruption: TI, EITI, and Civil Society,* in *Corruption, Global Security, and World Order, supra* note 32, at 416 (discussing anticorruption efforts of the World Bank, United Nations, Transparency International, and others).

116. *See, e.g.,* Pranab Bardhan, *Corruption and Development: A Review of the Issues,* 35 J. Econ. Lit. 1320, 1327–1330 (1997); Michael Johnston, *Syndromes of Corruption: Wealth, Power, and Democracy* 18 (2005); Susan Rose-Ackerman, *Corruption and Government: Causes, Consequences, and Reform* 3, 22–23 (1999).

117. *See* Robert I. Rotberg, *How Corruption Compromises World Peace and Stability,* in *Corruption, Global Security, and World Order, supra* note 32, at 1, 4 (discussing how "the moral fabric of any society is rent . . . [by] corruption"). *See also* Myrdal, *supra* note 109, at 238 (conditions for corruption include "stronger loyalty to less inclusive groups—family, caste, ethnic, religious, or linguistic 'community' . . ., and class," rather than to "the community as a whole, whether on the local or the national level").

118. Edward C. Banfield, *The Moral Basis of a Backward Society,* in *Political Corruption: Readings in Comparative Analysis, supra* note 1, at 129, 129 (emphasis deleted).

119. *Id.*

120. *Id.* at 133.

121. *See id.* at 131. *See also* Jeremy Boissevain, *Patronage in Sicily,* in *Political Corruption: Readings in Comparative Analysis, supra* note 1, at 138, 139 (in heavily patronage-dependent communities in Sicily, "[t]he central institution of . . . society is the nuclear family"; "[t]he rights and obligations which derive from membership in it provide the individual with his basic moral code." "Other values and organisational principles are of secondary importance.").

122. *See* Banfield, *supra* note 118, at 131. *See also* Ledivina V. Cariño, *Tonic or Toxic: The Effects of Graft and Corruption,* in *Bureaucratic Corruption in Asia: Causes, Consequences, and Controls* 163, 178 (Ledivina V. Cariño ed., 1986); Colin Leys, *What Is the Problem about Corruption?,* in *Political Corruption: Readings in Comparative Analysis, supra* note 1, at 31, 34.

123. *See, e.g.,* Bayley, *supra* note 108, at 527 ("Corruption in government, perceived by the people, lowers respect for constituted authority. It undercuts popular faith in government to deal evenhandedly.").

124. H. A. Brasz, *Administrative Corruption in Theory and Dutch Practice*, in *Political Corruption: Readings in Comparative Analysis, supra* note 1, at 243, 248. *See also* Gunnar Myrdal, *Corruption as a Hindrance to Modernization in South Asia*, in *Political Corruption: Readings in Comparative Analysis, supra*, at 229, 231–232 (describing the "folklore of corruption," which exaggerates the prevalence of corruption and encourages others to become corrupt).

125. For studies that associate corruption with political instability and regime change, *see, e.g.*, Michael Nacht, *Internal Change and Regime Stability*, in *Adelphi Papers No. 166: Third-World Conflict and International Security* 52 (1981); Klitgaard, *supra* note 108, at 45–46; McMullan, *supra* note 108, at 318; Sinnathamby Rajaratnam, *Bureaucracy versus Kleptocracy*, in *Political Corruption: Readings in Comparative Analysis, supra* note 1, at 546, 546–548.

126. *See, e.g.*, Rajaratnam, *supra* note 125, at 548.

127. Myrdal, *supra* note 124, at 229.

128. *See* Klitgaard, *supra* note 108, at 44–46.

129. *See, e.g.*, Huntington, *supra* note 113, at 493 ("Corruption may be the means of assimilating new groups into the political system by irregular means. . . ."); Walter Lippmann, *A Theory about Corruption*, in *Political Corruption: Readings in Comparative Analysis, supra* note 1, at 294, 296–297 (arguing that corrupt political machines in the United States enabled newly arrived immigrant groups to achieve political participation and influence); V. O. Key Jr., *Techniques of Political Graft*, in *Political Corruption: Readings in Comparative Analysis, supra*, at 46, 51 ("The patronage system [in the United States] has served, and still serves, as the principal method of consolidating into a cohesive mass the politically effective sector of the population."); Leff, *supra* note 114, at 512 (arguing that in underdeveloped countries, "graft may be the only institution allowing [out-of-power groups] . . . to achieve articulation and representation in the political process").

130. *See, e.g.*, Bayley, *supra* note 108, at 530–531; José Veloso Abueva, *The Contribution of Nepotism, Spoils, and Graft to Political Development*, in *Political Corruption: Readings in Comparative Analysis, supra* note 1, at 534, 534.

131. *See* Abueva, *supra* note 130, at 534.

132. Lippmann, *supra* note 129, at 294, 297. For instance, Lippmann continues, "I once heard the President of a Latin-American Republic explain that he was consolidating his regime at home by making ambassadors, with extra-large grants for expenses, out of his most dangerous political enemies. It had been the custom to shoot them." *Id.*

133. C. Raj Kumar, *Corruption and Human Rights in India: Comparative Perspectives on Transparency and Good Governance* 32–33 (2011).

134. Michael M. Calavan, Sergio Diaz Briquets, & Jerald O'Brien, *Cambodian Corruption Assessment* 3 (2004), available at http://www.usaid .gov/kh/democracy_and_governance/documents/Cambodian_Corruption_ Assessment.pdf (last visited Sept. 17, 2011) (quoted in Kumar, *supra* note 133, at 41).

135. *See* Kumar, *supra* note 133, at 42–43, 53–58.

136. *See* Rajaratnam, *supra* note 125, at 547–548.

137. *Id.* at 547.

138. *Id.* at 548.

139. Hartmut Schweitzer, *Corruption—Its Spread and Decline*, in *The New Institutional Economics of Corruption* 16, 36 (Johann Graf Lambsdorff, Markus Taube, & Matthias Schramm eds., 2005).

140. Larry Rohter & Juan Forero, *Unending Graft Is Threatening Latin America*, N.Y. Times, July 30, 2005, at A1.

141. *See, e.g.*, Robert Legvold, *Corruption, the Criminalized State, and Post-Soviet Transitions*, in *Corruption, Global Security, and World Order, supra* note 32, at 194, 195.

142. *See id.*

143. *See id.*

144. *See* Chapter 2.

145. For instance, as Jean-François Bayart described the problem of corruption in postcolonial Africa, "It would be a grave error to see all of these [corrupt] dealings simply as the corruption of the State. They are, conversely, the State's fabric." Jean-François Bayart, *The State in Africa: The Politics of the Belly* 89 (1993). *See also* Daniel Jordan Smith, *The Paradoxes of Popular Participation in Corruption in Nigeria*, in *Corruption, Global Security, and World Order, supra* note 32, at 283.

146. Jim Yardley, *The Chinese Go After Corruption, Corruptly*, N.Y. Times, Oct. 22, 2006, at BW 3.

147. Kelly M. Greenhill, *Kleptocratic Interdependence: Trafficking, Corruption, and the Marriage of Politics and Illicit Profits*, in *Corruption, Global Security, and World Order, supra* note 32, at 96, 100.

148. For instance, as Greenhill writes, "it would be misleading to call Russia corrupt. Corruption is what happens 'when businessmen offer officials large bribes for favors. Today's Russia is unique. The businessmen, the politicians, and the bureaucrats are the same people. They have privatized the country's wealth and taken control of its financial flows.'" *Id.* at 102 (quoting Andrei Piontkovsky).

149. Dennis F. Thompson, *Ethics in Congress: From Individual to Institutional Corruption* 28 (1995).

150. *United States v. Fenster*, 449 F. Supp. 435, 438 (E.D. Mich. 1978).

CHAPTER 6. COSTS AND BENEFITS EXAMINED

1. *See* Kareem Fahim, *Seeking Free Home, Ex-Legislator Will Get a Prison Cell Instead*, N.Y. Times, June 13, 2008, at C9.

2. *See id.*

3. *See id.*

4. Andy Newman, *Videotape at Trial Shows Legislator Discussing Deal*, N.Y. Times, Mar. 14, 2008.

5. *See* Fahim, *supra* note 1.

6. *See id.*; Newman, *supra* note 4.

7. *See* Michael Brick, *Brooklyn Legislator Charged with Taking Bribes to Aid Land Deal*, N.Y. Times, July 11, 2006.

8. *See* Fahim, *supra* note 1.

9. *Id.*

10. *Id.*

11. *Id.*

12. *See id.*

13. *Blagojevich Arrested on Federal Charges*, Dec. 9, 2008, articles .www.chicagobreakingnews.com/2008-12-09/news/28512776_1_political -corruption-crime-spree-pat-quinn-arrest (last visited Aug. 6, 2012).

14. Peter Slevin, *Barbs? Charges? Tapes? Blagojevich Sees Lies! Lies! Lies!*, Wash. Post, Sept. 9, 2009.

15. Monica Davey & Jack Healy, *Illinois Governor Charged in Scheme to Sell Obama's Seat*, N.Y. Times, Dec. 9, 2008.

16. *Id.*

17. Monica Davey, *Top Blagojevich Aide Pleads Guilty to Fraud*, N.Y. Times, July 9, 2009, at A18.

18. *Id.*

19. *Id.*

20. Slevin, *supra* note 14.

21. Mark Silva, *Blagojevich "Corrupt" Cloud over Illinois: Reid,* Jan. 4, 2009, www.swamppolitics.com/news/politics/blog/2009/01/blagojevich_corrupt_cloud_over.html (last visited Aug 6, 2012).

22. *Id.*

23. *See* Mike Dorning & Monique Garcia, *Senate Official Rejects Burris Paperwork,* Jan. 5, 2009, www.swamppolitics.com/news/politics/blog/2009/01/senate_secretary_rejects_burri.html (last visited Aug. 6, 2012).

24. Monica Davey & Susan Saulny, *Blagojevich Charged with 16 Corruption Felonies,* N.Y. Times, Apr. 3, 2009.

25. See Natasha Korecki, Chris Fusco, Dave McKinney, & Abdon Pallasch, *Blagojevich, Brother among Six Indicted,* Chi. Sun-Times, Apr. 3, 2009.

26. *Id.*

27. *Id.*

28. Davey & Saulny, *supra* note 24.

29. *See* Korecki et al., *supra* note 25.

30. The show was described as "a survival-style reality show" that featured "a 'Swiss Family Robinson'–type [of] competition in which 10 celebrities are dropped into the heart of the jungle 'to face fun and comedic challenges designed to test their survival skills.' American viewers decide which celebrities go, in addition to selecting the challenges used to earn food, supplies, and luxury items. The last celeb left is crowned King or Queen of the Jungle." Stacy St. Clair, *Former Gov. Rod Blagojevich Hoping to Appear on Reality Show,* Chi. Trib., Apr. 15, 2009.

The federal judge assigned to his case later rejected Blagojevich's travel request. "The judge denied the request even after NBC offered to hire two court-selected security guards to watch over Blagojevich while he filmed the show in Costa Rica." "Upon leaving the courthouse, Blagojevich said of the judge's denial: 'It's another day in the city.'" Natasha Korecki, *Judge Says "No" to Rod Blagojevich Reality Show,* Chi. Sun-Times, Apr. 21, 2009. "His wife, Patricia Blagojevich, went in his place, trying to garner sympathy for her husband's case while taking part in competitions in which she ate a tarantula and crawled through a mud pit." Emma Graves Fitzsimmons, *Lawyers Worry Blagojevich TV Role Will Taint Jury,* N.Y. Times, Oct. 20, 2009, at A19.

31. Jeff Coen & Lauren R. Harrison, *Rod Blagojevich: Former Governor Pleads Not Guilty at His Arraignment,* Chi. Trib., Apr. 15, 2009.

32. *See* Davey, *supra* note 17.

33. *See* Emma Graves Fitzsimmons, *Suicide of Fund-Raiser for Blagojevich Is Reported*, N.Y. Times, Sept. 16, 2009.

34. Judy Keen, *Blagojevich Book Offers His Side*, USA Today, Sept. 8, 2009.

35. *Id.*

36. Rod Blagojevich, *The Governor* (2009). Perhaps aptly published by Phoenix Books, *The Governor* enjoyed a three-and-a-half-star rating on Amazon.com after twenty-one reviews. It is available through Amazon in Kindle Edition, Hardcover, Audio, CD, Audiobook, and electronic Audio Download. *See* http://www.amazon.com/Governor-Rod-Blagojevich/dp /B006LWELLO/ref=sr_1_3?s=books&ie=UTF8&qid=1345563622&sr= 1-3&keywords=Blagojevich (last visited Aug. 21, 2012).

37. Monica Davey, *Ex-Illinois Governor Adds Author to His Resume*, N.Y. Times, Sept. 7, 2009.

38. *See* Fitzsimmons, *supra* note 30.

39. *Id.*

40. *Id.*

41. *Id.*

42. *See id.*

43. Keen, *supra* note 34.

44. Michael Tarm & Mike Robinson, *Blagojevich Corruption Trial Begins in Chicago*, Associated Press, June 8, 2010.

45. Monica Davey, *Blagojevich Was Led Astray, Lawyer Tells Jurors*, N.Y. Times, June 9, 2010, at A12.

46. *Id.* (quoting Blagojevich's lawyer).

47. Associated Press, *Blagojevich Team Plotted to Make Cash, Ex-aide Says*, USA Today, June 10, 2010.

48. *Id.*

49. Stacy St. Clair, *Blago's Lawyer Calls Ex-Governor Foolish But Not Corrupt*, Chi. Trib., July 27, 2010.

50. *Id.*

51. *Id.*

52. Natasha Korecki, Dave McKinney, & Sarah Ostman, *Blagojevich Defense Gives Theatrical Closing Argument*, Chi. Sun-Times, July 28, 2010.

53. *Editorial, Blagojevich 23, Fitzgerald 1*, Wall St. J., Aug. 19, 2010.

54. Suzanne Vranica, *Blago, Snooki to Pitch for Pistachios*, Chi. Trib., Nov. 1, 2010.

55. Natasha Korecki, *Rod Blagojevich Goes Nuts*, Chi. Sun-Times, Nov. 1, 2010.

56. Monica Davey & Emma G. Fitzsimmons, *Jury Finds Blagojevich Guilty of Corruption*, N.Y. Times, June 27, 2011.

57. *Id.*

58. *See United States v. Siegelman*, 561 F.3d 1215, 1220–1222 (11th Cir. 2009), *vacated sub nom. Siegelman v. United States*, 130 S.Ct. 3542 (2010); Kyle Whitmire, *Trial Begins for Former Alabama Governor*, N.Y. Times, May 2, 2006.

59. *See* Whitmire, *supra* note 58.

60. *See* Carrie Johnson, *Jury Acquits HealthSouth Founder of All Charges*, Wash. Post, June 29, 2005.

61. *See* Lawrence Viele Davidson, *HealthSouth Founder Scrushy Gets 6 Years, 10 Months for Bribery*, June 28, 2007, www.bloomberg.com/apps /news/news?pid=newsarchive&sid=avxz5qL9ZglA&refer=home (last visited Aug. 7, 2012).

62. Michael Kinsley, *The Lord and Richard Scrushy*, Wash. Post, July 3, 2005.

63. *See* Brian Grow, *Richard Scrushy's "Amen Corner,"* Bus. Wk., Jan. 20, 2006. *See also* Greg Farrell, *Former HealthSouth CEO Scrushy Turns Televangelist*, USA Today, Oct. 25, 2004.

64. Kinsley, *supra* note 62.

65. *See Siegelman*, 561 F.3d at 1223.

66. Kyle Whitmire, *Former Governor Convicted With Ex-Chief of HealthSouth*, N.Y. Times, June 30, 2006.

67. Adam Zagorin, *Rove Named in Alabama Controversy*, Time Mag., June 1, 2007.

68. *See Transcript of Interview of: Dana Jill Simpson, before the U.S. House of Representatives, Committee on the Judiciary*, Sept. 14, 2007, Wash., D.C.

69. *See* Zagorin, *supra* note 67.

70. *Transcript, supra* note 68, at 23.

71. *See id.* at 23–24.

72. *Id.* at 25–27.

73. *See id.* at 27.

74. *See id.* at 47.

75. *Id.* at 48.

76. *See id.* at 49.

77. *Id.* at 50–51.

78. *Id.* at 85.

79. *See id.* at 62–65, 79–84.

80. Zagorin, *supra* note 67.

81. *Siegelman*, 561 F.3d at 1244–1245.

82. *See United States v. Siegelman*, No. 2:05-CR-119 MEF, 2008 WL 45531, at 7 n.11 (M.D. Ala. Jan. 2, 2008).

83. *Editorial*, N.Y. Times, Aug. 6, 2007.

84. *Id.*

85. Adam Cohen, *The Strange Case of an Imprisoned Alabama Governor*, N.Y. Times, Sept. 10, 2007.

86. *See* Scott Horton, *CBS: More Prosecutorial Misconduct in the Siegelman Case*, Harper's, Feb. 24, 2008; *Did Ex-Alabama Governor Get a Raw Deal?*, CBS News, Feb. 24, 2008.

87. Horton, *supra* note 86. As one commentator has explained: "Patronage involves personal relationships of exchange characterised by inequality, reciprocity and personal contacts. In the political context it involves payoffs for favours and support. . . . Is patronage then a form of corruption? In the strictest sense, the answer would seem to be affirmative. . . . But such a conclusion would necessarily label a substantial proportion of political activity as corrupt." Morris Szeftel, *Corruption and the Spoils System in Zambia*, in *Corruption: Causes, Consequences and Controls* 163, 166 (Michael Clarke ed., 1983).

88. Horton, *supra* note 86.

89. *See Siegelman*, 561 F.3d at 1245. Scrushy's convictions and sentence were affirmed.

90. *See* John Schwartz, *Ex-Governor of Alabama Loses Again in Court*, N.Y. Times, May 16, 2009, at A9.

91. 130 S.Ct. 2896 (2010).

92. *See* 18 U.S.C. §§ 1341, 1346 (2006) (it is a crime to use the mails "to deprive another of the intangible right of honest services").

93. *See Skilling*, 130 S.Ct. at 2931.

94. *United States v. Siegelman*, 640 F.3d 1159 (11th Cir. 2011).

95. *See id.* at 1165.

96. Danny Hakim & William K. Rashbaum, *Spitzer, Linked to a Sex Ring as a Client, Gives an Apology*, N.Y. Times, Mar. 11, 2008, at A1.

97. *See id.*

98. *See id.*

99. William K. Rashbaum, *Revelations about Governor Began in Routine Tax Inquiry*, N.Y. Times, Mar. 11, 2008, at A1.

100. *See id. See also* David Johnston & Stephen Labaton, *The Reports That Drew Federal Eyes to Spitzer*, N.Y. Times, Mar. 12, 2008, at B1.

101. *See* Danny Hakim & Don Van Natta Jr., *U.S. Is Examining Spitzer's Funds*, N.Y. Times, Mar. 14, 2008, at A1.

102. *See* Johnston & Labaton, *supra* note 100.

103. David Kocieniewski & Danny Hakim, *Spitzer Resigns in Sex Scandal and Turns His Attention to Healing His Family*, N.Y. Times, Mar. 13, 2008, at A1.

104. Hakim & Rashbam, *supra* note 96.

105. *Id.*

106. *Id.*

107. *Id.*

108. Kocieniewski & Hakim, *supra* note 103.

109. *The Governor's Resignation Speech*, N.Y. Times, Mar. 13, 2008, at A20.

110. *Id.*

111. *Id.*

112. *See* N.Y. Times, Mar. 13, 2008, at A24.

113. Manny Fernandez, *Lamenting a Lost Trust, and Lost Opportunities*, N.Y. Times, Mar. 13, 2008, at B4.

114. *Id.*

115. *See* Ellen Goodman, *Editorial*, Boston Globe, Mar. 15, 2008.

116. *See* Susan Dominus, *Emperor's Club Sold as an Oxymoron: High-Class Prostitution*, N.Y. Times, Mar. 14, 2008, at B1.

117. Alex Williams, *I Agree, Dear, It Was Awful*, N.Y. Times, Mar. 16, 2008, at A8.

118. Natalie Angier, *In Most Species, Faithfulness Is a Fantasy*, N.Y. Times, Mar. 18, 2008, at F1.

119. Jan Hoffman, *Public Infidelity, Private Debate: Not My Husband (Right?)*, N.Y. Times, Mar. 16, 2008, at A1.

120. *Id.*

121. Jonathan Darman, *Spitzer in Exile: When Your Résumé Says "Disgraced Ex-Governor," What Do You Do Next?*, Newsweek Mag., Apr. 20, 2009, at 20, 22.

122. *See* Glenn Coin, *Can Spitzer Mend His Image? He's Back in the Public Eye, Including a Speech at SU Today, but His Scandalous Fall from Grace Still Shadows Him,* Syr. Post-Standard, Feb. 11, 2010, at A1.

123. This name is spelled "Bracy" in some court records and "Bracey" in others. To avoid confusion, I shall use "Bracy" throughout.

124. *See People v. Collins,* 478 N.E.2d 267, 272 (Ill.), *cert. denied,* 474 U.S. 935 (1985).

125. *See id.*

126. *See People v. Hooper,* 552 N.E.2d 684 (Ill. 1989), *cert. denied,* 498 U.S. 911 (1990).

127. *See Collins,* 478 N.E.2d at 272.

128. *See id.* "In fact, [Nellum] received only two and a half years . . . of probation, not prison." *Bracy v. Gramley,* 81 F.3d 684, 687 (7th Cir. 1996), *rev'd,* 520 U.S. 899 (1997).

129. *See Collins,* 478 N.E.2d at 272.

130. *See id.* at 272–273.

131. *See id.* at 273.

132. *See id.*

133. *See id.*

134. *See id.*

135. *See id.*

136. *See id.* at 273–274.

137. *See id.* at 274.

138. *See id.*

139. *Id.* at 276.

140. *Id.* at 277.

141. *Id.*

142. *See id.* at 279–280.

143. *See id.* at 280–282.

144. *See id.* at 283.

145. *Id.* at 284.

146. *Id.*

147. *See id.* at 282.

148. *See id.* Two justices did not agree, arguing in dissent that the seating of this juror was plain error that required a new trial. *See id.* at 290.

149. *See id.* at 285–287.

150. *See id.* Certiorari was subsequently denied by the United States Supreme Court. *See Collins v. Illinois*, 474 U.S. 935 (1985).

151. *Collins*, 478 N.E.2d at 289.

152. *See United States v. Maloney*, 71 F.3d 645, 649, 652 (7th Cir. 1995), *cert. denied*, 519 U.S. 927 (1996).

153. *See id.; Bracy v. Gramley*, 520 U.S. 899, 901 (1997).

154. *See Maloney*, 71 F.3d at 650.

155. *Brief for the United States in United States v. Maloney*, No. 94–2779, 1995 WL 17064156 (May 23, 1995), at 1, 2.

156. *See Maloney*, 71 F.3d at 650.

157. "Tr." refers to the trial transcript in the case.

158. *Brief for the United States, supra* note 155, at 2.

159. *Id.*

160. *Id.* at 3.

161. *Id.* at 3–4 (footnote omitted).

162. *Id.* at 5–6.

163. *Id.* at 6 (footnotes omitted).

164. *Id.* at 7 (footnote omitted).

165. *Id.* at 7 n.6.

166. *Id.* at 7–8.

167. *Id.* at 8–9.

168. *Id.* at 10–11 (footnotes omitted).

169. *Id.* at 11.

170. *Id.* at 16.

171. *Id.* at 17.

172. *Id.* at 18 (footnote omitted). *See also People v. Hawkins*, 690 N.E.2d 999, 1001–1002 (Ill. 1998). In postconviction proceedings, initiated after Maloney was convicted on corruption charges, Hawkins and Fields were granted a new trial on the ground that "Maloney possessed and actively cultivated a personal, pecuniary interest in the outcome" of their cases, which denied them a fair trial. *Id.* at 1002–1004.

173. *Proffer of the Government's Evidence in Aggravation and Memorandum Supporting Consideration of Proffered Evidence*, in *United States v. Thomas J. Maloney & Robert McGee*, No. 91 CR 477-1 (June 2, 1994), at 3.

174. *Bracy*, 81 F.3d at 696 (Rovner, J., dissenting).

175. *See Sentencing Transcript, United States v. Thomas J. Maloney & Robert McGee*, No. 91 CR 477, 1994 WL 96673 (July 21, 1994), at 634.

176. *See Bracy*, 520 U.S. at 901.

177. *Bracy*, 81 F.3d at 689.

178. *Id.* at 697 (Rovner, J., dissenting).

179. *Transcript of Oral Argument, Bracy v. Gramley*, No. 96-6133, 1997 WL 189276 (April 14, 1997), at 32.

180. *Bracy*, 81 F.3d at 702 (Rovner, J., dissenting).

181. No. 95 C 5034, 2004 WL 609308 (N.D. Ill. Mar. 23, 2004).

182. *See id.* at 1; *Guest v. McCann*, 474 F.3d 926, 929 (7th Cir.), *cert. denied*, 552 U.S. 824 (2007).

183. *Page*, 2004 WL 609308, at 6.

184. *See id.* at 7.

185. *See id.*

186. *See id.* at 6.

187. *Id.* at 6–7.

188. *Id.* at 6.

189. *Id.* at 7 (emphasis in original).

190. No. 98 C 2415, 1999 WL 98340 (N.D. Ill. Feb. 19, 1999). To a similar effect, *see People v. Fair*, 738 N.E.2d 500, 504–506 (Ill. 2000) (requiring establishment of a "nexus" between the judge's corruption and the outcome of the convicted defendant's trial); *United States v. Lucas*, 89 F. Supp.2d 976, 980 (N.D. Ill. 1999) (convicted defendant must show " 'actual prejudice' as a result of the [judge's] alleged corruption"); *Commonwealth v. Shaw*, 580 A.2d 1379, 1381 (Pa. Super. Ct. 1990), *appeal denied*, 580 A.2d 1379 (Pa. 1991) (convicted defendant must "establish actual prejudice resulting from the trial judge's extrajudicial conduct" (acceptance of bribes in other cases)). *Cf. Cartalino v. Washington*, 122 F.3d 8, 10–11 (7th Cir. 1997) (evidence that a codefendant, tried at the same time and by the same judge, bribed the judge for lenient treatment "does not in and of itself establish the judge's lack of impartiality in the [nonbribing] defendant's trial"; however, the case was remanded for the development of further evidence that part of the deal was that the defendant would "take the fall").

191. *O'Sullivan*, 1999 WL 98340, at 4.

192. *See, e.g., Bracy*, 520 U.S. at 904–905.

193. *See, e.g., Cartalino*, 122 F.3d at 9–10.

194. Linda Greenhouse, *Justices Weigh How to Deal with Taint of Corrupt Judge*, N.Y. Times, Apr. 15, 1997, at A9.

195. *Id.*

196. *See Bracy*, 520 U.S. at 902.

197. *Transcript of Oral Argument, supra* note 179, at 4, 10, 20 (emphasis added).

198. *Id.* at 26.

199. *See Vasquez v. Hillery*, 474 U.S. 254, 263 (1986).

200. *Id.* (emphasis added).

201. *Bracy*, 81 F.3d at 688 (emphasis added).

202. *See id.* at 689.

203. *See U.S. ex rel. Collins v. Welborn*, 79 F. Supp.2d 898, 907 (N.D. Ill. 1999), *aff'd and rev'd in part sub nom. Bracy v. Schomig*, 248 F.3d 604 (7th Cir. 2001), *aff'd*, 286 F.3d 406 (7th Cir.), *cert. denied*, 537 U.S. 894 (2002) (after his judicial appointment, "Thomas Maloney, the former champion of the defendant, became one of the most ruthless judges on the bench").

204. *See Bracy*, 81 F.3d 688–689.

205. *Bracy v. Schomig*, 286 F.3d 406, 422 (7th Cir.), *cert. denied*, 537 U.S. 894 (2002) (Posner, J., concurring in part and dissenting in part).

206. *Collins*, 79 F. Supp.2d at 909.

207. *Id.* at 907; *see also Sentencing Transcript, supra* note 175, at 607.

208. *Bracy v. Schomig*, 248 F.3d 604, 607 (7th Cir. 2001), *aff'd*, 286 F.3d 406 (7th Cir.), *cert. denied*, 537 U.S. 894 (2002).

209. *Bracy*, 81 F.3d at 690. This view is, of course, open to serious question. As the same court admitted in the review of a subsequent "Operation Greylord" case, "[I]t is irrelevant that [the defendant] . . . was convicted by a jury, . . . for the judge's role in presiding over a jury trial is obviously not of a merely ministerial character. . . ." *Cartalino*, 122 F.3d at 10. As a dissenting judge argued in Bracy's case, it is naive to "ignore the influence that the judge retains even in a jury trial. . . . I do not refer so much to the ability of the judge to communicate his opinions to the jury through raised eyebrows, choice bits of sarcasm, and questioning of the witnesses that strays into advocacy, although this happens. . . . I mean the extraordinary ability of the trial judge to shape the trial itself. It is she who decides what evidence the jury may hear, how counsel may behave in front of the jury, what arguments may be made, . . . what legal principles the jury must apply . . . ." *Bracy*, 81 F.3d at 701 (Rovner, J., dissenting).

210. *United States ex. rel. Collins v. Welborn*, 868 F. Supp. 950, 991 (N.D. Ill. 1994), *affd, Bracy v. Gramley*, 81 F.3d 684 (7th Cir. 1996), *rev'd*, 520 U.S. 899 (1997). The difficulty in proving judicial bias in these circumstances was raised in questioning of Bracy's counsel during oral argument in the Supreme Court: "Question: . . . I can imagine cases where . . . the case has gone to a jury trial, and there's no provable fault in the instructions given to the jury, and there was no single evidentiary ruling that could be said to be improper. . . . [W]hy should that case be upset, even though the judge turns out to have been a very bad actor?

"Mr. Levy: With all due respect, . . . it seems difficult to me to imagine a situation in a serious criminal matter where the judge is not making discretionary rulings all along the way which might in some fashion have an impact on the case. . . .

"Mr. Levy: . . . If you simply look at the correctness of the rulings that the judge made, then you insulate a whole category of judicial bias from appellate court scrutiny, because surely judges can influence or impact the outcome of cases without appearing to abuse their discretion." *Transcript of Oral Argument, supra* note 179, at 14–15.

211. *Bracy,* 81 F.3d at 691.

212. *Bracy,* 286 F.3d at 411.

213. *Bracy,* 81 F.3d at 689.

214. *Id.* at 691.

215. *Bracy,* 520 U.S. at 908.

216. *Bracy,* 81 F.3d at 702 (Rovner, J., dissenting).

217. *Bracy,* 248 F.3d at 608 (internal quotation marks omitted).

218. *Collins,* 79 F. Supp.2d at 907.

219. *Bracy,* 248 F.3d at 608 (internal quotation marks deleted).

220. *Bracy,* 520 U.S. at 906, 909.

221. *Bracy,* 81 F.3d at 700 (Rovner, J., dissenting).

222. *Id.* (Rovner, J., dissenting).

223. *Id.* at 700 n.2 (Rovner, J., dissenting). *See also Petitioner's Reply to the State's Response and Supporting Memorandum of Law,* in *United States ex rel. Bracy v. Gramley,* No. 93 C-5328 (N.D. Ill. Mar. 24, 1994) (Maloney "succumb[ed] to the temptation to abandon his impartiality. . . .").

224. *Bracy,* 81 F.3d at 700.

225. *See Sentencing Transcript, supra* note 175, at 560 (argument by prosecution that Maloney "was ruthless; . . . he heartlessly meted out sentences without any compassion." "Where do you see remorse? There is none. There is not any acceptance of responsibility." "Mr. Maloney is not reformable. . . .").

226. *Transcript of Oral Argument, supra* note 179, at 25–27.

227. *See Bracy*, 520 U.S. at 908–909; *Bracy*, 81 F.3d at 689.

228. *See Bracy*, 520 U.S. at 908–909; *Bracy*, 81 F.3d at 689. The United States Supreme Court held that Bracy was entitled to discovery, to see if he could prove Maloney's actual bias in his case. *Bracy*, 520 U.S. at 908–909. On remand, the federal district judge held that there was no evidence of pro-prosecution bias during the jury trial on the issue of guilt, but that there was sufficient evidence of pro-prosecution actions during the sentencing phase to justify vacating the sentences of death. *Collins*, 79 F. Supp.2d at 910–911. This relief was reversed by a panel of the Seventh Circuit, which held that there was no evidence that the convictions or sentences were tainted by Maloney's bribe taking. *See Bracy*, 248 F.3d at 604. This was in turn reversed in part by the Seventh Circuit sitting en banc. The en banc court held that "Bracy and Collins have the heavy burden of showing actual bias"; and that they failed to make this showing regarding the finding of guilt, but succeeded regarding the sanction of death. *Bracy*, 286 F.3d at 411, 415–419. The case was remanded for a new penalty proceeding, as directed by the trial court. *Id.* at 419.

229. *Collins*, 79 F. Supp.2d at 910.

230. *Bracy*, 81 F.3d at 689.

231. *Bracy*, 81 F.3d at 703 (Rovner, J., dissenting).

232. *See e.g., In the Matter of Peter J. Coruzzi*, 472 A.2d 546, 550 (N.J. 1984) ("[A] judge who accepts a bribe must be removed from office. There can be no exceptions whatsoever."). Indeed, as the New Jersey Supreme Court stated, "[r]emoval proceedings are unique. The interests involved are so great that the Legislature required that the matter be heard directly by the [state] Supreme court or through its designated three-judge panel. No other proceeding is given this primacy." *Id.* at 552.

233. *Bracy*, 81 F.3d at 689.

234. Joseph Borkin, *The Corrupt Judge: An Inquiry into Bribery and Other High Crimes and Misdemeanors in the Federal Courts* 10, 9 (1962). As stated at the sentencing of one corrupt judge: "Peter Coruzzi, you have defaced the image of justice in this case. You have done violence to your oath of office. You have undermined the public confidence in the judicial branch of government. . . . You have given in to temptation and you have abused the great power reposed in you as a judge of this state." *State v. Coruzzi*, 460 A.2d 120, 144 (N.J. Sup. Ct. App. Div. 1983).

235. *Borkin, supra* note 234, at 10.

236. For this reason, for instance, early English law regarded bribery of a judge as among the most heinous of crimes, and punished it as high treason. *See* Borkin, *supra* note 234, at 17. *See also* David H. Bayley, *The Effects of Corruption in a Developing Nation*, in *Political Corruption: Readings in Comparative Analysis* 521, 527 (Arnold J. Heidenheimer ed., 1978), and Gunnar Myrdal, *Corruption as a Hindrance to Modernization in South Asia*, in *Corruption: Readings in Comparative Analysis, supra*, at 231–232 (discussing the disproportionate, damaging, and contagious effects of the corruption of top public officials).

237. *Bracy*, 81 F.3d at 704 (Rovner, J., dissenting).

238. *Bracy*, 286 F.3d at 411. This majority still felt bound to honor the "actual bias" test in Bracy's case. *See id.* at 415.

239. *See* Chapter 3.

240. *See Borkin, supra* note 234, at 5.

241. *United States v. Manton*, 107 F.2d 834, 836–837 (2d Cir. 1939), *cert. denied*, 309 U.S. 664 (1940).

242. *Id.* at 845.

243. *Id.* at 846. *See also United States v. Jacobs*, 431 F.2d 754, 759 (2d Cir. 1970), *cert. denied*, 402 U.S. 950 (1971) (federal bribery statute, 18 U.S.C. § 201(b), "is violated even though the official offered a bribe is not corrupted, or the object of the bribe could not be attained"); *United States v. Thomas*, 916 F.2d 647, 651 (11th Cir. 1990) (success or failure of the corrupt endeavor is immaterial to the question of guilt of the offense).

244. *See United States v. Holzer*, 816 F.2d 304, 308 (7th Cir.), *vacated Holzer v. United States*, 484 U.S. 807 (1987).

245. *See* Michael Brick, *Former Judge Is Convicted of Bribery in Divorce Court*, N.Y. Times, Apr. 20, 2007.

246. *See id.*

247. *Id.*

248. *Id.*

249. *See id.*

250. *See* Ian Urbina, *Suit Names 2 Judges Accused in a Kickbacks Case*, N.Y. Times, Feb. 14, 2009, at A13.

251. Ian Urbina, *Despite Red Flags about Judges, a Kickback Scheme Flourished*, N.Y. Times, Mar. 28, 2009, at A1.

252. John Schwartz, *Clean Slates for Youths Sentenced Fraudulently*, N.Y. Times, Mar. 27, 2009, at A13. Both judges were later convicted on criminal racketeering charges.

253. Frank Mastropola, Lauren Pearle, & Glenn Ruppel, *Pennsylvania Supreme Court Throws Out Thousands of Juvenile Delinquency Cases*, ABC News, Nov. 10, 2009.

254. *See* William Ecenbarger, *Judge Tells of Perverted Justice in Luzerne Juvenile Cases*, Phila. Inquirer, Nov. 10, 2009.

255. *Id.*

256. *Id.*

257. *In Re: Expungement of Juvenile Records and Vacatur of Luzerne County Juvenile Court Consent Decrees or Adjudications from 2003–2008, Related to: In Re: J.V.R.*, No. 81 MM 2008 (Pa. Oct. 29, 2009), at 6 (emphasis in original).

258. *Id.* at 3, 4, 6.

259. *See id.* at 6–8.

260. *See id.* at 9.

261. Boston Globe.

262. Elizabeth Drew, *Politics and Money: The New Road to Corruption* (1983).

263. *See id.* at 1. For instance, money spent on congressional campaigns increased from $99 million in 1976 to $374 million in 1984. *See* Frank J. Sorauf, *Caught in a Political Thicket: The Supreme Court and Campaign Finance*, 3 Const. Commentary 97, 101 (1986).

264. Drew, *supra* note 262, at 3.

265. *Id.* at 49.

266. Fred Wertheimer & Susan Weiss Manes, *Campaign Finance Reform: A Key to Restoring the Health of Our Democracy*, 94 Colum. L. Rev. 1126, 1132 (1994).

267. *See id.*

268. *See id.*

269. *See* Daniel L. Boren, *A Recipe for the Reform of Congress*, in *The Constitution and Campaign Finance Reform: An Anthology* 5, 9 (Frederick G. Slabach ed., 1998).

270. *See id.* at 5.

271. David Matthews, *Foreword*, in Kettering Foundation, *Citizens and Politics: A View from Main Street America* v (1991) (quoted in Boren, *supra* note 269, at 10).

272. *Federal Election Campaign Act of 1971* (FECA), Pub. L. No. 92-225, 86 Stat. 3 (1972) (codified as amended at 2 U.S.C. §§ 431–455 and 18 U.S.C. §§ 591–610).

273. For a history of prior legislation, *see* Frank J. Sorauf, *Inside Campaign Finance: Myths and Realities* 1–8 (1992).

274. *See* Drew, *supra* note 262, at 1. *See also* Sorauf, *supra* note 273, at 98; J. Skelly Wright, *Money and the Pollution of Politics: Is the First Amendment an Obstacle to Political Equality?*, 82 Colum. L. Rev. 609, 610, 631 (1982).

275. 424 U.S. 1 (1976).

276. *See id.* at 39–59. The Court subsequently invalidated the Act's limits on expenditures by political parties, which are made "independently and without coordination" with any candidate, as well. *See Colorado Republican Fed. Campaign Comm. v. Federal Election Comm'n*, 518 U.S. 604 (1996).

277. *See Buckley*, 424 U.S. at 23–38. After *Buckley* and later cases, FECA contribution limits were described by the Court as follows: "[F]or present purposes, the Act now prohibits individuals and political committees from making direct, or indirect, contributions that exceed the following limits: (a) For any 'person': $1,000 to a candidate 'with respect to any election'; $5,000 to any political committee in any year; $20,000 to the national committees of a political party in any year; but all within an overall limit (for any individual in any year) of $25,000. . . . (b) For any 'multican-didate political committee': $5,000 to a candidate 'with respect to any election'; $5,000 to any political committee in any year; and $15,000 to the national committees of a political party in any year. . . ." *Colorado Republican Fed. Campaign Comm.*, 518 U.S. at 610 (opinion of Breyer, J.). Contribution limits imposed by state laws have also been upheld, *see, e.g., Nixon v. Shrink Mo. Gov't PAC*, 528 U.S. 377 (2000) (Missouri law), unless they are "dispro-portionately severe." *See Randall v. Sorrell*, 548 U.S. 230, 237, 247–248 (2006) (plurality opinion) (striking down a Vermont law) ("contribution limits might sometimes work more harm to protected First Amendment interests than their anticorruption objectives [can] . . . justify") (emphasis deleted).

278. *See Buckley*, 424 U.S. at 26.

279. *Id.* at 26–27.

280. *Id.* at 27 (footnote omitted).

281. *Id.*

282. *Id.* (quoting *United States Civil Serv. Comm'n v. National Ass'n of Letter Carriers*, 413 U.S. 548, 565 (1973)).

283. *See id.* at 27–28.

284. 494 U.S. 652 (1990), *overruled by Citizens United v. Federal Election Comm'n*, 130 S.Ct. 876 (2010).

285. *Id.* at 659, 660. *See also Federal Election Comm. v. Beaumont*, 539 U.S. 146, 152 (2003) (quoting *United States v. Automobile Workers*, 352 U.S. 567, 570 (1957)) (current prohibitions on corporate campaign contributions "grew out of a 'popular feeling' in the late 19th century 'that aggregated capital unduly influenced politics, an influence not stopping short of corruption'"). It must be noted, however, that to date the Court's explicit concern with "wealth effects" in campaign finance has been limited to the corporate form. *Cf. Buckley*, 424 U.S. at 48 (rejecting asserted government interest "in equalizing the relative ability of individuals and [noncorporate] groups to influence the outcome of elections").

286. 533 U.S. 431 (2001).

287. *Id.* at 453.

288. 540 U.S. 93 (2003), *overruled by Citizens United v. Federal Election Comm'n*, 130 S.Ct. 876 (2010).

289. *Bipartisan Campaign Reform Act of 2002 (BCRA)*, Pub. L. No. 107-155, 116 Stat. 81 (codified in scattered sections of 2, 18, 28, 36, 47 U.S.C.).

290. *McConnell*, 540 U.S. at 115 (internal quotation marks omitted).

291. *Id.* (internal quotation marks omitted).

292. *See id.* at 143.

293. *Id.* (internal quotation marks omitted). *See also Nixon*, 528 U.S. at 389–395 (corruption extends beyond explicit cash-for-votes to undue influence on an officeholder's judgment); *First National Bank of Boston v. Bellotti*, 435 U.S. 765, 788–789 (1978) (concern that large campaign expenditures will be perceived as having an "undue influence on the outcome" of an election with resultant loss of "the confidence of the people in the democratic process").

294. *See McConnell*, 540 U.S. at 143–144. *See also Nixon*, 528 U.S. at 390 (the perception that "large donors call the tune" might "jeopardize the willingness of voters to take part in democratic governance").

The Court's shifting majorities have distinguished situations where the spending is simple "issue advocacy," rather than campaign speech. *See, e.g., Federal Election Comm'n v. Wisconsin Right to Life, Inc.*, 551 U.S. 449, 456 (2007) (opinion of Roberts, C.J.) (anticorruption rationale does not justify restriction of corporate expenditures for political speech that is neither "campaign speech [n]or its functional equivalent"); *Citizens against Rent Control v. City of Berkeley*, 454 U.S. 290, 297–299 (1981) (state interest in preventing the corruption of officials—or the perception of corruption of officials—is not present in spending that advocates views on ballot measures); *Colorado Republican Fed. Campaign Comm.*, 518 U.S. at 609 (opinion of Breyer, J.) (purpose of federal campaign finance law was "to remedy the appearance of a 'corrupt' political process (one in which large contributions seem to buy legislative votes)"). Dissenters have argued that public confidence in the political process is undermined whenever big money is spent to influence politics. *See, e.g., Wisconsin Right to Life, Inc.*, 551 U.S. at 306–308 (White, J., dissenting).

295. Some commentators have argued—rather unconvincingly—that even the explicit exchange of a legislator's vote for a campaign contribution is not a "corrupt" transaction. *See, e.g.*, David A. Strauss, *What Is the Goal of Campaign Finance Reform?*, 1995 U. Chi. Legal F. 141, 143–144, and Bruce E. Cain, *Moralism and Realism in Campaign Finance Reform*, 1995 U. Chi. Legal F. 111, 116–117 (arguing that the exchange of votes for cash is simply another form of a citizen's expression of policy preferences). However, as Daniel Lowenstein responds, the "[b]artering of contributions for favorable official action diminishes the 'perceived legitimacy of the political system' and contradicts almost any 'logic of representation' [that can be] . . . imagin[ed]." "[F]or Demetrios to accept a large contribution from Bigbucks in exchange for agreeing to vote in her favor on a tax bill" is "unequivocal[ly] disapprov[ed of] . . . in the American political culture. . . ." And "Americans disapprove of this transaction because they recognize it as corrupt." Daniel H. Lowenstein, *Campaign Contributions and Corruption: Comments on Strauss and Cain*, 1995 U. Chi. Legal F. 163, 180, 172.

296. 130 S.Ct. 876 (2010).

297. An "electioneering communication" was defined as "any broadcast, cable, or satellite communication" that "refers to a clearly identified candidate for Federal office" and is made within thirty days of a primary or sixty days of a general election. 2 U.S.C. § 434(f)(3)(A) (2006). *See also Citizens United*, 130 S.Ct. at 887.

298. *See Citizens United*, 130 S.Ct. at 886.

299. *Id.* at 903 (quoting *Austin*, 494 U.S. at 660).

300. *See id.* at 909–911.

301. *See id.* at 911.

302. *Id.* at 910.

303. *Id.* at 961 (Stevens, J., concurring in part and dissenting in part).

304. *Id.* (internal quotation marks omitted). In support of this conclusion, the dissent cited district court findings in the *McConnell* case that " 'corporations and labor unions routinely notify Members of Congress as soon as they air electioneering communications relevant to the Members' elections' "; " 'that Members express appreciation to organizations for the airing of these election-related advertisements' "; that " 'Members of Congress are particularly grateful when negative issue advertisements are run by these organizations' "; that lobbyists testified that " 'these organizations use issue advocacy as a means to influence various Members of Congress' "; and that " '[a]fter the election, these organizations often seek credit for their support.' " *Citizens United*, 130 S.Ct. at 961–962 (Stevens, J., concurring in part and dissenting in part).

305. *Id.* at 963 (Stevens, J., concurring in part and dissenting in part) (quoting *Wisconsin Right to Life, Inc.*, 551 U.S. at 507 (Souter, J., dissenting)).

306. *See McConnell*, 540 U.S. at 117, 164.

307. *Austin*, 494 U.S. at 660.

308. *Buckley*, 424 U.S. at 259 (White, J., concurring in part and dissenting in part).

309. *McConnell*, 540 U.S. at 115. *See also id.* at 116 (money in politics is "one of the great political evils of [our] time") (internal quotation marks omitted); *Federal Election Comm'n v. National Right to Work Comm.*, 459 U.S. 197, 210 (1982) (Supreme Court will not "second-guess a legislative determination as to the need for prophylactic measures where corruption is the evil feared").

310. *McConnell*, 540 U.S. at 115. *See also id.* at 354 (Rehnquist, J., dissenting in part) (discussing whether federal candidates or officeholders "are corrupted or would appear corrupted" by contributions); *Bellotti*, 435 U.S. at 788 n.26 (discussing the "corruption of elected representatives" through the creation of political debts); *Buckley*, 424 U.S. at 259 (White, J., concurring in part and dissenting in part) (discussing corruption's "mortal danger," against which effective steps must be taken). Work by academic commentators in this field utilize these images as well. *See, e.g.,* Dennis F.

Thompson, *Ethics in Congress: From Individual to Institutional Corruption* 28 (1995) (private interests that attempt to achieve political influence through campaign contributions are "agents of corruption"); Samuel Issacharoff & Pamela S. Karlan, *The Hydraulics of Campaign Finance Reform,* 77 Tex. L. Rev. 1705, 1734 (1999) (reforms in the campaign finance area should be aimed at "the worst pathologies"); Amitai Etzioni, *Capital Corruption: The New Attack on American Democracy* xi (1988) ("Washington is corrupt to the core.").

311. *See* Bradley A. Smith, *Faulty Assumptions and Undemocratic Consequences of Campaign Finance Reform,* 105 Yale L. J. 1049, 1072–1075 (1996) (limitations on campaign contributions reinforce the status quo by hindering the ability of challengers to compete with incumbents on equal terms).

312. *See* Vincent Blasi, *Free Speech and the Widening Gyre of Fund-Raising: Why Campaign Spending Limits May Not Violate the First Amendment after All,* 94 Colum. L. Rev. 1281, 1283 (1994) (arguing that *Buckley*'s upholding of contribution limits, and invalidation of spending limits, forces candidates to spend an inordinate amount of time on fund-raising, which undermines representative government).

313. Issacharoff & Karlan, *supra* note 310, at 1714 (arguing that reforms will have the perverse effect of channeling money away from potentially mediating institutional buffers, such as candidates and political parties, and into the coffers of more extreme issue advocacy groups); Cain, *supra* note 295, at 117–140 (reformist visions assume an ideal of deliberative government that ignores the fact that money is simply another currency through which voters express their electoral preferences).

314. *See, e.g.,* Sorauf, *supra* note 273 (arguing that fears about the influence of money in politics is greatly exaggerated).

315. Nathaniel Persily & Kelli Lammie, *Perceptions of Corruption and Campaign Finance: When Public Opinion Determines Constitutional Law,* 153 U. Pa. L. Rev. 119, 124, 129 (2004). *See also* D. Bruce LaPierre, *Campaign Contribution Limits: Pandering to Public Fears about "Big Money" and Protecting Incumbents,* 52 Admin. L. Rev. 687, 688–690, 713–714 (2000) (the "appearance of corruption" is a "speculative," "amorphous," and "dangerous" standard for regulating political speech).

316. *See* Persily & Lammie, *supra* note 315, at 121.

317. For a review of this literature, *see, e.g.,* Sorauf, *supra* note 273; Thomas F. Burke, *The Concept of Corruption in Campaign Finance Law,* 14

Const. Commentary 127, 139 n.45 (1997); Daniel Hays Lowenstein, *On Campaign Finance Reform: The Root of All Evil Is Deeply Rooted,* 18 Hofstra L. Rev. 301, 313–322 (1989).

318. Paul H. Douglas, *Ethics in Government* 44 (1952). *See also* Wertheimer & Manes, *supra* note 266, at 1129.

319. Wertheimer & Manes, *supra* note 266, at 1140.

320. *Id.* at 1128.

321. Cong. Rec. S 7187 (daily ed. June 15, 1993) (statement of Senator Bumpers) (quoted in Wertheimer & Manes, *supra* note 266, at 1129).

322. *See, e.g.,* Persily & Lammie, *supra* note 315, at 135–136 (arguing that campaign finance reform is justified only if it is shown that campaign finance contributions "affect policy outcomes").

323. *See Buckley,* 424 U.S. at 265 (White, J., concurring in part and dissenting in part). As Michael Johnston has written, the primary concern in the United States is not that policies and roll-call votes are bought and sold, since there is little evidence on this point, but rather that the existing system "reduce[s] public trust and [creates] widespread perceptions of abuses of power and privilege." Michael Johnston, *Syndromes of Corruption: Wealth, Power, and Democracy* 43 (2005).

324. *See, e.g.,* Edward C. Banfield, *The Moral Basis of a Backward Society* (1958); Michael Johnston, *Patrons and Clients, Jobs and Machines: A Case Study of the Uses of Patronage,* 73 Am. Pol. Sci. Rev. 385 (1979).

325. Mitchell A. Seligson, *The Impact of Corruption on Regime Legitimacy: A Comparative Study of Four Latin American Countries,* 64 J. Pol. 408, 412 (2002).

326. *See* Donatella della Porta, *Social Capital, Beliefs in Government, and Political Corruption,* in *Disaffected Democracies: What's Troubling the Trilateral Countries?* 202 (Susan J. Pharr & Robert D. Putnam eds., 2000); Stephen D. Morris, *Corruption & Politics in Contemporary Mexico* 70–74 (1991); Susan J. Pharr, *Officials' Misconduct and Public Distrust: Japan and the Trilateral Democracies,* in *Disaffected Democracies: What's Troubling the Trilateral Countries?, supra,* at 173; Seligson, *supra* note 325; Benjamin I. Page & Robert Y. Shapiro, *The Rational Public: Fifty Years of Trends in Americans' Public Policy Preferences* 337–338 (1992). Typical is the conclusion of Morris: "Pervasive corruption produces a pernicious 'culture of corruption' among the public that includes widespread distrust and cynicism toward public officials. . . . [T]his distrust greatly magnifies the potential loss of legitimacy that is [necessary to] sustain the state's organizations." Morris, *supra,* at 18.

327. *Wisconsin Right to Life, Inc.*, 551 U.S. at 506–507 (Souter, J., dissenting) (citing Mark Mellman & Richard Wirthlin, *Public Views of Party Soft Money*, in *Inside the Campaign Finance Battles: Court Testimony on the New Reforms* 266, 267 (Anthony Corrado, Thomas E. Mann, & Trevor Potter eds., 2003)) (internal quotation marks omitted). *See also* Sorauf, *supra* note 263, at 115 ("[C]ampaign finance [is] . . . one element in a growing cynicism about American political institutions. . . . [A]ppearances and perceptions are a potent reality in themselves.").

328. *See* Boren, *supra* note 269, at 15 (it is "the perception of *corruption in the aggregate* that has alienated voters from Congress as an institution") (emphasis added).

329. Indeed, a prophylactic approach to the corruption of public officials is routine in other American contexts. *See, e.g.*, 5 U.S.C. § 7353(a)(2) (2006) (broadly prohibiting the giving of gratuities to employees of the executive, legislative, and judicial branches); 18 U.S.C. § 209(a) (2006) (broadly prohibiting the "supplementation" of an executive branch official's salary); 18 U.S.C. §§ 212–213 (2006) (broadly prohibiting the giving of any loan or gratuity by a bank employee to a bank examiner).

330. *See* David Barnhizer, *"On the Make": Campaign Funding and the Corrupting of the American Judiciary*, 50 Cath. U. L. Rev. 361 (2001); Paul D. Carrington, *Judicial Independence and Democratic Accountability in the Highest State Courts*, 61 Law & Contemp. Probs. 79 (1998): Jason Miles Levien & Stacie L. Fatka, *Cleaning Up Judicial Elections: Examining the First Amendment Limitations on Judicial Campaign Regulation*, 2 Mich. L. & Pol'y Rev. 71 (1997).

331. *See* William Glaberson, *State Chief Justices to Meet on Abuses in Judicial Races*, N.Y. Times, Sept. 8, 2000, at A14.

332. *See* Texans for Public Justice, *Texas Supreme Court Fundraising Closely Tied to Court's Case Load: 40% of Justices' Contributions Tied to Sources Litigating Supreme Court Cases*, Feb. 23, 1998 (quoted in Barnhizer, *supra* note 330, at 372).

333. William Glaberson, *State Judges Are Acting More Like Politicians as Challenges Grow*, J. Record (Oklahoma City), June 23, 2000 (quoted in Barnhizer, *supra* note 330, at 362 n.3).

334. *Frontline: Justice for Sale?*, PBS Broadcast, Nov. 23, 1999, available at http://www.pbs.org/wgbh/pages/frontline/shows/justice (quoted in Barnhizer, *supra* note 330, at 377).

335. Barnhizer, *supra* note 330, at 364.

336. Philip Rawls, *Big Spender Calls for Limits on Judicial Campaign Contributions*, AP Newswire, Nov. 12, 1999 (quoted in Barnhizer, *supra* note 330, at 364 n.8).

337. *See* Barnhizer, *supra* note 330, at 364 n.8.

338. Rawls, *supra* note 336 (quoted in Barnhizer, *supra* note 330, at 364 n.8).

339. Barnhizer, *supra* note 330, at 365 (footnote omitted).

340. *Id.* at 366 (footnote omitted). *See also* Peter D. Webster, *Selection and Retention of Judges: Is There One "Best" Method?*, 23 Fla. St. U. L. Rev. 1, 9–10 (1995); Scott D. Wiener, *Note, Popular Justice: State Judicial Elections and Procedural Due Process*, 31 Harv. Civ. R.-C.L.L. Rev. 187, 208–209 (1996).

341. *See* Adam Liptak & Janet Roberts, *Campaign Cash Mirrors a High Court's Rulings*, N.Y. Times, Oct. 1, 2006, at A1.

342. *Id.*

343. *See id.*

344. *Id.*

345. *See id.*

346. *Id.* (quoting Chief Justice Thomas Moyer of the Ohio Supreme Court).

347. 129 S.Ct. 2252 (2009).

348. *See id.* at 2257.

349. *See id.*

350. *Id.*

351. *Id.*

352. *See id.*

353. *Id.*

354. *See id.* at 2258.

355. *Id.* These grounds were "first, that a forum-selection clause contained in a contract to which Massey was not a party barred the suit in West Virginia, and second, that res judicata barred the suit due to an out-of-state judgment to which Massey was not a party." *Id.*

356. *Id.*

357. *See id.*

358. *See id.*

359. *Id.* at 2263.

360. *Id.* (quoting *Withrow v. Larkin*, 421 U.S. 35, 47 (1975)).

361. *Id.* at 2264.

362. *Id.* at 2265 (internal quotation marks omitted).

363. *See id.* at 2262.

364. *See, e.g.*, Smith, *supra* note 311, at 1071–1084; Lillian R. BeVier, *Campaign Finance Reform: Specious Arguments, Intractable Dilemmas*, 94 Colum. L. Rev. 1258, 1268 (1994).

365. *See* Stephen E. Gottlieb, *The Dilemma of Election Campaign Finance Reform*, 18 Hofstra L. Rev. 213, 216–228 (1989).

366. It has been suggested that the value of incumbency for a federal congressional campaign approaches $4 million. *Id.* at 222.

367. *See id.* at 216–228.

368. *See* Wertheimer & Manes, *supra* note 266, at 1135 ("For most PACs, contributions to challengers are seen as a waste of money. Moreover, few PACs are willing to run the risk of antagonizing an incumbent Member of Congress by contributing to his or her opponent.").

369. Smith, *supra* note 311, at 1072.

370. *McConnell*, 540 U.S. at 153.

371. *See* Persily & Lammie, *supra* note 315, at 124.

CHAPTER 7. CORRUPTION AND MORAL VALUES

1. See Chapter 5.

2. Li Xueqin, *Ruhe pingjia fan fubai douzheng de chengxiao* ([How to evaluate results in the anticorruption struggle], Neibu wengao (Internal manuscripts) no. 1: 21–22 (quoted in Melanie Manion, *Corruption by Design: Building Clean Government in Mainland China and Hong Kong* 84 (2004)).

3. Reuters, *Half of Russians Believe Bribery Solves "Problems,"* May 13, 2010, available at www.reuters.com/article/2010/05/13/us-russia-graft -poll-idUSTRE64C1ZD20100513 (last visited Aug. 8, 2012).

4. *Id.*

5. Robert Legvold, *Corruption, the Criminalized State, and Post-Soviet Transitions,* in *Corruption, Global Security, and World Order* 194, 197 (Robert I. Rotberg ed., 2009).

6. *Id.* at 196.

7. Manion, *supra* note 2, at 13. *See also* Susan Rose-Ackerman, *Corruption in the Wake of Domestic Conflict,* in *Corruption, Global Security, and*

World Order, supra note 5, at 66, 83 (in pre-independence Kosovo, the denial of government services to Kosovar Albanians "entrenched a culture of corruption in Kosovo, limited its moral stigma, and increased public tolerance of corruption").

8. Citizens must trust that others are adhering to the rules of the game. "[T]rust is a key dimension of the political capacities of civil society, which in turn reflects the capacities of individuals and groups to act for common ends. . . . [H]igh levels of distrust within society erode these capacities, the absence of which is one condition for detached, unresponsive, and corrupt governments. . . ." Mark E. Warren, *Introduction*, in *Democracy & Trust* 1, 12 (Mark E. Warren ed., 1999).

9. Daniel Kaufmann, *Revisiting Anti-Corruption Strategies: Tilt Towards Incentive-Driven Approaches?*, in United Nations Development Programme & OECD Development Centre, *Corruption & Integrity Improvement Initiatives in Developing Countries* 63, 79 (1998). *See also* Michael Johnston, *Public Officials, Private Interests, and Sustainable Democracy: When Politics and Corruption Meet*, in *Corruption and the Global Economy* 61, 61 (Kimberly Ann Elliott ed., 1997) ("Corruption occurs in many forms, with contrasting patterns and political implications.").

10. *See, e.g.,* Robert B. Charlick, *Corruption in Political Transition: A Governance Perspective*, 7 Corruption and Reform: An Int'l J. 177 (1993); Kimberly Ann Elliott, *Corruption as an International Policy Problem: Overview and Recommendations*, in *Corruption and the Global Economy, supra* note 9, at 175, 198; Patrick Glynn, Stephen J. Kobrin, & Moisés Naím, *The Globalization of Corruption*, in *id.* at 7, 8–10; Johnston, *supra* note 9, at 61, 65; Legvold, *supra* note 5, at 194; Quentin Reed, *Dysfunctionality and Change in the Czech and Slovak Republics*, 22 Crime, L., and Soc. Change 323, 326–331 (1994); Rose-Ackerman, *supra* note 7. In the past twenty years, corruption has also contributed to peaceful political change within existing regimes in India, Indonesia, Israel, Japan, Pakistan, Spain, the United Kingdom, and West Germany, among other countries. *See* Jennifer L. McCoy & Heather Heckel, *The Emergence of a Global Anti-Corruption Norm*, in *Global Society in Transition: An International Politics Reader* 217, 226 (Daniel N. Nelson & Laura Neack eds., 2002).

11. *See* Steve Askin & Carole Collins, *External Collusion with Kleptocracy: Can Zaire Recapture Its Stolen Wealth?*, 57 Rev. Afr. Pol. Economy 72 (1993); Glynn et al., *supra* note 10, at 10; Kaufmann, *supra* note 9, at 75; Rose-Ackerman, *supra* note 7, at 71, 76–82; Augustine Ruzindana, *The Importance* *of Leadership in Fighting Corruption in Uganda,* in *Corruption and the Global Economy, supra* note 9, at 133, 134–136; David Stasavage, *Causes and Consequences of Corruption: Mozambique in Transition,* in *Corruption and Democratisation* 65, 65 (Alan Doig & Robin Theobald eds., 2000).

12. *See* Glynn et al., *supra* note 10, at 8–10; Elliott, *supra* note 10, at 198.

13. Glynn et al., *supra* note 10, at 11.

14. *See id.;* Elliott, *supra* note 10, at 198. Michael Johnston explains the variable effect of democratic strategies on the existence of corruption in the following terms: "Checks and balances, accountable leaders, liberal markets, competitive elections, and administrative transparency do much to control corruption in countries where it is the exception rather than the rule, and where [governments] . . . enjoy broad-based legitimacy. It does not follow, however, that . . . putting [such factors] in place will control the problem." Michael Johnston, *Syndromes of Corruption: Wealth, Power, and Democracy* 22 (2005).

15. *See, e.g.,* Elliott, *supra* note 10, at 198; Glynn et al., *supra* note 10, at 8, 10; Legvold, *supra* note 5, at 201–202; Morris Szeftel, *Corruption and the Spoils System in Zambia,* in *Corruption: Causes, Consequences and Control* 163 (Michael Clarke ed., 1983).

16. *See, e.g.,* Charlick, *supra* note 10, at 183; Sarah Dix & Emmanuel Pok, *Combating Corruption in Traditional Societies: Papua New Guinea,* in *Corruption, Global Security, and World Order, supra* note 5, at 239; Nick Smart, *Classes, Clients and Corruption in Sicily,* in *Corruption: Causes, Consequences and Control, supra* note 15, at 127, 132–134.

17. *See, e.g.,* Rose-Ackerman, *supra* note 7; Stasavage, *supra* note 11, at 65–66, 85–86; Daniel Jordan Smith, *The Paradoxes of Popular Participation in Corruption in Nigeria,* in *Corruption, Global Security, and World Order, supra* note 5, at 283, 287–306; USAID, *Fighting Corruption and Restoring Accountability in Burundi* (2006). "The characteristic weakness of the functioning of post-authoritarian new democracies is often analyzed to be the scarcity of [inter-personal trust] and the prevalence of [ethical] cynicism. . . ." "[I]nstitutional regimes [often] consist of an incoherent patchwork of old and new rules without any evident underlying principle. The widely publicized and highly visible experience of corruption, inconsistency, fuzzily defined and hence often contested domains . . . [reflects the] failure to generate credible commitments to any meaningful Gestalt of principles, ideas, and [institutional] functions. . . ." Claus Offe, *How Can We Trust Our Fellow Citizens?*, in *Democracy & Trust, supra* note 8, at 42, 77–78.

18. *See, e.g.,* Johnston, *supra* note 14, at 195–199; Legvold, *supra* note 5; Ewa Letowska, *Corruption: Towards Greater Transparency?*, paper cited in Alexandra Mills, *Strengthening Domestic Institutions against Corruption: A Public Ethics Checklist,* in *Corruption & Integrity Improvement Initiatives in Developing Countries, supra* note 9, at 141, 142; Kim Lane Scheppele, *The Inevitable Corruption of Transition,* 14 Conn. J. Int'l L. 509 (1999). Robert Legvold describes the flourishing of corruption in the Soviet Union as a product of "scarcity and clientelism, . . . combined with the moral decay arising from the long-lost ideological idealism." "Hence, the Soviet Union provided a base for the criminalized state, but not its essence. That required the collapse of the Soviet Union, and the chaotic transition from one economic order to another." Legvold, *supra* note 5, at 204.

19. Manion, *supra* note 2, at 94–95 (quoting Wojtek Zafanolli, *A Brief Outline of China's Second Economy,* in *Transforming China's Economy in the Eighties,* vol. 2, *Management, Industry, and the Urban Economy* 138, 139 (Stephen Feuchtwang, Athar Hussain, & Thierry Pairault eds., 1988)).

20. Yan Sun, *The Chinese Protests of 1989: The Issue of Corruption,* 31 Asian Survey 762, 772 (1991).

21. Manion, *supra* note 2, at 94.

22. *See* Jim Yardley, *The Chinese Go After Corruption, Corruptly,* N.Y. Times, Oct. 22, 2006, at BW 3.

23. *See* Smith, *supra* note 17, at 283.

24. *Id.* at 289.

25. *Id.* at 305–306.

26. *Id.* at 305.

27. *See, e.g.,* Alan Doig & Stephen Riley, *Corruption and Anti-Corruption Strategies: Issues and Case Studies from Developing Countries,* in *Corruption & Integrity Improvement Initiatives in Developing Countries, supra* note 9, at 45, 50–55; Mills, *supra* note 18; W. Paatii Ofosu-Amaah, Raj Soopramanien, & Kishor Uprety, *Combating Corruption: A Comparative Review of Selected Legal Aspects of State Practice and Major International Initiatives* 5–7 (1999).

28. *See* Manion, *supra* note 2, at 27.

29. *Id.*

30. *See id.*

31. *Id.* at 43–44.

32. *Id.* at 47.

33. *See id.* at 47–48.

34. *Id.* at 48.

35. *Id.* (quoting Independent Commission Against Corruption, *Annual Report by the Commissioner of the Independent Commission Against Corruption* 8 (1977)).

36. *See, e.g.,* Doig & Riley, *supra* note 27, at 54; Alan Doig & Robin Theobald, *Introduction: Why Corruption?,* in *Corruption and Democratisation, supra* note 11, at 1, 7; Elliott, *supra* note 10, at 198, 208–209; Barbara Harriss-White & Gordon White, *Corruption, Liberalization and Democracy,* 27 IDS Bull. 1 (1996); Johnston, *supra* note 14, at 9; Kaufmann, *supra* note 9, at 72; Rose-Ackerman, *supra* note 7, at 77–78; Stasavage, *supra* note 11, at 69–70, 85–86; Hartmut Schweitzer, *Corruption—Its Spread and Decline,* in *The New Institutional Economics of Corruption* 16, 34–35 (Johann Graf Lambsdorff, Markus Taube, & Matthias Schramm eds., 2005).

37. *See* Elliott, *supra* note 10, at 208; Doig & Riley, *supra* note 27, at 50 ("For developing countries, [a] . . . consensus suggests that democratisation, public sector 'downsizing' and deregulation are . . . a useful means to reduce . . . corruption.").

38. *See, e.g.,* Elliott, *supra* note 10, at 198; Kaufmann, *supra* note 9, at 72–73.

39. *See* Robert Leiken, *Controlling the Global Corruption Epidemic,* 105 Foreign Pol'y 55, 68 (Winter 1996–1997). *See also* Kaufmann, *supra* note 9, at 72–73.

40. Leiken, *supra* note 39, at 72.

41. Elliott, *supra* note 10, at 209.

42. *See* Chapter 2. As Peter Euben has written, "[C]orruption is a disease of the body politic. It has less to do with individual malfeasance than with systematic and systemic degeneration of those practices and commitments that provide the terms of collective self-understanding and shared purpose." J. Peter Euben, *Corruption,* in *Political Innovation and Conceptual Change* 220, 222–223 (Terence Ball, James Farr, & Russell L. Hanson eds., 1989).

43. *See, e.g.,* Warren, *supra* note 8, at 12; Offe, *supra* note 17, at 47–49, 60–65.

44. *See* Johnston, *supra* note 14, at 36–48.

45. Manion, *supra* note 2, at 4.

46. *Id.*

47. *See* Johnston, *supra* note 14, at 9; Michael Johnston & Yufan Hao, *China's Surge of Corruption*, 6 J. Democracy 80 (1995).

48. *See* Johnston, *supra* note 14, at 9.

49. *Id.*

50. *Id.* at 8.

51. *Id.* at 73.

52. *See id.* at 162.

53. *See* Manion, *supra* note 2, at 94–95.

54. Manion, *supra* note 2, at 94–95 (quoting He Qinglian, *Zhongguo de xianjing* [China's pitfall] 195 (1997), and Andrew J. Nathan, *China's Crisis: Dilemmas of Reform and Prospects for Democracy* 108 (1990) (footnotes omitted)).

55. Yardley, *supra* note 22.

56. *See, e.g.*, Doig & Riley, *supra* note 27, at 54; Kaufmann, *supra* note 9, at 72–73; Rose-Ackerman, *supra* note 7, at 77–78; Stasavage, *supra* note 11, at 65–70, 85–86.

57. Stasavage, *supra* note 11, at 85.

58. *See id.* at 86.

59. *See* Scheppele, *supra* note 18, at 516.

60. *Id.* at 521–522.

61. *See id.*

62. Robert Williams, *Corruption: New Concepts for Old?*, 20 Third World Q. 503, 504 (1999).

63. *See, e.g.*, Colin Leys, *What Is the Problem about Corruption?*, 3 J. Mod. Afr. Stud. 215, 216 (1965); Bayless Manning, *The Purity Potlatch: Conflict of Interests and Moral Escalation*, in *Political Corruption: Readings in Comparative Analysis* 307, 307–312 (Arnold J. Heidenheimer ed., 1978). The statement by Victor LeVine is typical. In his view, there is no point in focusing on the "moral aspects of corrupt behavior" when an "empirical examination of consequences is certain to contribute more to an understanding of political corruption than the roundest [moral] condemnation." Victor T. LeVine, *Political Corruption: The Ghana Case* xii–xiii (1975).

64. *See, e.g.*, Manning, *supra* note 63.

65. Frank Anechiarico & James B. Jacobs, *The Pursuit of Absolute Integrity: How Corruption Control Makes Government Ineffective* (1996).

66. *See id.* at xiii.

67. *Id.*

68. *Id.* at xiv–xv.

69. *See, e.g., id.* at 50–62, 69–72, 123–138.

70. *See id.* at 12.

71. *See id.* at 7–13.

72. *Id.* at 9.

73. *Id.* at 11.

74. *Id.* at 12.

75. *See* Chapter 5.

76. *See* Anechiarico & Jacobs, *supra* note 65, at 11.

77. *See id.*

78. *See, e.g.,* Transparency International Corruption Perceptions Index 2010, http://www.transparency.org/policy_research/surveys_indices/cpi /2010/results (last visited Sept. 15, 2011).

79. *See* Anechiarico & Jacobs, *supra* note 65, at 14, 153. *See also* Doig & Theobald, *supra* note 36, at 6 ("It is widely accepted that the measurement of crime in general is fraught with difficulty. Even more is this the case with [corruption,] a pattern of behaviour which in many countries is neither illegal nor even regarded as illegitimate. Our thinking about the level of corruption in this or that society tends therefore to be somewhat impressionistic. . . .").

80. Anechiarico & Jacobs, *supra* note 65, at 153.

81. *See id.*

82. *Id.* at 156–157.

83. *See, e.g.,* Michel Cahen, *Nationalism and Ethnicities: Lessons from Mozambique,* in *Ethnicity Kills? The Politics of War, Peace, and Ethnicity in Sub-Saharan Africa* 163, 163 (Einar Braathen, Morten Boas, & Gjermund Saether eds., 2000); Doig & Riley, *supra* note 27, at 50–55; Manion, *supra* note 2, at 27–48; Jeremy Pope, *Enhancing Accountability and Ethics in the Public Sector,* in *Curbing Corruption: Toward a Model for Building National Integrity* 66 (Rick Stapenhurst & Sahr J. Kpundeh eds., 1999); Ruzindana, *supra* note 11, at 138–145; Smith, *supra* note 17, at 301–307; David Watt, Rachel Flanary, & Robin Theobald, *Democratisation or the Democratisation of Corruption? The Case of Uganda,* in *Corruption and Democratisation, supra* note 11, at 37, 60–61.

84. *See* Robert I. Rotberg, *Leadership Alters Corrupt Behavior,* in *Corruption, Global Security, and World Order, supra* note 5, at 341, 341–343, 350.

85. *See id.* at 157–158; Yong-Lin Moon & Gary N. McLean, *The Nature of Corruption Hidden in Culture: The Case of Korea*, in *Fighting Corruption in Asia: Causes, Effects and Remedies* 297, 303 (John Kidd & Frank-Jürgen Richter eds., 2003).

86. Schweitzer, *supra* note 36, at 26.

87. Herbert C. Kelman & V. Lee Hamilton, *Crimes of Obedience* (1989).

88. *See id.* at 333.

89. *See id.*

90. *Id.*

91. Johnston, *supra* note 14, at 192.

92. *See, e.g.*, McCoy & Heckel, *supra* note 10, at 220–239 (discussing this effort on an international level).

CHAPTER 8. CODA

1. *See* Noel B. Reynolds, *Constitutionalism and the Rule of Law*, in *Constitutionalism and Rights* 79, 80, 90 (Gary C. Bryner & Noel B. Reynolds eds., 1987).

2. *Id.* at 90–91.

3. *Cf.* Richard H. Fallon Jr., *"The Rule of Law" as a Concept in Constitutional Discourse*, 97 Colum. L. Rev. 1, 50–51 (1997) (discussing the idea of standards as a part of the rule of law).

4. See Chapter 5.

5. Kenneth Anderson, *Nuremberg Sensibility: Telford Taylor's Memoir of the Nuremberg Trials*, 7 Harv. Hum. Rts. J. 281, 290 (1994).

6. Bob Dylan, *Gotta Serve Somebody* (1979).

INDEX

Abramoff, Jack, 61–62, 65–66, 80–81, 270n71
Abu Ghraib atrocities, 270n63
Abuse of power as a theory of corruption, 37–40; definition of corruption in, 38–39; distinctive aspects of, 38–39; insufficient to describe corruption, 39–40
Acts as focus of law, 5, 9, 69, 114; character vs. acts, 113–121
Administration of law and equality in bureaucratic dealings, 30–34; transparency requirements, effect of, 237, 242. *See also* Bureaucratic corruption
Africa, corruption and political instability in, 226, 235, 291n145
Agents' (agentic) role of judges, juries, and legislators, 125–126
Agnew, Spiro T., 55–56, 81
Alabama: judicial races in, 214; political corruption in, 155–164
Alatas, Syed Hussein, 47–48, 58–59, 104
Alexander, Jeffrey, 98

Ames, Albert Alonzo, 283n45
The Anatomy of Disgust (Miller), 108
Ancient Greeks: on democratic government, 57; on evil, 103; on political corruption, 97
Anechiarico, Frank, 236, 238–239
Anselm of Canterbury, 59
Anticorruption machinery in U.S., critique of, 236–242
Aquinas, Thomas, 59
Augustine, St., 59
Austin v. Michigan Chamber of Commerce (1990), 204–205, 207, 208–209
Authoritarian regimes, 131, 227

Bacon, Francis, 78–79, 82, 194
Baden, John, 7, 41
Barnhizer, David, 213–214
Batheja, Ranjan, 141–142
BCRA (Bipartisan Campaign Reform Act of 2002), 205, 207
Beasley, Jere, 214

208–209, 211–212, 215, 218, 221, 256*n*30, 259*n*47, 307–308*n*295; secrecy as element of, 23; state judicial elections, 213–221; subtle process of, 210, 214, 256–257*n*30; and theory of equality, 260*n*52; understandings, U.S. Supreme Court, 206–207

Canary, Bill, 157–158, 160

Caperton v. A. T. Massey Coal Co. (2009), 215–217

Capture-by-evil, 4–5, 54–73, 106–140; character vs. acts, 5, 113–121; and collateral punishment, 127–128; conferring irrevocable moral status, 80, 99–101; costs and benefits, 107–140; as a degenerate concept, 5, 244–247; and denial of variable criminal culpability, 121–124; and emotion entwined with law, 5, 107–113; evidence of, 83–86, 97–99; as an explicitly moral notion, 55–64; as an external force, 64–68, 115; involving loosening of social bonds, 58, 232; as a moral injunction, 136–138, 249, 254*n*13; religious roots, 59, 63–64, 101–102; requiring moral suasion, 102–104; and responsibility for acts, 86–89; and the rule of law, 244–247; and standardlessness in law, 124–127, 246, 249; as a statement of

disposition, 74–89; as a statement of status, 68–72; and systemic harm, 6, 139–140; transaction-based corruption, compared, 185; undermining prosecutions, 112–113

Catts, Sidney Johnston, 284*n*45

Cellini, William, 147

Chen Xitong, 61

Chicago, examples of public corruption in, 145–155, 169–197

Chile, treatment of bribery in, 273*n*100

China: corruption-fighting efforts in, 11–12; crisis of values due to rise of market capitalism in, 234–235; culture of corruption in, 224, 228; examples of political corruption in, 60–61, 85

Choice. *See* Moral choice

Chow Murder Case, 174–176

Christian teachings on evil, 92

Ciavarella, Mark A., Jr., 198–200

Citizens United v. Federal Election Commission (2010), 207, 208–209

Clientelism, 211–212

Clinton, Bill, 85

Coelho, Tony, 210

Collins, Roger, 170–173

Collor de Mello, Fernando, 61

Combination theories of corruption, 46–50; examples of, 47–48; insufficient to describe corruption, 48–50

Compensatory bias, 182–183, 187–188

Conahan, Michael T., 198–200

Conduct: acts as focus of law, 5, 9, 69, 114; character vs. acts, 113–121; insufficient to describe corruption, 69–72

Conflict of interest, 216–217, 237

Conscientic model of law, 126

Consumption of individual by corruption, 81–82

Convictions tainted due to corrupt judges, 184–201

Cooke, Maeve, 77, 81

Cooley, Robert, 174–176

Corporate speech, 207

Corruption: as alternative moral system, 223–226, 232; as capture-by-evil, 54–73; concept of, 1–2, 7–8; as a degenerate concept, 2; early definitions of, 57; international consequences of, 135; and knowable and articulated standards, 1–2; and morality, skeptics, 236–242; and move to a market economy, 231–236; norm-changing powers, 138; and political instability and regime change, 226–231; race and allegations of, 112; and the rule of law, 244–247; status conferred by, 69–71; traditional theories of, 2–3, 7–53, 51–52f; as virus or cancer, 66–68, 224. *See also* Capture-by-evil; Traditional theories of corruption

"Corruption of the blood," 120, 285n79

Coruzzi, Peter, 275–276n26, 303n234

Costs of corruption, 2, 5, 42, 128–136, 222, 263nn105–106; anticorruption costs, 236–237

Country-specific understanding of corruption, 226

Crimes: correlated with corruption, 9–10; of immorality, 55–64, 99; status conferred by, distinguished from corruption, 74–77, 81. *See also* Punishment of crime; Responsibility for corruption

Criminal culpability, degree of, 121–124, 273n100, 286n84. *See also* Punishment of crime

Culture of corruption, 6, 138, 224–225, 239

Cunningham, Randy "Duke," 62

da Silva, Luiz Inácio Lula, 134

Davis, John Warren, 284n45

Democratic government: and inequality, 24–25; and market system, 233; and regime change as opportunity for corruption, 226–227; and rule of law, 244; secrecy as incompatible with, 24

De Sade, Marquis, 60

Dews, Peter, 96

Le Dictionnaire de l'Académie Françoise, dedié au Roi (1694), 57

Disgust, 108–110

Dispositional nature of corruption, 3, 74–89; definition of dispositions, 75, 274n1; and evidence of corruption, 83–86;

evidence of dispositions, 75–76; homosexuality's treatment as analogous to, 116–119; implications of, 75–82; and irrevocable moral status, 80–81, 100; and personal vices, 84–85; and responsibility for crime, 86–88, 115; and systemic damage, 82; and total consumption of individual, 81–82, 83–84.
See also Evil disposition
Distortion of political process, 206, 209
Distrust of government. *See* Public opinion of government
Dower, Frank, 184
Drew, Elizabeth, 201–202
Duty, breach of. *See* Breach of duty

Eastern Europe, corruption and political instability in, 226, 235, 271*n*83
Economic theories of corruption, 2–3, 8–9; 40–46; definition of corruption in, 8–9; "good" economic corruption, 129–132; insufficient to describe corruption, 45–46; and market economy, 231–236; as a normative theory, 43–46; as rectification of market failure or reallocation of undesirable power arrangements, 40–43; as rent seeking, 43
Edwards, Jonathan, 59–60
Elections. *See* Campaign corruption

Emotion and law, 107–112
Equality, principle of. *See* Inequality
Ethical imperative, public interest as, 36
Evidence of corruption, 83–86
Evil, nature of, 91–97; and relativism, 94–97
Evil disposition, 90–105; historical association with corruption, 59–60, 97, 103; implications of corruption as evil, 97–105; moral suasion as means to defeat, 102–104; "no account and no expiation" for, 99–101; religious explanations and condemnations of, 101–102
Exploitation of power. *See* Abuse of power
External evil as corruptive force, 3–4, 64–68, 195
Extortion, defined, 260*n*53
Extralegal nature of capture-by-evil, 250

Federal Election Campaign Act (FECA), 203, 205, 306*nn*276–277
Federal Election Commission, 203, 205
Federal Election Commission v. Colorado Republican Federal Campaign Committee (2001), 205
Fisher, Helen, 167
Flood, Daniel John, 284*n*45
Foreign Corrupt Practices Act, 67, 265*n*5, 286*n*84

Misuse of authority. *See* Breach
of duty
Money laundering, 254–255*n*15
Monk, Lon, 147
Moral choice: duty to resist
temptation, 88–89; and
normative system, 242–243; not
to act corruptly, 251; and
obedience to orders by superiors,
241–242; and rule of law, 247
Moral entrepreneurs, 237
Moral injunction, need for,
136–138, 249
Moral turpitude, 275*n*15
Moral values, 223–243; alternative
moral system, corruption as,
223–226; and breach of duty, 18;
critics of analyses involving,
236–242, 319*n*63; and regime
change, 226–231; and transition
to market economy, 231–236
Mozambique, corruption and
political instability in, 226, 235
Murphy, Jeffrie, 110
Myrdal, Gunnar, 131

Neiman, Susan, 99
Nellum, Morris, 170–172
Neo-liberal political reform,
226–231
New York (state), examples of
public corruption in, 164–169
New York City, examples of public
corruption in, 61, 65, 141–144
New York Times: on Blagojevich
trial, 153; on Bracy trial by
corrupt judge, 184–185; on

campaign contributions and
Ohio judicial elections, 214–215;
on Siegelman trial, 159–160; on
Spitzer's case, 166
Ney, Bob, 66
Nigeria, culture of corruption in,
228–229
Noonan, John, 56
Normative economic theories of
corruption, 43–46
Nussbaum, Martha, 109

Obedience to orders by
superiors, 241
O'Donnell, Terrence, 215
Ohio judicial elections, 214–215
"Operation Greylord," 173, 183,
301*n*209
O'Sullivan, United States v. (1999),
184

Parker, Wilmer, 57
Patronage, 133, 296*n*87
Pennsylvania, judicial corruption
in, 197–200
Pennsylvanians for Effective
Government, 213
Personal vice, 58–59, 84–85, 97,
99, 127, 155, 169, 249. *See also*
Luxuriousness
Peters, John, 123, 124
Philippines, corruption in, 129
Philosophers' view of evil and
corruption, 59–60, 91–92, 103
Philp, Mark, 47, 48–49
Place, U. T., 75
Pocock, J. G. A., 60

Rose-Ackerman, Susan, 44
Rosenberg, Tina, 25
Rotberg, Robert, 239–240
Rousseau, Jean-Jacques, 60
Rove, Karl, 161
Rule of law, 5–6, 244–247; costs of delegitimation of, 43; dispassionate nature of, 110–111; governing corruption, 9–14; inadequate to control corruption, 247
Russia and former Soviet Union: corruption and political instability in, 226, 317n18; culture of corruption in, 224–225, 291–292n148; market transition in, 235
Ryle, Gilbert, 83

Schmitz, Eugene, 276n27
Schweitzer, Hartmut, 133, 241
Scott, James C., 9, 11, 13, 37
Scrushy, Richard M., 155–158, 160, 162–163
Secrecy as part of corrupt transaction, 22–24; in combination theories of corruption, 48; and democratic government, 24; and equal opportunity, 26; insufficient to describe corruption, 23–24
Self-indulgence as corruption, 58, 143, 232
Self-interest as motivator, 44, 227, 232–237
Shell theories of corruption, 2–3, 9–20; breach of duty, 14–20;

definition of corruption in, 8; and public-interest theory, 35; violation of law, 9–14, 41–42
Siegelman, Don, 155–164
Simon, Robert, 102
Simpkins, Edgar, 57
Simpson, Dana Jill, 157–159, 160, 163
Skilling v. United States (2010), 162
Smalls, Robert, 112
Social benefits from corruption, 132–135
Social bonds, disregard for, 58
Souter, David, 212
Soviet Union. *See* Russia and former Soviet Union
Spanish Inquisition, 276n34
Speaking with the Devil (Goldberg), 102
Speed money for performance of bureaucratic tasks, 30, 31–34, 138
Spitzer, Eliot, 164–169
Standardlessness in law and corruption, 124–127, 246, 249
Stasavage, David, 235
Status conferred by corruption, 68–72; difference from status conferred by other crimes, 74–77, 81; irrevocable moral status, 80–81, 100
Stigmatization, 113–121
Stone, Michael, 97
Stone, W. Clement, 203
Structuralists, 104
Substantive theories of corruption, 2–3, 8, 20–40; abuse of power,

37–40; betrayal and secrecy, 20–24; definition of corruption in, 8; inequality, 24–35; public-interest theories, 35–37

Subversion of public interest. *See* Public-interest theories of corruption

Sulzer, William, 276*n*29

Summa Theologica (Aquinas), 59

Susceptibility of humans to corruption, 64–68. *See also* Temptation

Swano, William, 176–180, 182

Systemic harm of corruption, 6, 82, 139–140, 143, 194–195, 211–212, 224, 249–250

Tainted convictions due to corrupt judges, 184–201

Temptation, 64–68, 101, 109, 137, 251

Tertullian of Carthage, 92

Texas judicial elections, 213

Theories of corruption. *See* Traditional theories of corruption

Thomas Aquinas, 59

Thompson, Dennis, 140

Tilman, Robert, 41

Tokars, Frederic W., 71–72

Traditional theories of corruption, 2–3, 7–53; combination theories, 46–50; economic theories, 2–3, 8–9, 40–46; overall shortcomings of, 50–53; overlaps, 51–52*f*; shell theories, 2–3, 8, 9–20; substantive theories, 2–3, 8, 20–40

Transaction-based corruption, 185

Transparency requirements, effect of, 237, 242

Trust relationships, 21–23, 232, 256*n*28. *See also* Breach of duty; Public opinion of government

Undue influence, 206, 220

United States: anticorruption machinery, critique of, 236–242; number of corruption prosecutions in, 238

United States v. See name of opposing party

van Klaveren, Jacob, 43

Vice. *See* Personal vice

Violation of law, 9–14; acts as focus of law, 5, 9, 69, 114; and combination theories, 48; crimes correlated with corruption, 9–10; distinguished from corruption, 13, 69, 254*n*14; and economic theories, 41–42; insufficient to describe corruption, 12–14; and moral values, 13–14; overlap with other theories, 51–52*f*; safeguards from rule of law applied to, 10

Visa processing, equal treatment in, 31–32

Wall Street Journal on Blagojevich trial, 152

Wang Baosen, 60–61

Watergate, 203